ECONOMISM

ALSO BY JAMES KWAK

(with Simon Johnson)

White House Burning

13 Bankers

JAMES KWAK

ECONOMISM

Bad Economics and the Rise of Inequality

FOREWORD BY SIMON JOHNSON

PANTHEON BOOKS, NEW YORK

Library of Congress Cataloging-in-Publication Data
Name: Kwak, James, author.
Title: Economism : bad economics and the rise of inequality /
James Kwak.
Description: First edition. New York : Pantheon Books, [2016]. Includes
bibliographical references and index.
Identifiers: LCCN 2016024099. ISBN 9781101871195 (hardcover : alk.
paper). ISBN 9781101871201 (ebook).
Subjects: LCSH: Economics. Economics—Sociological aspects.
Economics—United States. Economic policy.
United States—Economic policy.
Classification: LCC HB71 .K893 2016. DDC 330—dc23.
LC record available at lccn.loc.gov/2016024099.

www.pantheonbooks.com

Jacket design by Janet Hansen

Printed in the United States of America
First Edition
2 4 6 8 9 7 5 3 1

For Sylvia, my favorite economist

My dear brothers, never forget, when you hear people praising the advances of the Enlightenment, that the Devil's greatest trick is convincing you that he does not exist!

—Charles Baudelaire[1]

Contents

Foreword

by Simon Johnson

Why are we so angry? Prospective international trade agreements attract widespread objections, attempts to balance budgets draw thousands into the streets, and people are outraged about issues such as pollution, corruption, and the power of big banks. Protest votes of all kinds are growing in number, and frustration with our economic system seems to be spreading across much of the world. Yet according to basic economics, we—citizens of the world—have never had it so good.

The fundamental intuition of economics is simple and powerful: markets are good, and free exchange without coercion and based on strong property rights is even better. The government, in this view, mostly just gets in the way.

Since at least 1980, government has been in retreat in the United States and many other relatively rich countries. This change became more global with China's gradual shift away from central planning and with the sudden collapse of the Soviet Union in 1991. Globalization—meaning freer trade in goods and services but also greater mobility for capital and ideas—has become the prevailing paradigm of this century.

We have experienced episodes of greater cross-border integration before, including in the late nineteenth century, when more than forty million Europeans crossed the oceans to find better opportunities, along with more personal freedom and security.

And we should not exaggerate the importance of the latest technological innovations; after all, the biggest shrinking of distance arrived more than 150 years ago with railroads, steamships, and the telegraph. Still, recent decades have undoubtedly brought us closer than ever together as a world. And, more than ever, we transact with each other through national and international markets in which there is little or no government intervention.

There is a lot of truth to the idea that free markets can produce good outcomes. If you have a brilliant new technical idea, you can persuade a U.S. venture capitalist to fund it, you can hire engineers from around the world to build it, and you can pay a company in a faraway country to mass-produce it. Look at your TV, your laptop, and (everyone's favorite piece of modern technology) your mobile phone; they all came to you along some version of this route.

But, as James Kwak explains carefully in this book, there is a catch, and it turns out to be a big one. The way we typically think and talk about economics is seriously incomplete. This problem—hiding in plain sight—increasingly distracts or even blinds us, particularly when it comes to assessing public policy options.

The market is a great mechanism for allocating resources. You prefer one type of mobile phone over another—perhaps you abandoned BlackBerry for an iPhone—and this sends a powerful signal. Apple's profits increase, and it produces more phones. This creates jobs both in the United States, where Apple workers earn good wages, and in the countries where assembly takes place (partly in China). The American consumer gains, and so does the American and the Chinese worker. People working at the Canadian company that produces BlackBerry smart phones have obviously done less well. But in a properly functioning market economy, they get new good jobs elsewhere in the tech sector or (until recently) in the booming Canadian energy sector. In terms of the elegant workhorse models that all professional economists have deeply imprinted on their brains, resources—capital and people—move smoothly between sectors. Economic growth brings higher incomes and better opportunities.

Except of course when it doesn't. The failure of growth to translate into higher living standards has been the bitterly disappointing experience of recent decades for many people in the United States and other industrialized countries.

If you only know about very basic economics—perhaps the first year of a university textbook, without paying attention to any of the nuance—the answer would be "remove any and all government intervention" and everything will get better. The paradigm of "more markets" is a powerful pedagogical allegory that has impressed many people, including those who now hold the reins of power in the United States. But stopping with only the simplest economic concepts not only gives you an incomplete picture of how the world works; it is also seriously misleading. The most basic introductory framework is really only a reference point around which more accurate description and analysis are built.

Economists disagree just as much as other people. And there are profound arguments about public policy—including many issues covered in this book—in which people with impressive credentials are on both sides of the debate. But a great deal of economics research in recent decades has established at least five main modifications to the Economics 101 view of the world. There is more on each of these and related topics in this book, but here are some points to whet your appetite.

First and perhaps foremost, people do not make decisions in the hyperrational manner—based on full and accurate information—that underlies Economics 101. Government intervention makes a lot more sense when people would not otherwise become well-informed, for example regarding the precise nature of risks in the financial securities that they buy. (This was a big problem in the 1930s and again in 2008.) The next time you see an advertisement from a for-profit university (or a nonprofit, for that matter) look very carefully at what it is claiming, and then check the specifics against what the Department of Education says are the actual results. When we make infrequent complex decisions—about mortgages, education, pension savings, or health care—we often get it wrong and end up being overcharged, or worse.

Second, politics matter. Again, this is an obvious thought, but it is typically completely missing from the first year of economics (and, to be honest, often from some later years also). If you can capture the government or persuade officials to see things your way, this can be worth billions of dollars. Financial regulation has failed repeatedly and in many countries precisely because the regulators became too close, in their worldview, to the people over whom they were supposed to be watching.

Third, more devious strategies also work well. Create misperceptions of quality and you can overcharge people. This is obvious to you in a grocery store, because you can figure out at home the same evening if items are overhyped. But did you know that some important parts of professional money management operate on exactly the same basis? Principal-agent theory may sound like irrelevant jargon, but in fact the core idea—that the people you hire do not necessarily have your best interests at heart—is the dominant organizing principle of modern finance.

Fourth, the distribution of income can be tilted in your favor. Modern international trade deals are incredibly detailed and complex. Companies work long and hard to get a seat at or close to the negotiating table, to frame the issues in their favor, and to make sure they have enough votes in Congress to get what they want. "Get a bigger subsidy" is an entirely feasible and appealing corporate strategy, and everything that has been done to undermine and delegitimize government really just makes it easier for well-funded lobbyists to win the day. And there are many clever ways to get your hands on what are effectively subsidies, including various forms of implicit or explicit government guarantee.

Fifth, not all property rights are created equal. Many people do not benefit from economic growth, because they start out with little or because they are expropriated as soon as their property (a small business or a claim on a piece of real estate) becomes valuable. As we get richer as a society, the barriers to individual success also rise: the real cost of completing college has increased dramatically at the same time that the rewards of a good education (or the penalty for lacking such an education) have jumped upward.

Putting this together leads to an uncomfortable thought for an economist or anyone else paying attention. Basic economics is today more than a tool kit or a structure upon which you can build deeper knowledge. It has also become, particularly in the United States, the raw material for a deliberately created ideology and a powerful belief system. (If you don't believe me, you need to read chapter 3.)

Economists like to think they are scientists or, failing that, at least engineers who can build systems that work well. And there is real value to the logic of economics, including some of its mathematical tools. But simplistic economic stories are also used—day in and day out—to defend a particular set of policies, which really amount to allowing rich and powerful people to do well while ensuring that everyone else gains less. Increasingly, the understanding that economics is used in this way has spread throughout society, reinforced by the global financial crisis of 2008 and the disappointing economic recovery.

Too many people just get angry and vote in favor of someone with no coherent plan for real change. This is populism in a potentially dangerous form. It is never a good idea to elect people who promise as many as six impossible things before breakfast.

My very strong alternative recommendation is this: read this book, understand better how the world really operates, and work to change everything—by supporting political agendas that are rooted in sensible economic analysis but without the blinkers of

Economics 101 as ideology. "More government" or "more regulation" is not necessarily the answer. But nor is "less government" or "more markets" or "greater competition." You may agree or disagree with James Kwak on the myriad points of substance covered here. But take this opportunity to think more deeply about how you live—including when, where, and how someone is taking advantage of you.

Simon Johnson is the Ronald A. Kurtz (1954) Professor of Entrepreneurship at MIT's Sloan School of Management and former chief economist and director of the research department at the International Monetary Fund.

ECONOMISM

1

The Best of All Possible Worlds

It is proved that things cannot be other than they are, for since everything was made for a purpose, it follows that everything is made for the best purpose.

—Pangloss, in Voltaire's *Candide*, 1759[1]

Gottfried Wilhelm Leibniz was one of the most brilliant people of any age—an inventor of calculus, an expert in virtually all of the natural sciences, and a pioneer of modern philosophy. One of his central preoccupations, however, was a fundamentally religious question: If God is both benevolent and all-powerful, why do evil and suffering exist? In his 1710 *Theodicy*, Leibniz answered, "There is an infinitude of possible worlds among which God must needs have chosen the best, since he does nothing without acting in accordance with supreme reason." If a better world were possible, God would have created that one instead; therefore, we live in the best of all possible worlds.[2]

Unfortunately for Leibniz, his philosophy is best known as the subject of Voltaire's satirical novel *Candide*, a manifesto of the French Enlightenment. In Voltaire's story, Pangloss proves to his student Candide that we live in the "best of all possible worlds," and Candide cheerfully repeats the mantra "all is for the best" as he suffers an increasingly fantastic succession of misfortunes.[3]

Voltaire was mocking not just Leibniz but also the use of religion to justify the social order of the time. Early modern Europe was a world of widespread material hardship in which a privileged few lived in relative comfort while the masses struggled to make ends meet—an archaic order that was upended by the French Revolution of 1789. If you were a landowning aristocrat in pre-revolutionary Europe—when the "1 percent" owned something like 60 percent of everything there was to own[4]—how would you have explained the vast gulf in living standards between you and the common people? You might not have been a strict Leibnizian Optimist, but most likely you would have taken refuge in a religious understanding of the social order. Depending on your denomination, you might have believed that the socioeconomic hierarchy was dictated by God or that the virtuous poor would earn their just deserts in a kingdom to come. According to the sociologist Max Weber, we owe the rise of capitalism to Calvinist Protestants who saw their material success as proof of their personal salvation.[5] One way or another, religion provided a ready justification for a vastly unequal society.

Fast-forward to the late nineteenth century. The Western world has been utterly transformed by industrialization and the growth of the urban working class. But society once again appears dominated by a small number of extraordinarily wealthy families with names like Rockefeller, Carnegie, Mellon, and Morgan. On the eve of World War I, the 1 percent own more than 40 percent of total wealth in the United States.[6] If you are a rich industrialist living in a Hudson Valley mansion, how do you rationalize an economic system that allows you and your peers to live like French monarchs while books like *How the Other Half Lives* are exposing the squalor of urban slums?

In a post-Enlightenment world, traditional religion is unlikely to do the trick. Instead, you can appeal to modern science in the form of Darwinian evolution, metaphorically applied to human society. Herbert Spencer, who was enormously influential in the

United States after the Civil War, claimed that societal evolution required the "survival of the fittest": "the poverty of the incapable, the distresses that come upon the imprudent, the starvation of the idle, and those shoulderings aside of the weak by the strong" all ultimately serve the long-term progress of humanity.[7] William Graham Sumner translated this doctrine into a celebration of the wealthy: "[The millionaires] may fairly be regarded as the naturally selected agents of society for certain work. They get high wages and live in luxury, but the bargain is a good one for society." Any attempt to tinker with this natural order of things would be doomed to failure.[8] For the businessmen who emerged victorious from the "evolutionary" struggle, this worldview provided a convenient justification for their riches and social standing. In the words of the historian Richard Hofstadter, Social Darwinism "was seized upon as a welcome addition, perhaps the most powerful of all, to the store of ideas to which solid and conservative men appealed when they wished to reconcile their fellows to some of the hardships of life."[9]

Now fast-forward to today. Across the developed world, vast fortunes are again ascendant. In the United States, the top 1 percent take home a larger share of total income than at any time except the late 1920s. The total wealth of the world's billionaires has quadrupled in the past two decades (even when the definition of "billionaire" is adjusted for inflation).[10] The signs of excess are visible everywhere, from Stephen Schwarzman's $3 million birthday party to Bill Ackman's $90 million New York apartment that he doesn't plan to live in.[11] In the meantime, ordinary people are struggling. In the United States, the average family makes only 8 percent more money (after adjusting for inflation) than it did in the early 1970s, and even that meager increase is due to the fact that more people work today, whether by choice or by necessity; median income for men has actually fallen.[12] In the 1950s, a typical CEO of a large company took home as much money as twenty average employees; today he makes as much as two hundred workers. The percentage of families in poverty has remained essentially unchanged for the past half century.[13] A rising tide no longer lifts all boats.

If you are a Wall Street master of the universe or a billionaire hedge fund manager, you face the same challenge as the aristocrats and industrialists of centuries past: How do you justify the vast economic chasm that separates you from the people you pass on the street every day? Appeals to Christian theology or evolutionary necessity are unlikely to be convincing today. Instead, you can turn to another source of absolute truth: Economics 101. According to an introductory economics class, each person's income is equal to her marginal product: you are necessarily paid the value of your work. Inequality simply reflects the fact that some people are smarter, more skilled, or more hardworking than others. Tinkering with the natural distribution of income— say, through taxes—would reduce the incentive to work, making everyone worse off. The law of supply and demand ensures that all resources are put to their optimal use, maximizing social welfare. Attempts to interfere with these fundamental principles— regulations, for example—only create "deadweight losses" that reduce the total output of the economy. We live in the best of all possible worlds (or we would, if only we could get rid of those taxes and regulations), not because God would otherwise have made a different one, but because any other world would make everyone worse off.

THE KEY TO ALL THINGS

This invocation of basic economics lessons to explain all social phenomena is *economism*.* It rests on the premise that people,

---

* "Economism" is a somewhat obscure academic term, generally used to criticize someone for overvaluing economics—by overestimating the importance of material condi-

companies, and markets behave according to the abstract, two-dimensional illustrations of an Economics 101 textbook, even though the assumptions behind those diagrams virtually never hold true in the real world. Economism is an interpretive lens through which people make sense of reality. Like any such framework, it also implies a certain set of value judgments and policy choices. For example, if a simple supply-and-demand model shows that taxes reduce employment, then it follows that high tax rates are bad and should be lowered. Because it claims the authority of "economics," economism can be a powerful rhetorical tool. And while superficial economic arguments can serve multiple purposes, in today's world they most often justify the existing social order—and the inequality that it generates—while explaining the futility of any attempt to change it.

For every well-intentioned proposal to help ordinary working people, economism provides an answer. Raise the minimum wage so the working poor take home more money? That's a nice idea, but that's not how the world works. According to Jude Wanniski, one of the pillars of *The Wall Street Journal*'s editorial page in the 1970s, "Every increase in the minimum wage induces a decline in real output and a decline in employment." Wanniski was an adviser to Ronald Reagan, who echoed, "The minimum wage has caused more misery and unemployment than anything since the Great Depression." Raise taxes on the rich to pay for services for everyone else? Good try, but, Gregory Mankiw (author of one of the world's most popular economics textbooks) explains, "as [high-income taxpayers] face higher tax rates, their services will be in shorter supply." Or, in the words of the 2012 vice presidential candidate Paul Ryan, "if you want faster economic growth,

---

tions, focusing exclusively on economic metrics, applying economic methodologies when they are inappropriate, or accepting economic theory too readily.[14] In this book, I use "economism" in a more specific sense, as the belief that a few isolated Economics 101 lessons accurately describe the real world. The economist Noah Smith calls this phenomenon "101ism."[15]

more upward mobility, and faster job creation, lower tax rates across the board is the key."[16] The examples go on and on. The problems of financial markets, health care, education, and many other fields can all be reduced to economic first principles that dictate simple solutions.

These claims are made so often in the media and by politicians that they appear to be a natural feature of the landscape. But they all come from somewhere. They are based on a lesson that economics students learn in their first semester: the model of a competitive market driven by supply and demand. In this model, the supply and demand for any product determine its price; prices create incentives for individuals and businesses; and those incentives ensure that consumers get what they want, companies are as efficient as possible, and resources are allocated optimally across the economy. As the pathbreaking economist Paul Samuelson wrote in 1948, this basic lesson is "all that some of our leading citizens remember, 30 years later, of their college course in economics."[17] (Samuelson was well aware of the power of introductory courses: "I don't care who writes a nation's laws—or crafts its advanced treatises," he once said, "if I can write its economics textbooks."[18])

This elegant model, however, rests on a set of highly unrealistic assumptions. The definition of a competitive market requires that all suppliers offer the same product—there are no differences in features, quality, or anything else—and that each company is so small that its behavior has no effect on overall supply. If this assumption does not hold—such as in the market for cell phone service, or air travel, or automobiles, or books, or almost anything—then supply and demand do not necessarily produce the optimal price, and the allocation of resources may be distorted.[19] The argument that a minimum wage increases unemployment assumes that employees are currently being paid the entire value of their work; otherwise, employers would be willing to pay slightly higher wages in order to keep them. Again, this

premise is unlikely to be true in the real world of fast-food restaurants or hotels, where workers have little bargaining power
and companies are therefore able to claim most of the value that
their employees create.

Economism ignores these uncooperative facts and assumes
the necessary assumptions, reducing all real-world questions to
simple models and answering them in the same terms. In this
sense, economism is like an ideology. Communism explained
industrial society as the product of class struggle, with the inevitable outcome of proletarian revolution. Nationalism, the other
great European ideology of the nineteenth century, saw rivalry
between groups of people with a common background as the
motor of history. Its lesson was that each nation should achieve
political unity to promote its interests in the world.

Communism and nationalism were popular because they were
timely: each provided an explanation of the world that appealed
to the interests of an important interest group. Today, economism
is the perfect way to justify our new gilded age. "The fortunate is
seldom satisfied with the fact of being fortunate," Weber wrote a
century ago. "Beyond this, he needs to know that he has a right
to his good fortune."[20] Many people feel uncomfortable driving
past slums on the way to tropical beach getaways. What they
need is a model of society in which the inequality they observe is
part of a larger design that works to the betterment of all people.

The common justification for great disparities of wealth is no
longer that the social hierarchy was dictated by God or that the
survival of the fittest is required for the progress of the species.
Instead, inequality is necessary, even celebrated, because it is the
natural outcome of an economic system that provides the greatest
good to the greatest number. If the government tries to mitigate
the stark disparities produced by inequality of talent, educational
achievement, or hard work, it will only make things worse for
everyone by sapping incentives and creating deadweight losses.
Instead, the problems facing society in areas such as health care,

education, poverty, and crime are best solved by unleashing the forces of supply and demand.

When deployed as a defense of the existing social order, economism shares with Leibnizian Optimism and Social Darwinism the conclusion that we must accept the world as it is, because our attempts to make it better are doomed to fail. It improves on its predecessors, however, because it doesn't require you to believe in God, or even in evolution—only to accept the principles of Economics 101. This makes economism a supremely convenient tool for the 0.1 percent, the perfect comeback to the Occupy Wall Street protesters. You understand why well-meaning dogooders want to make taxes more progressive, subsidize health care, provide free higher education, and regulate Wall Street. But they simply don't understand economics. As William Baumol and Alan Blinder write in their textbook, "Attempts to repeal the laws of supply and demand usually backfire, and sometimes produce results virtually the opposite of those that were intended."[21] The pleasure of pointing out the counterintuitive—of showing, using economic logic, how good intentions will necessarily be frustrated—even contributes to the allure of economism.

Economism, however, is not a fully fledged political ideology like communism or nationalism. Economism provides a vocabulary for explaining the world, but it lacks a comprehensive doctrine, a political program, and even self-professed adherents. People claim to understand economics, but no one claims to believe in economism. Instead, it functions as an unspoken worldview: a framework that people use for interpreting social reality, a style of thinking that shapes, consciously or unconsciously, their values and preferences.

The fact that economism is *not* a recognized ideology is one source of its influence. An ideology like liberalism or conservatism is easily identified as a set of value judgments that you can agree or disagree with. If you believe that people of the same sex should be able to get married, it's easy to write off someone who says that marriage should be reserved for the union of a man and a woman. You just don't share the same values. But even if you believe that everyone should have access to health care, it's hard to write off someone who explains, using the concepts of supply and demand, that universal coverage will lead to excess consumption. You either have to find a flaw in her economic argument, or you have to come up with a reason why economics is not the appropriate way to approach this issue.

People with a wide range of affiliations resort to economism both to analyze the world and to act on it. In the United States today, conservatives, neoliberals, and libertarians all rely on Economics 101 concepts when it serves their purposes—as do Clintonian "New Democrats" or even big-government liberals, albeit less often. The frequency with which different types of people make these appeals to abstract economic truth has helped naturalize them in contemporary American culture. When Karl Marx wrote, "Workers of the world, unite! You have nothing to lose but your chains!" capitalists knew they had a problem on their hands.[22] By contrast, when Gregory Mankiw writes in his textbook today, "The market outcome makes the sum of consumer and producer surplus as large as it can be. In other words, the equilibrium outcome is an efficient allocation of resources," tens of thousands of students memorize the concept for a final exam.[23] The ability of economism to pass as abstract science rather than rhetorical device is one source of its strength.

Economism is also influential because of its seductive elegance and explanatory power. It presents a model of the world in which policy outcomes are determined by theoretical axioms as inevitably as mathematical proofs flow from their assumptions. In his 1946 book, *Economics in One Lesson*, the journalist Henry Hazlitt put it this way:

[Economics] is a science of recognizing inevitable *implications*. We may illustrate this by an elementary equation in algebra. Suppose we say that if $x = 5$ then $x + y = 12$. The "solution" to this equation is that y equals 7; but this is so precisely because the equation *tells* us in effect that y equals 7. . . . *The answer already lies in the statement of the problem*. . . . All this is equally true of economics.[24]

This appeal to the powers of pure logic is a hallmark of economism. The model says that international trade makes everyone better off; therefore international trade makes everyone better off. The model says that increasing taxes on investments reduces savings and hence economic growth; therefore increasing taxes on investments reduces growth. (Pangloss would have been proud.) Economism presents a clean, uncluttered picture of the world stripped to its bare essentials, which can be communicated quickly and easily, dispensing with messy and uncooperative facts. If you are trying to understand the world, this is a major failing. If you are trying to win a debate, it is a huge benefit.

This elegant reduction of complex social phenomena to supply and demand curves can have a real impact on impressionable students, who sometimes believe that they are seeing the world clearly for the first time. Robert Bork described his experience taking economics in law school as "a religious conversion" that "changed our view of the whole world." He went on to rewrite antitrust law and become an influential appeals court judge. Jeb Hensarling, now chair of the House Financial Services Committee, recalled his undergraduate studies this way: "I suddenly saw how free-market economics provided the maximum good to the maximum number, and I became convinced that if I had an opportunity, I'd like to serve in public office and further the cause of the free market." Popular economics books can have the same effect. Keli Carender said, "I started reading books, started reading blogs, and really started to get into it. The first one I read was *Basic Economics* by Thomas Sowell, and I'm a ginormous Thomas Sowell fan." Carender began blogging and was one of the initiators of the Tea Party movement.[25]

ECONOMISM AND ECONOMICS

Yet economism is not the same thing as economics, or even "neoclassical" economics.[26] Good textbook writers and teachers are careful to highlight the assumptions and limitations of the abstract concepts presented in introductory courses. As the columnist Matthew Yglesias has noted, someone who pays attention carefully during an Economics 101 course will learn plenty of "liberal" lessons—for example, that natural monopolies need to be regulated and that markets tend to produce too much pollution.[27] Used properly, the model of a competitive market driven by supply and demand can be a powerful explanatory tool, which economists often use as their starting point for thinking about an issue. Even economists who favor the minimum wage, for example, will begin by considering how it affects the supply of and demand for labor. But they don't stop there; they study the differences between the real world and the assumptions of the model, develop additional theories that take those differences into account, and test those theories using empirical data.

Most advanced economics, you could say, is about making distinctions between abstract markets and the real world. Industrial organization deals with markets in which the assumption of perfect competition does not hold. Environmental economics is devoted to goods that are not optimally "produced" in an unregulated market. Behavioral economics illustrates the ways in which people violate the assumption of rational behavior. And so on. "Academic reputations are built on new and imaginative demonstrations of market failure," writes the economist Dani Rodrik.[28] To take just a few examples: George Akerlof, Michael Spence, and Joseph Stiglitz won a Nobel Prize for showing how information disparities affect market outcomes; Robert Shiller won a Nobel Prize for research demonstrating that securities markets can be driven by irrational investor behavior; and Elinor Ostrom won a

Nobel Prize for describing how real-world institutions can solve certain problems better than abstract markets. In each case, their theories build on the models taught in Economics 101 to provide a richer, more accurate description of behavior. "Although economists believe in markets in general," writes the economist Mark Thoma, "they are continuously identifying instances of market failure and then designing government policy responses that can make these markets work better."[29]

Experienced economists also know that the assumptions of any model rarely hold in the real world. Many of them study markets for actual goods and services, using large data sets and increasingly sophisticated statistical techniques. Today, the ability to collect and analyze data is a requirement for anyone seeking a job as an economics professor. As the columnist Justin Fox puts it, "Economics is now really all about the data."[30] A large body of empirical research has advanced our understanding of issues ranging from the impact of taxes on savings to the long-term value of early childhood education to the relationship between guns and crime. There are certainly different ways to analyze and interpret data. But on the whole, the profession has made vast strides forward in being able to separate real-world fact from theoretical fiction. In recent years, cutting-edge research has even made minor celebrities of academic economists such as Steven Levitt, of *Freakonomics* fame, and Thomas Piketty, whose six-hundred-page book on the distribution of wealth created a sensation in 2014.

The problem, as the economist John Komlos puts it, is that "most students of Econ 101 do not continue to study economics so they are never even exposed to the more nuanced version of the discipline and are therefore indoctrinated for the rest of their lives." As a result, writes the economist Noah Smith, "if economics majors leave their classes thinking that the theories they learned are mostly correct, they will make bad decisions in both business and politics."[31] Discussion of complex policy questions on the airwaves and the Internet is dominated not by careful

economic research but by economism, which reduces complicated issues to a single, abstract model that is immune to facts.
Its simple, catchy arguments are not published in peer-reviewed
journals; they are generated by politically motivated think tanks,
amplified by the media, repeated by lobbyists, and adopted by
politicians as applause lines in stump speeches. Economism is
Economics 101 retold as fable—as "narratives that lodge easily
in the popular consciousness," in Rodrik's words. He continues,
"These fable-like narratives often have morals that can be formu-
lated in catchy terms (for example, 'taxation kills incentives') and
also sync up with clear political ideologies."[32] Economism is what
you are left with if you learn the first-year models, forget that
there are assumptions involved, and never get your hands dirty
with real-world data. This is one case in which a little knowledge
is a dangerous thing.

IDEAS IN THE WORLD

This is a book about economism: how it simplifies and distorts
economic thinking, why it has become so influential today, and
what damage it has done to policy debate in the United States.
My goal is not to argue that Economics 101 models are "wrong"
but to ask why those models are taken at face value so often and
by so many people. Similarly, this is not an "anti-free market"
book. Competitive markets can be a wonderful thing. The problem is that the popular case for free markets is too often applied
unthinkingly to virtually the entire sphere of social interaction,
with little or no regard for the complexity of the real world.

This book describes the path that a certain set of ideas has
taken, originating in basic economic theory and spreading
through our social and political institutions to shape the way we
understand the world. It asks why a small set of abstract concepts based on admittedly unrealistic assumptions has become so
widespread in contemporary society. It asks why influential com-

mentators and politicians so confidently hold out these concepts as the key to difficult social challenges instead of investigating the facts on the ground. It asks why the prestige of the economics discipline has been successfully harnessed by a worldview that most professional economists do not adhere to. And it asks who benefits from the systematic overvaluation of Economics 101 principles.

Economics is intrinsically intimidating to many people, and the basic mathematics it requires makes it particularly impressive to the layperson. This is one reason why the claims of economism can be so persuasive: most people have little idea how to contest an argument that dresses itself up as pure mathematical reason. The next chapter provides a primer introducing the fundamental concepts of supply and demand, market equilibrium, and social welfare—Economics 101 in a nutshell, if you will—to help you understand the logic of most popular economic arguments.

After the primer, I provide a historical account of how economism became a central mode of thinking in the contemporary United States, particularly among people critical of government intervention in the private sector. In telling this story, I focus on some of the economists, institutions, media figures, and politicians who packaged Economics 101 into sound bites for mass consumption and repeated them until they took on the appearance of self-evident truths.

The subsequent chapters describe the impact that economism has had on particular issues that are of central importance to contemporary society: labor markets, taxes, health care, finance, and international trade. These chapters assess the role of Economics 101 concepts in shaping some of the most pressing debates of our time. Should the minimum wage be raised? Are tax rates too high? Should people pay more for their health care? Do we need tighter regulations on Wall Street? Should we adopt the latest "free trade" agreement? Other chapters could be written: about school reform, where the movement for accountability and school choice is based on the idea that education should be distributed like any other service; about macroeconomic policy, which is often based on simple models in which printing money generates inflation or government spending cancels out recessions; or about criminal law, where harsher sentencing policies were intended in part to "increase the price" of committing a crime. I have chosen the topics for this book because they are directly relevant to just about everyone, they clearly illustrate the limitations of textbook models, and they show the impact that a few simple ideas have had on the distribution of power and wealth in contemporary society.

Each case study shows how the basic tools of Economics 101 can be formulaically applied to a particular policy issue—usually to show that the forces of supply and demand produce the best of all possible worlds. It then explains why these simple models fail to accurately represent our complicated society, briefly presenting some of the detailed empirical research proving that reality is much stranger than the introductory textbook. My goal is not to show that one side is right and the other is wrong, but to demonstrate that an unwavering adherence to simplistic models has had a pernicious impact on debates and policies that affect hundreds of millions of people. Most of the time, that impact has the effect of increasing inequality or legitimizing the inequality generated by our economic system.

This book will not make you an economics expert, but it will help you see through the misleading half-truths that are recklessly propagated by an entire class of self-styled experts. We all perceive our environment through a variety of lenses. It is impossible to make sense of a complex social order without some sort of explanatory framework that organizes our vision. The best we can do is become aware of the interpretive systems, such as economism, that compete to impose their structure and meaning on the reality that surrounds us. Only then can we escape the fantasy that we live in the best of all possible worlds and set about the task of improving this one.

2

The Magic of the Marketplace

Catch a parrot and teach him to say "supply and demand" and you have an excellent economist.

—Irving Fisher, 1907[1]

What is "Economics 101," anyway? Maybe you took economics a long time ago and blocked it out of your memory. Maybe you never took economics. Whatever the case, this quick primer will teach you the key lessons that, as Paul Samuelson said, are all that most people remember from Economics 101, anyway.

Introductory economics begins with the basic model of a competitive market driven by supply and demand. The short summary goes like this: Both individuals and firms possess useful things of value, and they trade with each other in a "market" to get other useful things. Because nobody is ever forced to make a trade (in theory, at least), a transaction occurs only if it makes both parties better off. Under these conditions, prices naturally adjust until supply equals demand. The resulting set of prices makes everyone as well-off as possible. In other words, markets produce the best of all possible worlds.

Let's take snow shovels as an example. If snow shovels are very cheap—say, $1 each—people will want to buy a lot of them. If your current shovel is beginning to wear out, you'll buy a new

Figure 2.1: The Demand Curve

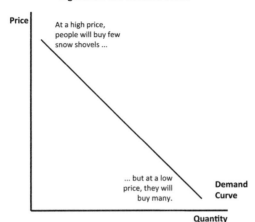

one. You might buy one for your kid to play with. You might get an extra in case you lose one. But if snow shovels are expensive— say, $100—then few people will buy them. You'll keep using your old one even when it's rusty, or you'll buy a snowblower instead, or you'll pay someone to plow your driveway. In general, the higher the price of a thing, the less of that thing people want to buy. This is the logic behind the *demand curve* shown in Figure 2.1. For any given *price* (on the vertical axis), the graph shows the total *quantity* of snow shovels (horizontal axis) that people would want to buy.* (Note that the demand curve doesn't have to be a straight line; for most goods, though, it does slope down and to the right.)

Next is the *supply curve*, shown in Figure 2.2, which is the opposite of the demand curve: at a higher price, companies that manufacture snow shovels will want to make and sell more of them. There are two main reasons why total supply increases at higher prices. The first is that, at any moment, companies have

---

* For the mathematically inclined, yes, this seems backward, at least if we think of quantity as a function of price. But this is how economists always do it.

Figure 2.2: The Supply Curve

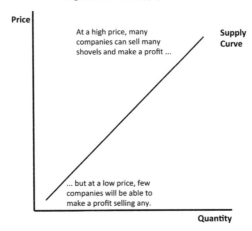

already decided how much factory space to rent, how many machines to buy, and how many workers to employ. If they want to increase production quickly, they have to find more space, buy more machines, hire more workers, or pay overtime, all of which are expensive to do on short notice. Therefore, additional shovels are increasingly costly to manufacture, at least in the short term. The second reason is that the supply curve includes all of the companies that can make snow shovels. Some are more efficient than others: some can produce shovels for $10 each, while others can only produce them at a cost of $20. If the price is between $10 and $20, only the former will make shovels; if the price is more than $20, both will make shovels, so the total supply will be larger. For these reasons, the supply curve roughly reflects the cost of production: as the total quantity increases, so does the cost to produce each unit.

The market price of snow shovels, then, is the price at which the demand and supply curves cross: $15 in Figure 2.3. If the price starts off higher (say, $20), supply exceeds demand and manufacturers make too many snow shovels; then, stuck with unsold inventory, they discount the shovels, bringing the price down

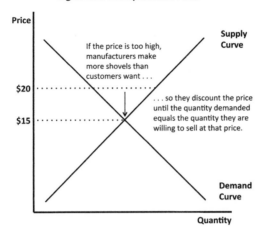

Figure 2.3: The Equilibrium Price

toward $15. If the price starts off lower, demand exceeds supply; manufacturers realize that they can raise prices and still sell all of their inventory, bringing the price up toward $15. Fifteen dollars is the *equilibrium price* because, at that price, manufacturers make exactly the number of snow shovels that consumers want to buy.

This is a good thing. Think about what the demand and sup-

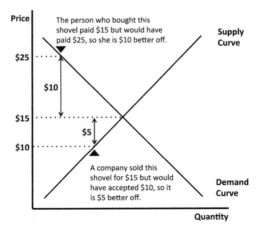

Figure 2.4: Trade Makes Everyone Better Off

ply curves mean. The demand curve, to the left of the equilibrium (where the curves cross), represents people who value a shovel at more than $15. (Imagine tiny people lined up on the demand curve; the height of the curve shows how much each of them would pay for a shovel.) The difference between the value they get from their purchase and what they actually pay is the benefit that they gain from trade. If a shovel is worth $25 to you but only costs $15, then you are $10 better off than before, as shown in Figure 2.4. The supply curve, again to the left of the equilibrium, represents shovels that manufacturers would have sold for less than $15; because they can in fact sell them for $15, the difference is additional profit.

The benefits of trade for buyers are collectively called *consumer surplus*, shown in Figure 2.5; the benefits of trade for suppliers are called *producer surplus;* and the sum of consumer and producer surplus is *social welfare.* A market governed by supply and demand makes social welfare as big as possible. Every snow shovel that can be brought to market for less than someone is willing to pay for it is produced. And no more should be made, because they

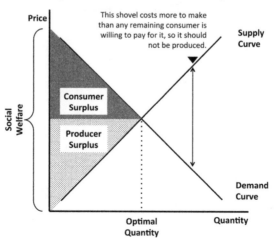

Figure 2.5: Consumer and Producer Surplus

would cost more to make than anyone would be willing to pay for them (as shown on the right side of Figure 2.5). We live in the best of all possible worlds.

That world is getting better all the time. At the equilibrium, remember, manufacturers are exactly breaking even on the last shovel they make before they stop production—the marginal shovel, in economics-speak. That must be true because otherwise they would make more shovels and sell them at a profit. So the price of shovels must equal their *marginal cost*—the amount it costs to make and sell the last (most costly) one.

What if some entrepreneur comes up with a cheaper way to make snow shovels that are just as good? Then she can start a new company. As her company grows, and as her competitors imitate her methods, the supply curve will shift "outward" (to the right): at any given price, the industry will be willing to sell more shovels than before, because it can make them at lower cost. The result is a new equilibrium at a lower price and higher quantity. Total social welfare—the sum of consumer surplus and producer surplus—is now greater than before, as seen in Figure 2.6. Over

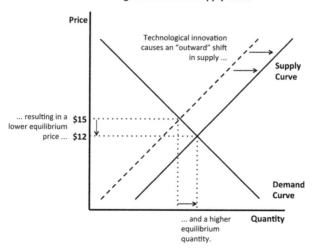

Figure 2.6: Shift in Supply Curve

the long term, the forces of innovation and competition ensure that products get better and cheaper, while wasteful firms are replaced by more efficient ones. Even better, when visionary entrepreneurs identify and deliver new products or services— mobile phones, new medicines, robot pets, or any of the other marvels of modern life—they create new markets, each with a demand curve, a supply curve, and plenty of new social welfare in between.

So far we've been looking at individual markets. Now let's zoom out to look at the economy as a whole. The price of every product or service is determined by supply and demand, and the interactions of those prices determine how resources are allocated across the economy. Assume (for simplicity) that snow shovels are made from only two materials, wood and aluminum. When our story begins, a certain amount of wood and a certain amount of aluminum are being turned into snow shovels. But then let's say that automobile manufacturers begin using more and more aluminum in their cars to make them lighter and more efficient. This means that the demand curve for aluminum shifts outward (to the right) and prices go up. That makes it more costly to produce snow shovels, so the supply curve for snow shovels shifts inward (to the left). Snow shovels become more expensive, so people buy fewer of them. (This is just the opposite of Figure 2.6.)

But this is a wonderful thing. Automobile manufacturers have found a way to make aluminum more valuable, so, as a society, we want more aluminum to go into cars and less to go into snow shovels. Prices send signals across individual product markets, and those signals affect how resources are allocated across different possible uses. It's not just that innovation in the automobile market causes aluminum to shift from snow shovels to cars. The higher price of aluminum causes mining companies to increase investment in discovering and exploiting sources of bauxite (the ore used to produce aluminum), which increases demand for mining equipment, and so on. Expensive aluminum also encourages

snow shovel manufacturers to design products with less aluminum, and it motivates scientists to invent new types of materials.
Supply, demand, and prices together ensure that labor and capital
are constantly being directed to where they can do the most good
for society as a whole.

So far, this sounds like the best of all possible worlds. But
some people—those who haven't taken Economics 101—might
not agree. Say a hardware store has been selling shovels for
$15. Then one night there is a major snowstorm. What will (or
should) happen?

In the very short term and in a confined area like a small town,
the supply curve for snow shovels is vertical and unchanging:
inventory is fixed at any price, because whatever the hardware
store has in stock is all that is available. The demand curve, however, can change quickly: after a snowstorm, you need to clear
your driveway. At any given price, then, more people will want
to buy shovels when a snowstorm is forecast than before. The
demand curve shifts to the right, as in Figure 2.7. The new equilibrium price— the price at which supply equals demand—is $20.
Therefore, the hardware store should increase the price to $20.

Figure 2.7: Snowstorm!

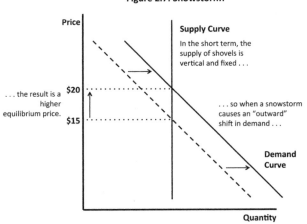

That's the only way to ensure that the shovels are going to the people who value them the most—more than $20, that is—in order to maximize social welfare. If the price stays at $15, there will be a shortage. Demand will exceed supply; some people who value shovels at only $16 will get them, while some who value shovels at $26 won't get them, reducing social welfare.

Now, there's a name for raising prices in times of disaster-related scarcity: price gouging. It's against the law in many states, and most people think it's immoral. When the pioneering scholars Daniel Kahneman, Jack Knetsch, and Richard Thaler surveyed randomly selected people, 82 percent thought it was unfair for a hardware store to raise prices from $15 to $20 after a snowstorm. But that's not what people think after studying economics. When Thaler asked his students at the University of Chicago's business school, 76 percent thought it was fine for stores to boost prices after storms. And a panel of economists surveyed by the Chicago Booth School of Business strongly opposed a proposed state law making price gouging illegal.[2]

So who's right? If the supply is truly fixed, then higher prices will not encourage more suppliers to enter the market, so the question is purely one of distribution: Who gets the shovels? The price mechanism decides based on people's willingness to pay, which is partly based on the benefit they receive from a shovel but also reflects how rich they are. So the venture capitalist who works at home can afford a shovel, but not the single mother who will be fired if she can't get to work. In most cases, we rely on prices because alternate means of distributing goods have their own problems: Could you imagine if the hardware store asked people to apply for snow shovels by explaining how much they needed them? But sometimes, when it comes to particularly valuable products, we don't allocate them via the price mechanism, because most people agree that wouldn't be fair. During the 2009 H1N1 influenza pandemic, for example, vaccines were distributed in the United States by the Centers for Disease Control and by state agencies with the goal of targeting people in high-risk groups, such as pregnant women—instead of letting the price system allocate the vaccines to rich hypochondriacs.[3]

There is a reasonable argument in favor of price gouging, because supply is rarely perfectly fixed. When a natural disaster strikes, it may be possible to bring in additional supplies of water, flashlights, batteries, and other necessities, but only at a high cost; store owners will only make the effort if they are allowed to raise prices. Alternatively, if they have the opportunity to earn high profits during an emergency, they may keep larger inventories on hand, which would be good when the disaster does occur.[4]

What the controversy over price gouging really illustrates is the fundamental tension between efficiency and fairness. The competitive market model, under certain important assumptions, will maximize productive and allocative efficiency: resources will be transformed into products and those products will be distributed in the way that maximizes social welfare—defined as consumer surplus plus producer surplus. The resulting outcomes, however, many not seem fair according to ordinary people's intuitions. As Paul Samuelson wrote in his influential textbook, "John D. Rockefeller's dog may receive the milk that a poor child needs to avoid rickets. Why? Because supply and demand are working badly? No. Because they are doing what they are designed to do, putting goods in the hands of those who can pay the most."[5] This is true all the time; price gouging during a hurricane only makes it more evident.

The lesson of John D. Rockefeller's dog is that the competitive market model is blissfully unconcerned with inequality. Or, more to the point, if inequality results from the workings of competitive markets, then it must be for the best. The magic of the model is that it takes a phenomenon that most people accept but have misgivings about—rich people get more and better stuff than poor people—and transforms it into a crucial driving factor behind overall prosperity. Inequality is not merely something we have to live with; it is a central reason why we live in the best of all possible worlds. This is why Economics 101 has become the preferred conceptual vocabulary for people who defend and even celebrate the high levels of inequality in the rich world today.

If introductory economics were merely propaganda for the economic elite, its influence would be limited. The key insights of the competitive market model, however, are deeply seductive to many people who become privy to its secrets. This elegant framework promises to explain virtually all social phenomena with a handful of diagrams; in addition, it appeals to the know-it-all contrarian in many of us, eager to explain why she is right and everyone else is wrong. Learn how to manipulate the concepts of supply and demand, and you can master a long list of provocative cocktail party arguments: CEOs of large companies are underpaid, rich people should pay even lower taxes on their investments, Americans don't pay enough for their health care, and so on.

It's not hard to win debates by making these simple arguments. It's a lot easier to make a case in the abstract world of supply and demand curves than it is in the real world of people and institutions. That's a major reason why economism is so widespread and powerful. But it's the real world that we live in, not a textbook. The rest of this book looks at the influence that economism has had on major policy debates that matter to hundreds of millions of people—and the tremendous damage that it has done in the process.

3

The Long March of Economism

Each new class which puts itself in the place of one ruling before it, is compelled, merely in order to carry through its aim, to represent its interest as the common interest of all the members of society, that is, expressed in ideal form: it has to give its ideas the form of universality, and represent them as the only rational, universally valid ones.

—Karl Marx and Friedrich Engels, ca. 1846[1]

Ideas matter. They do not matter because they are incontrovertibly right, like mathematical theorems. Whether Karl Marx's analysis of the contradictions of capitalism was accurate is, from the standpoint of history, beside the point. Ideas matter because they have the power to shape the way people see the world around them.

Ideas can be most influential not when they appear as clear propositions that can be accepted or rejected but when they become part of the background conceptual vocabulary that we use to talk about the world. John Maynard Keynes and Friedrich Hayek, two great economists who agreed on little within their field, both believed in this subtle power of ideas. "Practical men, who believe themselves to be quite exempt from any intellectual influences, are usually the slaves of some defunct economist,"

wrote Keynes in 1936. "I am sure that the power of vested interests is vastly exaggerated compared with the gradual encroach-
ment of ideas." A decade later, Hayek echoed his rival: "What
to the contemporary observer appears as the battle of conflicting
interests has indeed often been decided long before in a clash of
ideas confined to narrow circles."[2]

As men of ideas, however, both Keynes and Hayek were
biased—or at least they did not tell the whole story. Ideas may
shape history, but rarely on their own. Instead, they are just one of
the weapons with which Hayek's "battle of conflicting interests"
is fought. Ideas gain power precisely when they become useful to
an important segment of society—when they support the interests of that group or provide it with a favorable interpretation of
the world. To be effective weapons, ideas must be more than brilliant or insightful. They must be refined into easily understood
form, applied to the issues that people care about, and repeated
through multiple channels to diverse audiences until they appear
self-evident. That unglamorous work requires money and man-
power, which will rarely be expended without the expectation of
some return.* Marx himself saw his own theories not as an independent force that could change history but as one manifestation
of an underlying class struggle: "A distinction should always be
made between the material transformation of the economic conditions of production . . . and the legal, political, religious, aes-
thetic or philosophic—in short, ideological forms in which men
become conscious of this conflict and fight it out."[4] Marx might
have been wrong about the outcome of that class struggle, but he
was right that the history of ideas cannot be separated from the
history of social and political movements.

For a worldview like economism to take root and grow, it must

---

* Hayek understood the need for "secondhand dealers in ideas" to spread the insights of
original thinkers. But he seems to have thought that they would be motivated solely by
belief in the ideas themselves: "We need intellectual leaders who are willing to work for
an ideal, however small may be the prospects of its early realisation."[3]

serve a significant social group. Communism became important because it reflected the growth of the industrial working class in Europe and explained how the proletariat could overthrow "bourgeois" governments and create a new economic order. Even in countries without a large manufacturing workforce— Russia, China, and Vietnam, for example—communism served as a useful explanatory tool for harnessing and organizing opposition to an autocratic government or a foreign colonial power. Marx's ideas mattered because they were perfectly suited to a particular historical context. Similarly, economism matters today not because the competitive market model taught in first-year economics classes is intrinsically correct. It matters because it is one important vehicle that interest groups have used to pursue their objectives during the past half century.

IDEAS AND INTERESTS

Economism exists because people and organizations saw how they could use basic economic principles to their advantage. Its first prerequisite was intellectual raw material: the underlying economics. In 1776, Adam Smith described the price mechanism in *The Wealth of Nations*, the founding text of modern economics: "The market price of every particular commodity is regulated by the proportion between the quantity which is actually brought to market, and the demand of those who are willing to pay the natural price of the commodity." In the short term, shortages or surpluses of goods cause prices to rise or fall, but in the longer term firms either increase or reduce supply. The result is that "the whole quantity of industry annually employed in order to bring any commodity to market . . . naturally aims at bringing always that precise quantity thither which may be sufficient to supply, and no more than supply, that demand."[5] Smith continues, however, by discussing many reasons why this general principle may not hold; he certainly did not believe that market forces, acting alone, would produce the best of all possible worlds.

In 1838, Antoine-Augustin Cournot first illustrated Smith's insights with supply and demand curves, which were later popularized by Alfred Marshall, particularly in his 1890 textbook, *Principles of Economics*.[6] According to historian Daniel Rodgers, Marshall and his contemporaries "made a pair of intersecting lines on a two-axis diagram into the great visual-conceptual engine of economics pedagogy, unforgettable to even the rankest beginner in a modern economics course."[7] In his textbook, Marshall showed how supply and demand interact to produce a stable equilibrium price that maximizes social welfare—but only "in this limited sense, that the aggregate satisfaction of the two parties concerned increases until [a position of equilibrium] is reached; and that any production beyond the equilibrium amount could not be permanently maintained so long as buyers and sellers acted freely as individuals." He rejected the idea that the resulting equilibrium was necessarily optimal for society. Because people differ in wealth, "the aggregate satisfaction can prima facie be increased by the distribution, whether voluntarily or compulsorily, of some of the property of the rich among the poor."[8]

Although the competitive market model was fully developed by the late nineteenth century, the historical and intellectual conditions for economism did not yet exist. At the time, unchecked market forces seemed to be producing social instability, not universal prosperity. The major political issue facing industrialized countries was the growth of the working class and, along with it, the socialist and communist movements. If political elites simply insisted that markets would produce the best of all possible worlds, they ran the risk that workers would seek to overthrow the entire system. Confronted by an increasingly militant labor movement, governments in both Europe and the United States instead attempted to accommodate the working class. Beginning with Prussia in the 1880s, many countries introduced social insurance programs such as pensions and workers' compensation insurance, although the United States was a relative laggard in building a social safety net.[9] Rather than insisting on the universal truth of the competitive market model, governments adopted these interventionist policies in order to defuse class struggle and ensure the survival of capitalism.

The need to dissuade the working class from giving in to the temptations of communism was exacerbated by the Great Depression of the 1930s, which produced widespread hardship and political turmoil around the globe. In the United States, the banking system virtually collapsed, and the unemployment rate reached 25 percent. The idea that unregulated markets could maximize prosperity for all seemed discredited once and for all. Franklin Delano Roosevelt and the Democratic Party swept to victory in the 1932 elections and launched an unprecedented program of government intervention in the economy. These policies, collectively known as the New Deal, included financial regulations, public works programs, controls on wages and prices, a safety net centered on Social Security, and union-friendly labor laws. The national mobilization required by World War II further expanded the federal government's role in the economy.

The 1930s also produced a major shift in economic thinking. In 1936, John Maynard Keynes published *The General Theory of Employment, Interest, and Money*, which claimed to explain why the Depression happened, what to do about it, and how to prevent it from recurring. According to Keynes, on the level of the economy as a whole, leaving markets to operate on their own can create a vicious cycle of underconsumption by households and underinvestment by businesses, resulting in "a chronic condition of sub-normal activity for a considerable period"—such as the Great Depression. (Keynes even criticized "the celebrated *optimism* of traditional economic theory, which has led to economists being looked upon as Candides, who . . . teach that all is for the best in the best of all possible worlds provided we will let well alone." He continued, "It may well be that the classical theory represents the way in which we should like our Economy to behave. But to assume that it actually does so is to assume our difficulties away."[10]) Keynes's solution was that the government should manage the overall demand for goods and services in the economy. In a depression, it should stimulate economic activity by cutting taxes or increasing its own spending. This enlarged role for the state, he believed, was necessary to preserve the capitalist system against the threats of fascism and communism: "It is certain that the world will not much longer tolerate the unemployment which, apart from brief intervals of excitement, is associated . . . with present-day capitalistic individualism. But it may be possible by a right analysis of the problem to cure the disease whilst preserving efficiency and freedom."[11]

Keynes's ideas were perfectly suited to the political landscape of the postwar United States, after the New Deal and World War II had given the federal government a central role in the economy. The Democratic coalition that emerged from the 1930s, including both unionized labor and large segments of big business, supported continued government activism to increase material prosperity and expand the safety net.[12] In the 1950s, President Dwight Eisenhower's moderate policies showed that mainstream Republicans were largely reconciled to this expanded role for the state.[13] The idea that the government should sit back and let competitive markets do their magic seemed hopelessly obsolete. The Keynesian approach to economics was codified in Paul Samuelson's 1948 introductory textbook, which dominated first-year classes until the 1970s. It focused on the key questions of macroeconomic management—"the causes on the one hand of unemployment, overcapacity, and depression; and on the other of prosperity, full employment, and high standards of living"— and endorsed activist government policies to minimize both unemployment and inflation.[14] President John F. Kennedy—who turned to Samuelson for economic advice—thought the issue settled once and for all in 1962: "What is at stake in our economic decisions today is not some grand warfare of rival ideologies which will sweep the country with passion but the practical management of a modern economy."[15]

Kennedy was wrong. Depression and war, by vastly expanding the reach of government throughout society, had reversed the political conditions that existed at the beginning of the century. No longer was a disaffected working class threatening to revolt, particularly in the United States. Now it was the old economic elite that saw itself as powerless, beset by labor unions, government bureaucracies, social insurance programs, and high taxes. Some corporations and their executives publicly endorsed the expanded role of government, but many stood to gain from a reversal of the New Deal. A smaller government would also benefit the wealthy, who would no longer have to pay taxes for programs they did not need, such as Social Security.

The business community and the rich, which obviously overlapped, formed the major interest groups contesting the economic order of postwar America, when tax rates as high as 91 percent funded federal government programs aimed at helping the poor, protecting ordinary families from economic risks, and regulating the private sector. But corporate executives and the wealthy couldn't just demand a better deal for themselves. Instead, they needed a conceptual framework that showed why their preferred policies were good for society as a whole (and only incidentally good for them).

Economics 101 provided that framework: because competitive markets regulated by supply and demand produce the best of all possible worlds, the government should let markets be "free." Without the New Deal and the success of Keynesianism, there would have been no need for economism. In the late nineteenth century, much of the working class adopted socialism or communism to contest an unequal political and economic order; in the mid-twentieth century, the rich and powerful created and adopted economism to combat what they saw as an oppressive government sustained by a coalition of Democrats and Eisenhower Republicans.

What these interest groups supplied was money and organizational support. The money first came from individual businessmen who controlled significant funds through corporations, trusts, or personal fortunes.[16] As economism became more popular, financing was contributed by flagship American corporations, including General Motors, Ford, Chrysler, General Electric, Consolidated Edison, U.S. Steel, Socony Mobil (later known simply as Mobil), and Procter & Gamble. Business associations such as the U.S. Chamber of Commerce and the Business Roundtable joined the fight, while corporate executives—particularly those in industries most affected by government regulation—took stands in favor of "free enterprise" and against big government.[17] As wealthy family foundations became more engaged in politics in the 1970s, many devoted considerable resources to economic ideas.[18] These people and organizations all shared the conviction that ideas were a crucial front in the battle to reshape American society. As the billionaire businessman and political entrepreneur Charles Koch explained in 1974, "Any program adopted should be highly leveraged so that we reach those whose influence on others produces a multiplier effect. That is why educational programs are superior to political action, and support of talented free-market scholars is preferable to mass advertising."[19]

Most important, economism was taken up by the broader conservative political movement. The competitive market model appealed to most elements of the emerging conservative coalition because it provided an intellectual alternative to the New Deal consensus. People with diverse ideological affiliations— libertarian, social conservative, or pro-business—adopted the argument that economic activity should be governed by supply, demand, and the price mechanism, not by politicians and bureaucrats. As economism became popular on the right, a growing number of interest groups and their affiliated organizations devoted resources to developing and propagating its central ideas. The competitive market model enabled conservatives to say that they were "pro-market" rather than simply "antigovernment," in a period when public opinion regarding government programs was largely favorable. In short, economism thrived because it served the interests of a large and dynamic political movement. And as conservatism grew in strength and shifted the political center of gravity, moderates and even liberals internalized the worldview of economism, at least in part.[20]

This confluence of ideas and interests is the fundamental reason for the rise of economism. The political scientists Jacob Hacker and Paul Pierson describe it this way: "New understandings swept the field because they intersected with and guided powerful economic interests that were becoming more and more influential within American politics."[21] Ideas and interest groups, however, accomplish their work through people. The remainder of this chapter describes some of the individuals and organizations that played key roles in developing and popularizing economism: intellectual pioneers who transformed economic concepts into a universal theory of society; think tanks and academic centers that industrialized the analysis of social and economic questions and the production of policy proposals; journalists and media figures who repackaged ideas for lay readers and broadcast them to mass audiences; and politicians who distilled those ideas into campaign slogans and reshaped society in their image. Behind all of them stood the executives, corporations, business organizations, and family foundations that funded the enterprise. This is the story of economism.

CREATORS

In 1948, Paul Samuelson buried supply and demand curves and the price mechanism more than four hundred pages into the first edition of his textbook. Around the same time, however, a handful of intellectual pioneers turned those same concepts into the key building blocks of a new theory of society and a comprehensive handbook for public policy. For them, the competitive market model was not just a useful abstraction and teaching tool but also the secret to freedom and prosperity.

Every idea has its roots in another idea. Our story, however, can begin during World War II with two Austrian economists, Ludwig von Mises and Friedrich Hayek. Mises, who moved to the United States in 1940, feared that increasing government control over economic affairs would necessarily lead to socialism. The only alternative, he argued, was competitive markets governed by the price mechanism and ultimately driven by consumer choice. "The real bosses, in the capitalist system of market economy, are the consumers," he wrote in his 1944 book, *Bureaucracy*. Market prices, which are based on "the valuation of all consumers' goods on the part of all the people," allocate resources by identifying "which of the indefinite multitude of thinkable processes of production are more advantageous and which less." When entrepreneurs come up with ways to provide more value at lower cost, they generate profits for themselves and increase the aggregate satisfaction of consumers' desires. A planned economy, by contrast, cannot ensure the optimal distribution of resources for the greatest benefit of society.[22]

Mises was a crucial influence for many conservative and libertarian thinkers, but his ideas did not directly reach a broad audience. The role of intellectual celebrity fell instead to Hayek, his student in interwar Austria, who spent World War II at the London School of Economics. Like Mises, Hayek feared that liberal, democratic countries risked a descent into socialism. "If we take the people whose views influence developments, they are now in the democracies in some measure all socialists," he wrote in *The Road to Serfdom*, his 1944 critique of central planning—communist, fascist, or social democratic.[23] Hayek echoed Mises's central argument: in a competitive economy, prices automatically direct effort and investment where they can do the most good—a feat that no government agency can match. "The more complicated the whole," he wrote, "the more dependent we become on that division of knowledge between individuals whose separate efforts are coordinated by the impersonal mechanism for transmitting the relevant information known by us as the price system."[24]

The Road to Serfdom received a boost in the United States from a glowing review in *The New York Times* by Henry Hazlitt. It was also promoted by business organizations, including the National Association of Manufacturers (NAM) and the Chamber of Commerce.[25] In 1945, a condensed version was featured in the politically conservative but enormously popular magazine *Reader's Digest*, which had a circulation of close to nine million.[26] Hayek became a sensation, particularly among opponents of the New Deal consensus.

On the speaking tour to promote his book, Hayek met Harold Luhnow, a businessman who would soon control the William Volker Fund. Luhnow suggested that Hayek write an American version of *The Road to Serfdom*, spelling out an alternative vision of "a workable society of free enterprise." In 1948, the Volker Fund financed a position for Hayek at the University of Chicago. The fund also paid for the Free Market Study research project, based at Chicago, which helped cement the university's reputation as the foremost center of academic research based on competitive market principles.[27]

In his 1960 book, *The Constitution of Liberty*, Hayek developed his core beliefs into a comprehensive economic and political program. He argued against labor union monopolies, government-provided social insurance, progressive taxation, activist monetary policy, public housing, environmental conservation, and public schooling.[28] If a minimal government and unregulated markets produced extreme inequality, Hayek saw that as a virtue, not a failing; as the political scientist Corey Robin has argued, Hayek thought that concentrated wealth was necessary for economic innovation and for cultural progress.[29] His ideas would become highly influential: after becoming leader of the Conservative Party in the United Kingdom, Margaret Thatcher brandished *The Constitution of Liberty* in an internal meeting, saying, "This is what we believe."[30]

Hayek sought not only to create ideas but also to promote them. He envisioned an international network of leading thinkers who would champion competitive market principles. The Mont Pelerin Society, founded in 1947 and still active today, brought together academics, journalists, and businessmen in a cosmopolitan alliance against the threat of socialism. In its early years, the group received financial support from think tanks and foundations such as the Foundation for Economic Education and the Volker Fund, as well as rich American businessmen.[31] They understood the importance that Hayek's ideas could have in the battle against the New Deal consensus.

The other intellectual founder of economism was Milton Friedman, who joined the University of Chicago economics department in 1946. Like Hayek—whose *Road to Serfdom* he called "an extraordinarily insightful and prescient book"—Friedman was a world-class economist who believed in the power of ideas to produce long-term political change. "The stage is set for the growth of a new current of opinion to replace the old," he wrote early in his career, "to provide the philosophy that will guide the legislators of the next generation."[32] Friedman was a founding member of the Mont Pelerin Society. Beginning in 1956, he gave lectures at conferences organized by the Volker Fund; he first reached a large audience when he and his wife, Rose Friedman, compiled those lectures into a book published in 1962.[33]

In *Capitalism and Freedom*, Milton Friedman argued that competitive markets are the best mechanism for delivering prosperity and ensuring political freedom.[34] Most of the book consists of simple, elegant arguments that different types of government intervention are bound to backfire. For example, public schools limit choices for parents and suppress competition among schools and teachers; a voucher system, by contrast, would create a competitive market for schools, encouraging innovation and attracting better teachers. "Here, as in other fields," Friedman wrote, "competitive enterprise is likely to be far more efficient in meeting consumer demand." Mandatory licensing (such as that required for medical doctors) restricts supply, which reduces consumer choice, increases prices, and reduces quality. Unions try to raise wages, but this only reduces employment (because employers demand less labor at a higher price), pushing excess workers into other industries where they depress wages by increasing the labor supply.[35] *Capitalism and Freedom* was a practical handbook for using basic economic concepts to show why we would all be better off if left to our own devices. In style, it was the American version of *The Road to Serfdom* that Luhnow had hoped for, its optimism and pragmatism contrasting with the gloomy, philosophical tone of Hayek's original.

The success of *Capitalism and Freedom* helped make Friedman a public figure. Beginning in 1966, he wrote a popular column in *Newsweek* that applied economic principles to a wide range of topics from monetary policy to the draft to drug legalization. In 1980, Milton and Rose Friedman addressed an even larger audience in *Free to Choose*, a ten-part television series. The first episode, "The Power of the Market," taught the audience the essentials of Economics 101: how prices ensure that supply matches demand and that resources are allocated to their best uses, all through voluntary interactions between buyers and sellers.[36] Other episodes applied these tools to different aspects of modern society, including Social Security, public education, unions, and consumer protection. In each case, the lesson was that competitive markets would produce ideal outcomes, if only the government would stop intervening. Television is an expensive medium, but by then many foundations, corporations, and business organizations were eager to finance the Friedmans' attack on big-government liberalism.[37] The book version of the TV series was an instant hit, selling 400,000 copies in its first year.[38]

Mises, Hayek, and Friedman were by no means the only important thinkers who contributed to the development of economism. Friedman was a central figure in the "Chicago School" of economists (named after the University of Chicago, where many of them taught), who applied the logic of prices and incentives to virtually every domain of human experience. Gary Becker, for example, described family interactions in economic terms; George Stigler showed how the incentives of industry groups, legislators, and bureaucrats combine to enable businesses to capture regulatory policy for their own benefit; and Richard Posner recast multiple fields of the law, including contracts, torts, and antitrust, in economic terms. Together, they transformed the Economics 101 model of competitive markets into a simple yet powerful intellectual weapon to aim at New Deal liberalism—at a time when many businesses and wealthy people were looking for one.

INDUSTRIALISTS

The arguments of people like Hayek and Friedman, standing on their own, would not have reached millions of people and reshaped the way Americans talk about politics and policy. Fortunately for them, however, their ideas were adopted, repackaged, and redistributed by a network of institutions—often backed by people and companies with their own economic interests in mind. In the years after World War II, a handful of relatively obscure think tanks took the lead in disseminating the competitive market critique of New Deal liberalism. As the ideas of Hayek and

Friedman seeped into the mainstream conservative movement, they were amplified by a widening circle of institutions, including think tanks, academic centers, trade associations, and political advocacy groups. When communicating with the media, politicians, and the public, these organizations leaned heavily on the Economics 101 model of the perfectly competitive market. In the process, they propagated economism to a far broader audience than a few intellectuals could have found on their own.

One of the first think tanks that supported economism was the Foundation for Economic Education (FEE), founded in 1946. FEE was headed by Leonard Read and funded by leading businessmen as well as some of America's largest corporations, including Consolidated Edison, U.S. Steel, General Motors, and Chrysler. Read admired Mises and Hayek, both of whom were associated with FEE in its early years, and helped fund Mises's position at NYU.[39] The think tank's premise was that if people understood economics, they would see the follies of the New Deal. Its mission was to educate businessmen in basic economics and its political implications—in Read's words, to "give the haven of liberty an intellectual lighthouse that persons may be attracted from the sea of socialistic error."[40] FEE sponsored and distributed papers, pamphlets, and books arguing that economic affairs should be left to the market. For example, its second publication, "Roofs or Ceilings?" by Milton Friedman and George Stigler, argued that rent control reduced the supply of affordable housing by distorting the all-important relationship between demand and supply.[41] Through its efforts, FEE introduced the competitive market model and its political applications to many future activists and important figures in the conservative movement.

While FEE focused on economics education, the model for the conservative policy think tank was established by the American Enterprise Institute (AEI). Founded in 1943, AEI was a firm proponent of free-market economic ideas; Friedman himself became an adviser to the organization in the early 1960s.[42] AEI translated general concepts into concrete policy positions and analyses of proposed bills, now a staple of inside-the-Beltway think tanks. In the 1940s and early 1950s, it published a series of pamphlets devoted to "national economic problems," attacking government intervention in the economy in any form. By the end of the 1950s, it was supplying legislative analyses to a large majority of Congress, bridging the gap between ideological principles and practical policy making. At the time, AEI counted more than half of the fifty largest industrial corporations as donors; by 1980, it had more than six hundred institutional sponsors, including several major conservative foundations.[43] Today, AEI remains a consistent source of studies, congressional testimony, and op-ed articles that favor competitive markets over various forms of government action, ranging from the minimum wage to financial regulation to Obamacare.

As the conservative movement gained strength, think tanks sprang up to fill every available ideological niche, many adopting the rhetoric of economism. The Heritage Foundation was founded in 1973 as a more militant, more relevant alternative to AEI. Heritage made the economic case for free markets a central theme of its work; in its first years, it argued for school choice, elimination of the minimum wage, and large cuts in marginal tax rates.[44] The Cato Institute, founded in 1977, focused on economic policy rather than the social and foreign policy issues also popular among conservatives. It initially made its mark with a proposal to privatize Social Security that began on the extreme fringes of political debate and finally became a centerpiece of President George W. Bush's second-term agenda.[45] The Manhattan Institute, also founded in the late 1970s, was dedicated to "a belief in the power of free markets and low taxes to deliver prosperity."[46] It consistently favors policies that rely on free choice in private markets, whether for educating children, delivering public services, or helping the poor. These and other similar organizations were funded by a network of wealthy family foundations and corporations: Heritage was initially bankrolled by Joseph Coors of the Coors brewing family, Cato by the Koch family, and Manhattan by Antony Fisher, an English business-man who was inspired to invest in ideas by an early meeting with Hayek; each think tank was soon supported by many other like-minded donors.[47]

The corporate and foundation executives who backed these think tanks also tried to build academic institutions that could develop the critique of New Deal liberalism and provide a coun-terweight to the predominantly liberal American academic com-munity. Their greatest success was the formation of the "Chicago School," in which the Volker Fund played an important role. The longtime domination of the University of Chicago's economics department and law school by Friedman and his allies provided a supportive environment for original research dedicated to the merits of competitive markets.

In addition, conservative funders created distinct research in-stitutes within leading universities. The Olin Foundation and the J. Howard Pew Freedom Trust contributed to the Center for the Study of American Business at Washington University in St. Louis—headed by Murray Weidenbaum, who served as Ronald Reagan's first chair of the Council of Economic Advisers—which produced studies consistently criticizing government regulation on economic grounds.[48] Money from the Koch family has estab-lished or supported academic centers at George Mason, Troy, Clemson, and Texas Tech Universities, each dedicated to com-petitive market principles; for example, the Manuel H. Johnson Center for Political Economy at Troy is "committed to advanc-ing our understanding about the role free markets and capital-ist institutions play in promoting prosperity." A grant to Florida State University's economics department was particularly con-troversial because it gave the foundation the power to screen candidates for the professorships it was funding.[49] These invest-ments generate new research arguing that markets are the right solution for society's ills and also increase the number of students learning the Economics 101 model of society.

Economism had particular success in penetrating law schools. Beginning with Aaron Director, who was brought to the University of Chicago Law School by the Volker Fund, professors in the classical law and economics movement rethought many areas of legal doctrine using Economics 101 concepts. The idea that legal rules should incorporate economic principles—or better yet serve economic objectives—spread throughout legal academia via the University of Chicago–published *Journal of Law and Economics*, fellowships sponsored by the Volker Fund, and the work of leading professors such as Guido Calabresi and especially Richard Posner.[50] In his *Economic Analysis of the Law*, Posner addressed a wide range of legal questions, concluding that "in every case the equitable answer lay in following out which course maximized the aggregate social wealth, measured by the prices economic actors put on it," in the words of Daniel Rodgers.[51] The expansion of the law and economics movement was accelerated by institutional programs that taught economics to law professors and judges. Henry Manne, who had studied with Director at Chicago, started a series of Economics Institutes for Law Professors, funded by ten corporations. These programs have taught two weeks of economics to hundreds of academics, many of whom joined the law and economics movement despite having little or no other training in economics. Manne later founded the Law and Economics Center (LEC), with funding from corporations concerned about the growth of the regulatory state. The LEC runs the Economics Institute for Federal Judges, which has so far taught two weeks of economics to thousands of judges—at one point more than 40 percent of the federal judiciary.[52]

These investments have paid off handsomely. As an Olin Foundation report noted, "It is especially important that every sitting judge who is even slightly receptive to the law and economics approach be given every chance to become familiar with it."[53] Douglas Ginsburg studied law at the University of Chicago and later attended the Economics Institute for Law Professors, which (according to Manne) helped convince him of the importance of law and economics.[54] Ginsburg later became chief judge of the D.C. Circuit Court of Appeals, which has become known for overruling federal regulations on economic grounds. Posner and Frank Easterbrook (another graduate of the University of Chicago Law School) both became judges on the Seventh Circuit Court of Appeals, where they drew on basic economic principles to rewrite many areas of the law. Elementary economic concepts have also reshaped the way the law is taught, particularly in fields such as contracts, torts, and antitrust.

These think tanks and academic institutions helped build a critical mass of researchers, white papers, and books explaining how markets governed solely by supply and demand could solve virtually any problem. From the blueprint set out by economists like Hayek and Friedman, they constructed a wide range of intellectual products ranging from research papers to congressional briefing documents to workshops for federal judges. Their work gave commentators and politicians the ammunition to criticize the New Deal and its descendants, such as President Lyndon Johnson's Great Society. They also supplied off-the-shelf policy proposals based on private sector firms and market incentives. For the most part, however, their messages were aimed at policy experts, politicians, and intellectuals—not the general public.

PROMOTERS

With the political elites supposedly converted to the gospel of Keynes, some intellectuals and businessmen sought to take the case for competitive markets directly to ordinary people. Befuddled by the popularity of progressive taxes, social insurance, and welfare programs, these entrepreneurs concluded that Americans just didn't understand economics—and set out to educate them. The journalist Henry Hazlitt announced in the opening line of his 1946 book, *Economics in One Lesson*, "This book is an analysis of economic fallacies that are at last so prevalent that they have almost become a new orthodoxy."[55] A quarter of a century later, William Simon, then a Nixon administration official, blamed the "economic illiteracy of the American people" for big government and the nation's economic ills.[56] In 1972, the CEO of PepsiCo identified "economic illiteracy" among young people as the most fundamental threat to the business community and the capitalist system.[57] Today, commentators continue to blame unfamiliarity with economics for the popularity of policies they oppose; during the 2016 presidential primaries, a hedge fund manager writing in *The Wall Street Journal* concluded that millennials only supported Bernie Sanders and Donald Trump because their generation was "economically clueless."[58]

For decades, corporations and business organizations have attempted to solve this problem by teaching Americans basic economics. "The story of business economics and philosophy needs to be told," said an executive at the National Association of Manufacturers shortly after World War II, "simply, understandably, repetitiously and without dilution or distortion—to broad masses of the people." Major corporations such as Johnson & Johnson, IBM, DuPont, Westinghouse, U.S. Steel, and General Electric created and shared economic educational materials that were rolled out to captive audiences of millions of workers. Their key themes included the profit motive, individual initiative, and the superiority of competitive markets over government intervention.[59] Big business also reached out beyond the workplace to the public at large. In the late 1940s, the NAM spent millions of dollars on advertisements highlighting profits as the driving force behind material progress. Individual companies ran their own print, radio, and television ads, highlighting their own contributions to the community while emphasizing the importance of free markets, competition, and profits.[60] Decades later, the Friedmans' *Free to Choose* was a much more successful variation on the same theme. And today, the campaign continues on the Internet. In 2016, the Council for Economic Education promoted an online "economic literacy" quiz. As the financial commentator Matthew Klein pointed out, many of the questions were "either wrong or deeply misleading"—usually because they were based on simple Economics 101 models, without recognizing that those models often fail to describe the real world accurately.[61]

Corporate America sought to insert its brand of economics directly into schools and colleges. In the late 1940s and the 1950s, business organizations and corporations cultivated classroom teachers directly, hosting hundreds of thousands of them at company sites and supplying schools with educational booklets, teaching aids, and films that reached millions of students. Similarly, the Foundation for Economic Education created a fellowship program that matched young professors with large companies in order to familiarize academics with the business world while teaching them basic economic principles. Business associations sent speakers to college campuses to explain the "economic facts of life," reaching hundreds of thousands of students each year by the mid-1950s. Both NAM and the American Economic Foundation (AEF) designed economics courses for school classrooms and trained teachers to deliver them; by the mid-1950s more than 12 percent of all secondary schools had adopted the AEF's program.[62] As the conservative movement gained strength, so did efforts to bring economics to the classroom. In the 1970s, the U.S. Chamber of Commerce distributed "Economics for Young Americans" teaching kits to twelve thousand schools. During the same decade, more than twenty states passed laws making economics a requirement for high school graduation. In the 1980s, the student group Students in Free Enterprise—backed by Coors, Dow Chemical, Walmart, and other companies—even reinterpreted *Free to Choose* as a series of skits for elementary school students.[63]

In addition to educational programs, another way to reach ordinary people is through the media—the newspapers, magazines, and radio and television shows that shape public perceptions of the important questions of the day. Hayek, Friedman, and some other Chicago School economists were highly effective popularizers of their own ideas; as we have seen, *The Road to Serfdom* and *Free to Choose* were both mass-market hits. Their voices were amplified many times over, however, by influential media figures who distilled their ideas into easily digestible form for mass consumption. Here it is possible to discuss only a few of these important popularizers.

Henry Hazlitt—the *New York Times* reviewer who helped make Hayek a celebrity—was an early and influential advocate of the Economics 101 worldview, as well as a member of the Mont Pelerin Society and one of the first executives of the Foundation for Economic Education. His *Economics in One Lesson* was an easy-to-read introduction to economics as an all-purpose explanatory tool. Its "one lesson" is the so-called law of unintended consequences: "The art of economics consists in looking not merely at the immediate but at the longer effects of any act or policy."[64] So, for example, Hazlitt criticized agricultural price supports for reducing production, aid to specific industries for diverting resources to less profitable sectors, and the minimum wage for creating unemployment. All of these policy mistakes, Hazlitt argued, ultimately follow from a failure to understand the price mechanism. Echoing Mises and Hayek, he wrote, "It is only the much vilified price system that solves the enormously complicated problem of deciding precisely how much of tens of thousands of different commodities and services should be produced in relation to each other."[65] Hazlitt's portrayal of economics as both easy and powerful was highly seductive. Since its publication, *Economics in One Lesson* has sold more than one million copies, and Hazlitt repeated its messages as an editor of *The Freeman*, an important journal in early 1950s libertarian circles, and as a columnist for *Newsweek* for twenty years.

When William F. Buckley Jr. founded *National Review* in 1955—with money from his family's oil fortune and from the Lynde and Harry Bradley Foundation—his goal was to create a unified conservative movement that brought together anti-communists, traditionalists, and libertarians.[66] Buckley is widely credited with successfully brokering an alliance between the different ideological strains that make up American conservatism.[67] In the process, he made competitive market principles part of the working vocabulary for conservatives of all stripes.

On economic questions, Buckley followed in the path of Hayek and Friedman (himself a good friend of Buckley's[68]). In his 1951 book, *God and Man at Yale*, Buckley described himself as "committed to the classical doctrine that the optimum adjustment—private property, production for profit and by private ownership, and regulation by a free competitive economy—brings not only maximum prosperity, but also maximum freedom." He continued, "I therefore consider any infringement upon the component parts of the free economy to be unsound economics." One of the principles in the founding manifesto of *National Review* reads, "The competitive price system is indispensable to liberty and material progress." In concluding his 1959 book, *Up from Liberalism*, Buckley warned of tinkering with competitive markets: "Deal high handedly . . . with the mechanisms of the marketplace, and the mechanisms will bind." Instead, we should

let the natural desire of the individual for more goods, and better education, and more leisure, find satisfaction in individual encounters with the marketplace, in the growth of private schools, in the myriad economic and charitable activities which . . . take organic form.[69]

Buckley's syndicated column—picked up by more than three hundred newspapers by the 1970s—and his television show, *Fir-*

ing Line, ensured that his arguments reached far more people than just the loyal subscribers to *National Review*.

While Hazlitt helped popularize economism in the 1940s and Buckley integrated it into the conservative movement in the 1950s and 1960s, Jude Wanniski came onto the stage when the movement was in full force in the 1970s. Hired by Robert Bartley to write for the editorial page of *The Wall Street Journal*, Wanniski packaged the ideas of the economists Arthur Laffer and Robert Mundell into what came to be known as supply-side economics. According to this doctrine, reducing barriers to "supply," such as taxes and regulations, is the key to unleashing entrepreneurial activity and boosting economic growth. In particular, lower tax rates could increase growth enough to generate higher tax revenues—an idea now referred to as the Laffer Curve (supposedly originally sketched on a restaurant napkin). The general idea that lowering taxes would increase growth by encouraging more people to save, invest, and work came straight out of Economics 101, although few people at the time thought tax revenues would actually rise as a result.*

Wanniski was an archetypical proponent of economism: a person with little training in economics who believed that a few concepts and a diagram on a napkin could explain all of social and political reality.[70] He developed his ideas in his 1978 book, *The Way the World Works*, written at AEI and funded by the Smith Richardson Foundation.[71] Wanniski's economic theory boils down to a few Economics 101 lessons: individuals have the incentive to work in order to maximize personal welfare; output will increase only if that incentive is strengthened; and therefore government policy should aim to reduce taxes and regulations that discourage work. Wanniski then used those tools to explain

---

* Supply-side economics was unorthodox at the time, but that was primarily because it drew on only one part of the Economics 101 textbook while ignoring other parts—particularly those concerned with the role of aggregate demand in macroeconomics.

everything from the Great Depression and the rise of Hitler (caused by an increase in U.S. tariffs) to the communist takeover of Vietnam (caused by high tax rates in South Vietnam).[72]

On his own, Wanniski might have been a historical curiosity. But with Bartley's backing, he was able to use the editorial page of *The Wall Street Journal*—the newspaper of American business—to promote his ideas. His 1974 article "It's Time to Cut Taxes," for example, popularized the idea that tax cuts could increase growth by strengthening the incentive to produce: "With lower taxes, it is more attractive to invest and more attractive to work; demand is increased but so is supply."[73] One of his readers was a congressman from Buffalo named Jack Kemp, who became a leading advocate for supply-side economics and helped convince Ronald Reagan of the need for across-the-board tax reductions—eventually resulting in the massive 1981 tax cut.[74]

While Hazlitt, Buckley, and Wanniski played historic roles in the popularization of economism, the more common function of the media has been to repeat talking points based on Economics 101 models until they become part of our everyday vocabulary. Since the days of Bartley and Wanniski, the editorial and op-ed pages of *The Wall Street Journal* have welcomed articles arguing that prosperity can be achieved by recognizing the laws of supply, demand, and competition. Many influential commentators who do not specialize in economic issues also routinely adopt the vocabulary of economism. For almost four decades, the syndicated columnist George Will has been teaching simple parables based on Economics 101. He has argued that school vouchers are good because they "will enable demand for private schools to match the supply," for example, and that Social Security should be privatized because competition among fund managers is preferable to a "government monopoly on income transfers from workers to retirees."[75] Similarly, the *New York Times* columnist David Brooks has often resorted to the tropes of economism. For example, he has praised an approach to government that "gives people access to markets," while hesitating to intrude on those markets or raise taxes, and criticized an alternative approach that "more aggressively raises taxes to shift money down the income scale, opposes trade treaties and meddles more in the marketplace." He has advocated for eliminating taxes on investments in order to encourage people to save more—an idea straight out of Economics 101. He has cautioned against raising the minimum wage because doing so would run afoul of the "laws of economic gravity."[76] Columnists may very well know that there is more to the world than the simple stories they tell—it's hard to fit caveats into eight hundred words—but by repeating these simple lessons, they popularize and legitimate economism's simplistic mode of thinking.

In recent decades, the influence of print journalists has probably been eclipsed by that of radio and television personalities, many of whom have also adopted the language of economism. An early pioneer, Ronald Reagan drew on Economics 101 in the syndicated radio addresses he delivered after leaving the California governor's office in 1975. In one talk, for example, he quoted Milton Friedman: "When you start paying people to be poor you wind up with an awful lot of poor people."[77] But the importance of broadcast media increased significantly with the rise of superstar radio personalities such as Rush Limbaugh beginning in the 1980s.

Conservative talk show hosts generally air a wide range of opinions, but when it comes to economic issues, they rely on talking points ostensibly based on Economics 101. Limbaugh, for example, maintains that lower taxes are the key to prosperity: a lower top tax rate "is quite motivating to go ahead and go out there and earn dollars . . . The way it works is the low rate creates economic growth, which creates jobs, which creates more taxpayers, which spreads the taxation burden across more people." On health care, he explains that people should get different services based on their ability to pay; the problem with health-care politics is that "the only way you can fully understand why some-body has to pay for it is to get some kind of a basic understanding of economics 101." Indeed, one of Limbaugh's recurring themes is that people need to learn economics, which he describes as a personal revelation: "Economics, it really takes the right person to explain it to you. . . . I will never forget when I learned how lowering taxes raises revenue. . . . You need somebody to explain it to you. And once somebody can, it makes total sense."[78] Lim-baugh even periodically recommends an online Economics 101 course, taught by Hillsdale College, one of his sponsors.

Limbaugh is only one of several popular talk show person-alities who invoke the authority of textbook economics to sup-port their political positions. The rise of the Fox Broadcasting Company created an enormous platform for hosts and commen-tators who cite competitive markets as the answer to all social and political questions. Even leaving aside right-leaning media outlets, Economics 101 is commonly used as a journalistic device. American Public Media's popular show *Marketplace*, for example, regularly describes economic phenomena such as rising rents or Uber surge pricing as the product of supply and demand.[79] While these explanations are often roughly correct—remember, the competitive market model can be a useful analytical tool—they reinforce the overall impression that the world can be adequately understood through the lens of simple models. The more that talk show banter, like op-ed articles, exposed growing audiences to supposed eternal laws of supply and demand, the more this type of simplistic economic reasoning came to seem like a natural way of explaining the world.

POLITICIANS

The media normalize economism by making it a standard way of presenting and discussing social and economic issues. Politicians provide a different kind of legitimation by incorporating econ-omism's central principles into their platforms and campaigns. National figures such as major party presidential candidates com-mand huge audiences, and the conceptual vocabulary they use to think about the world influences their followers directly. More subtly, when a leading politician adopts a program that assumes that the world behaves like an economics textbook, economism gains credibility even among people who may not agree with her, simply by virtue of being taken seriously on the national stage. The fact that candidates can win office using sound bites from Economics 101 demonstrates the political viability of econo-mism, inspiring others to adopt the same rhetoric. Finally, the eventual implementation of new laws based on the competitive market model serves as the ultimate validation of economism—because it will always be possible to argue that those policies were successful and that any failings were due to other, complicating causes.

National politicians in early postwar America had little use for unrestrained markets. President Dwight Eisenhower was a pragmatist in economic affairs, the archetype of the Republican reconciled to the New Deal. In 1954, he wrote,

> Should any political party attempt to abolish social secu-rity, unemployment insurance, and eliminate labor laws and farm programs, you would not hear of that party again in our political history. There is a tiny splinter group, of course, that believes you can do these things. . . . Their number is negligible and they are stupid.[80]

Richard Nixon, Eisenhower's vice president and the 1960 Repub-lican presidential nominee, was similarly uninterested in abstract economic principles.

As doctrinaire conservatives replaced moderates within the Republican Party, however, competitive markets became an increasingly important part of their political vocabulary. The Arizona senator Barry Goldwater was the first national champion of the postwar conservative movement. His political philosophy drew mainly on anticommunism and a kind of natural law—principles "derived from the nature of man, and from the truths that God has revealed about his creation"—but when it came to economic questions, he faithfully championed the law of supply and demand. "[Man] cannot be economically free, or even economically efficient, if he is enslaved politically," he wrote in his 1960 manifesto, *The Conscience of a Conservative*, echoing the ideas Milton Friedman was then developing.[81] Goldwater's criticism of federal farm policy showed his faith in competitive markets:

> If the nation's farmers are permitted to sell their produce freely, at price[s] consumers are willing to pay, they will, under the law of supply and demand, end up producing roughly what can be consumed in national and world markets. . . . Is it heartless to permit the natural laws of economics to determine how many farmers there shall be in the same way that those laws determine how many bankers, or druggists, or watchmakers there shall be?

"The way to build a strong economy," Goldwater concluded, "is to encourage the free play of economic forces: free capital, free labor, a free market."[82] When he ran for president in 1964, his chief policy adviser was William Baroody, the head of AEI, and Friedman served as an economic adviser.

Goldwater's campaign ended in a crushing defeat.[83] But it provided the coming-out party for a supremely gifted politician and communicator. Ronald Reagan was himself a product of the corporate offensive against the New Deal. He worked as a spokesman for General Electric in the 1950s, precisely when the company was attempting to sway its employees to the ideology of the free market, and his speeches at GE factories grew increasingly political over his tenure. By the 1960s, he was an avid reader of both Hayek and Mises.[84] A week before the 1964 election, Reagan endorsed Goldwater in a television speech known as "A Time for Choosing." The choice he posed was between freedom and totalitarianism, by which he primarily meant federal government programs that constrained individual choices. Reagan's criticism of New Deal policies echoed Hayek's and Friedman's warnings that government activism would inevitably lead to socialism.[85] It was too late to save Goldwater, but the speech put Reagan on the national stage. Only two years later he was elected governor of California.

Through the 1960s and 1970s, conservatives battled moderates for control of the Republican Party. Nixon, who was in neither camp, cultivated enough conservative support to win the 1968 nomination and the general election. But both he and his successor, Gerald Ford, pursued generally moderate economic policies while in office. It was only in 1980 that the conservatives, led by Reagan, seized control of their party and the White House. Although Reagan embraced the entire spectrum of conservative values, competitive market principles played a central role in his presidential campaign and his policy program, particularly after he was won over to supply-side tax cuts by Kemp and Wanniski.[86] In the presidential race, Reagan leaned heavily on the idea that lower taxes would strengthen incentives and produce economic growth. "I believe that when something is taxed, you get less of it," he said in one television commercial. "We're taxing work, savings, and investment [like] never before. So we have less work, less savings, and less investment."[87] During the campaign, Reagan cited Friedman as an important economic adviser; after his victory, he paid tribute to Hayek, Friedman, and Mises as intellectual forefathers.[88]

As president, Reagan backed up words with action. The centerpiece of his first year in office was the Economic Recovery Tax Act of 1981, which slashed income taxes, with the top rate falling from 70 percent to 50 percent. (The Tax Reform Act of 1986 later lowered the top rate to 28 percent.) Reagan pressed his staff to reduce the burden of government regulation. For example, Treasury Secretary Donald Regan's top priority was "the deregulation of financial institutions . . . as quickly as possible."[89] In the late 1970s, President Jimmy Carter had begun deregulating the trucking and commercial air travel industries. Reagan, however, made reducing government's role in the economy a matter of grand principle, famously proclaiming in his first inaugural address, "Government is not the solution to our problem; government is the problem."[90]

Reagan showed that it was possible to gain power and govern on the strength of a blueprint drawn largely from Economics 101. More important, the "Great Communicator" was able to take what might seem merely commercial or even tawdry— exchanges of labor, goods, and capital—and elevate it into a mystical talisman. "The societies which have achieved the most spectacular broad-based economic progress," he said in 1981, are those that "believe in the magic of the marketplace."[91] Although he rarely deigned to go into the details of any particular market, he stood for the principle that markets are both omnipotent and benevolent—that "millions of social interactions among free individuals and institutions can do more to foster economic and social progress than all the careful schemes of government planners."[92] By humanizing the competitive market model and blending it into a heady ideological potion along with freedom, national strength, and moral virtue, Reagan paved the way for a generation of followers to make economism part of their everyday platform.

After Reagan, the integration of economism into the American political landscape became a bipartisan affair. As Republican conservatives embraced the logic of supply and demand, competition, and incentives, they put pressure on Democrats, whose economic principles were a complicated and unsatisfying jumble of Keynesian demand management, social insurance, welfare, consumer protection, and industrial policy. In order to compete, Democratic politicians began adopting the vocabulary of economism. In the 1980 election, President Carter channeled Hayek's description of a market economy: "Every day millions of economic decisions are made in factories, in automobile showrooms, in banks and in brokerage houses, on farms and around kitchen tables . . . according to private needs and private individual judgments."[93] He could not compete with Reagan's full-throated advocacy of free markets, but this rhetorical shift would be an important part of his party's resurgence a decade later.

Bill Clinton won the presidency in 1992 as a former chair of the Democratic Leadership Council, an organization formed in the 1980s to move the party toward more centrist, business-friendly positions. Although some of Clinton's policies, such as his proposed overhaul of the national health-care system, were anathema to free-market purists, he was able to deploy the language of incentives and free enterprise to his advantage. It was Clinton who declared, in his 1996 State of the Union address, that "the era of big government is over."[94] Later that year, he followed through on his earlier campaign pledge to "end welfare as we know it" by signing a welfare reform bill that, among other things, was intended to strengthen the incentive to work.

Democratic attempts to co-opt the language of economics, however, have been complicated by the fact that many of their preferred policies—such as government health insurance, food stamps, and increases in the minimum wage—are hard to justify using the simple lessons of Economics 101. Increasingly conservative Republicans face no such constraint. In 1995, the House majority leader, Dick Armey, could simply say, "The market is rational and the government is dumb."[95] On the national level, President George W. Bush pressed for sweeping tax cuts with two different Economics 101 arguments. He started with the supply-side logic that "lower taxes and greater investment will help this economy expand," but, as the economy slipped into recession in 2001, he pivoted to the Keynesian position usually favored by Democrats: "A way to stimulate growth during recession is to give people—let them keep their own money. That's Economics 101."[96]

The younger Bush typically maintained his folksy way of talking about economic issues. By 2012, the Republican presidential nominee, Mitt Romney, was more explicit about the implications of economic logic. Unemployment insurance benefits, for example, "serve to discourage some individuals from taking jobs, especially when the benefits extend across years." On taxes, he argued that "high marginal tax rates . . . discourage work and entrepreneurship, as well as savings and investments." Health care, the candidate said, should be left to market forces, because "competition drives improvements in efficiency and effectiveness, offering consumers higher quality goods and services at lower cost."[97]

These invocations of Economics 101 concepts are now the bread and butter of most Republican economic policies. For example, the 2012 budget proposal produced by the House Budget Committee—then chaired by Paul Ryan, Romney's running mate in 2012 and later Speaker of the House of Representatives—reduced most of the nation's challenges to two-dimensional analyses worthy of a first-year economics class. The proposal justified slashing tax rates for the wealthy because "economic theory suggests, and most empirical studies prove, that marginal tax-rate hikes—tax increases that reduce incentives to work, save and invest for additional income above a certain cutoff—reduce economic output, while marginal rate reductions increase output." It opposed taxing investments because "mainstream economics, not to mention common sense, teaches that raising taxes on any activity generally results in less of it," and "tax reform should promote savings and investment because more savings and more investment mean a larger stock of capital available for job creation." In addition, Medicare plans should be privatized because "putting patients in charge of how their health care dollars are spent will force providers to compete against each other on price and quality. That's how markets work: The customer is the ultimate guarantor of value."[98]

Economism's successful penetration of the political landscape has had a profound impact on American society. Beginning with the Reagan administration, economic policy has been largely shaped by people who believed that it was necessary to "cut back all forms of government regulation and interference with the marketplace, open the markets so that entrepreneurs would rush in, innovate, grow, and in so doing reinvigorate and reshape the economy," as summarized by the economists Stephen Cohen and Brad DeLong. Why did they believe that? "They 'knew'— without looking at the world at all," say Cohen and DeLong.[99] All they needed to justify their choices was Economics 101.

When Hayek wrote *The Road to Serfdom* in 1944, it was by no means evident that the model of a competitive market driven by supply and demand would become a ubiquitous, all-purpose framework for understanding modern society. Few people thought such an approach would make sense, let alone be comprehensible and persuasive for the general public. The intervening decades, however, have seen the institutionalization, popularization, and legitimation of economism—thanks to the concerted efforts of business leaders, funders, intellectuals, journalists, and politicians. One of their successes was recapturing the terrain of introductory economics itself. By the 1990s, virtually every first-year textbook began not with the economy-wide problems of unemployment and depression, but with the competitive market model; even the fourteenth edition of Samuelson's textbook embraced the new order, describing it as the "rediscovery of the market."[100] More important, economism's sponsors succeeded in making it seem a natural part of our culture—a common lens through which to see the world, a set of arguments whose premises need no justi-fication. In the words of the economist David Kotz, "Ideas are an important part of the glue that holds an institutional form of capitalism together and renders it viable."[101] Economism plays that role today, justifying a particular economic system and the unequal outcomes that it produces.

The explicit values of American conservatism remain as con-tested as ever. The idea of the all-powerful competitive market, however, piggybacked on the spread of conservative ideology and now claims the status of incontestable logic. In that guise, econo-mism has warped the public understanding of many issues of cen-tral importance to our society, from labor markets to health care to financial regulation. The remainder of this book examines the impact that economism has had in these domains—most often to the benefit of businesses and the wealthy and to the detriment of ordinary families.

4

You Get What You Deserve

Society rewards those who give it what it wants. That is why how much people have earned is a rough measure of how much they gave society what it wanted.

—Ray Dalio, 2011[1]

In a rich, post-industrial society, where most people walk around with supercomputers in their pockets and you can have virtually anything delivered to your doorstep overnight, it seems wrong that people who work should have to live in poverty. Yet in America, there are more than ten million members of the working poor: people in the workforce whose household income is below the poverty line. If you look around, it isn't hard to understand why. The two most common occupations in the United States are retail salesperson and cashier. Eight million people have one of those two jobs, which typically pay about $9–$10 per hour.[2] It's hard to make ends meet on such meager wages. A few years ago, McDonald's was embarrassed by the revelation that its internal help line was recommending that even a full-time restaurant employee apply for various forms of public assistance.[3]

Poverty in the midst of plenty exists because many working people simply don't make very much money. This is possible because the minimum wage that businesses must pay is low: only

$7.25 per hour in the United States in 2016 (although it is higher in some states and cities). At that rate, a person working full-time for a whole year, with no vacations or holidays, earns about $15,000—which is below the poverty line for a family of two, let alone a family of four. A minimum-wage employee is poor enough to qualify for food stamps and, in most states, Medicaid. Adjusted for inflation, the federal minimum is roughly the same as in the 1960s and 1970s, despite significant increases in average living standards over that period.[4] The United States currently has the lowest minimum wage, as a proportion of its average wage, of any advanced economy, contributing to today's soaring levels of inequality.[5] At first glance, it seems that raising the minimum wage would be a good way to combat poverty.

THE PROBLEM WITH A PRICE FLOOR

Not according to economism, however. A pair of supply and demand curves proves that a minimum wage increases unem-

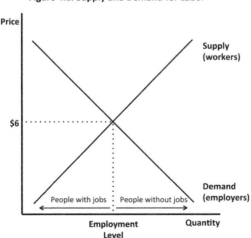

Figure 4.1: Supply and Demand for Labor

ployment and hurts exactly the low-wage workers it is supposed to help. The argument goes like this: Low-skilled labor is bought and sold in a market, just like any good or service. The sellers are workers, the buyers are employers, and the price of labor is the wage. The supply curve slopes upward because people want to work more hours if you pay them more, at least in theory. To see this, think about why people work in the first place. According to Economics 101, all of our actions have the goal of increasing our *utility*—well-being, satisfaction, happiness, or something like that. When deciding whether to work one more hour, you are really deciding whether you would gain more utility from your wages (and the things you can buy with that money) or from an hour of leisure time, which you might spend playing with your kids, watching the latest episode of *Game of Thrones*, or reading this book. The higher the wage rate, the more things you can buy, the more utility you gain from those things, and the more attractive work becomes relative to leisure.*

The demand curve slopes downward because, at higher wage levels, employers will not want to hire as many employees. Some companies may be able to replace workers with machines (substituting capital for labor). Others may scale back their operations or even go out of business. As in any market, the natural price ($6 per hour in Figure 4.1) is the one at which supply equals demand: the number of people willing to work for $6 per hour equals the number of jobs available at that wage. The people to the left of the supply-demand intersection—those willing to work for $6 per hour or less—have jobs. The people to the right, who demand more than $6 to give up one hour of their time, are not employed; but this is actually a good thing, because they prefer one hour of leisure time to $6. If one of them were to get a

---

* Ordinary demand curves themselves are based on the concept of utility. The demand curve for snow shovels shows, for each price, how many people get more utility from owning a shovel than from owning the other things they could buy with the money.

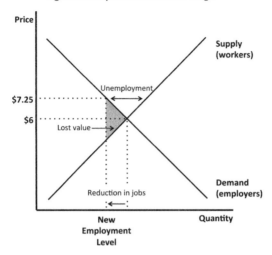

Figure 4.2: Impact of a Minimum Wage

job, society would actually be worse off: either that person would be earning less than the value she places on her own time, or her employer would be paying her more than her work is worth. This is the best of all possible worlds.

A minimum wage upsets this happy equilibrium because it sets a price floor in the market for labor. If it is below the natural wage rate, then nothing changes. But if the minimum is above the natural wage (say, $7.25 per hour), as in Figure 4.2, it distorts the market. More people want jobs at $7.25 than at $6, but companies want to hire fewer employees. The result: more unemployment. The people who are still employed are better off, because they are being paid more for the same work; their gain is exactly balanced by their employers' loss. But society as a whole is worse off. That little shaded triangle of "lost value" in Figure 4.2 represents transactions that would have benefited both buyers and suppliers of labor but that will not occur because of the minimum wage. These are jobs that someone would have been willing to do for less than $6 per hour and for which some company would have been willing to pay more than $6 per hour. Now those jobs are gone, as well as the goods and services that they would have produced. A minimum wage is a law that "prohibit[s] mutually beneficial exchanges between buyers and sellers," write William Baumol and Alan Blinder in their textbook, and so "a willing worker is condemned to remain unemployed because the wage she is offered is 'too low.'"[6]

The minimum wage has been a hobgoblin of economism since its origins. Henry Hazlitt wrote in *Economics in One Lesson*, "For a low wage you substitute unemployment. You do harm all around, with no comparable compensation." In *Capitalism and Freedom*, Milton Friedman patronizingly described the minimum wage as "about as clear a case as one can find of a measure the effects of which are precisely the opposite of those intended by the men of good will who support it." Because employers will not pay people more money than their work is worth, he continued, "insofar as minimum wage laws have any effect at all, their effect is clearly to increase poverty." Jude Wanniski similarly concluded in *The Way the World Works*, "Every increase in the minimum wage induces a decline in real output and a decline in employment." On the campaign trail in 1980, Ronald Reagan said, "The minimum wage has caused more misery and unemployment than anything since the Great Depression."[7] Cato, Heritage, and the Manhattan Institute have reliably attacked the minimum wage for decades, all the while emphasizing the key lesson from Economics 101: higher wages cause employers to cut jobs.[8]

In today's environment of increasing economic inequality, the minimum wage is a centerpiece of political debate. California, New York City, and Seattle are all raising their minimums to $15, and President Barack Obama called for a federal minimum of $10.10. An army of commentators has responded by reminding us of what we should have learned in Economics 101. In *The Wall Street Journal*, the economist Richard Vedder explained, "If the price of something rises, people buy less of it—including labor.

Thus governmental interferences such as minimum-wage laws lower the quantity of labor demanded." Writing for *Forbes*, Tim Worstall offered a mathematical proof: "A reduction in wage costs of some few thousand dollars increases employment. Obviously therefore a rise in wage costs of four or five times that is going to have significant unemployment effects. QED: A $15 minimum wage is going to destroy many jobs." (Of theoretical arguments in favor of a higher minimum wage, he continued, "I'm afraid I really just don't believe those arguments.") Jonah Goldberg of the American Enterprise Institute and *National Review* chimed in, "A minimum wage is no different from a tax on firms that use low-wage and unskilled labor. And if there's anything that economists agree upon, it's that if you tax something you get less of it."[9]

IN THE REAL WORLD

The real impact of the minimum wage, however, is much less clear than these talking points might indicate. Looking at historical experience, there is no obvious relationship between the minimum wage and unemployment: adjusted for inflation, the federal minimum was highest from 1967 through 1969, when the unemployment rate was below 4 percent—a historically low level.[10] When real economists try to tackle this question, they come up with all sorts of results. In 1994, David Card and Alan Krueger evaluated an increase in New Jersey's minimum wage by comparing fast-food restaurants on both sides of the New Jersey–Pennsylvania border. They concluded, "Contrary to the central prediction of the textbook model . . . we find no evidence that the rise in New Jersey's minimum wage reduced employment at fast-food restaurants in the state."[11]

Card and Krueger's findings have been vigorously contested across dozens of empirical studies. Today, people on both sides of the debate can cite papers supporting their position, and reviews of the academic research disagree on what conclusions to draw. David Neumark and William Wascher, economists who have long argued against the minimum wage, reviewed more than one hundred empirical papers in 2006. Although the studies had a wide range of results, they concluded that the "preponderance of the evidence" indicated that a higher minimum wage does increase unemployment. On the other hand, two recent meta-studies (which pool together the results of multiple analyses) have found that increasing the minimum wage does not have a significant impact on employment.[12] In the past several years, a new round of sophisticated analyses comparing changes in employment levels between neighboring counties also found "strong earnings effects and no employment effects of minimum wage increases." (That is, the number of jobs stays the same and workers make more money.) Not surprisingly, Neumark and Wascher have contested this approach.[13] The profession as a whole is evenly divided on the topic: when the University of Chicago Booth School of Business asked a panel of prominent economists in 2013 whether increasing the minimum wage to $9 would "make it noticeably harder for low-skilled workers to find employment," the responses were split down the middle.[14]

The idea that a higher minimum wage might not increase unemployment runs directly counter to the lessons of Economics 101. According to the textbook, if labor becomes more expensive, companies buy less of it. But there are several reasons why the real world does not behave so predictably. Although the standard model predicts that employers will replace workers with machines if wages increase, additional laborsaving technologies are not available to every company at a reasonable cost. Small employers in particular have limited flexibility; at their scale, they may not be able to maintain their operations with fewer workers. (Imagine a local copy shop: no matter how fast the copy machine, you still need one person to deal with customers.) Therefore, some companies can't lay off employees if the minimum wage is increased. At the other extreme, very large employers may have enough market power that the usual supply-and-demand model doesn't apply to them. They can reduce the wage level by hiring fewer workers (only those willing to work for low pay); a minimum wage forces them to pay more, which makes it profitable for them to hire more employees.

In the above examples, a higher minimum wage will raise labor costs. But many companies can recoup cost increases in the form of higher prices; because most of their customers are not poor, the net effect is to transfer money from higher-income to lower-income families. In addition, companies that pay more often benefit from higher employee productivity, offsetting the growth in labor costs.* Justin Wolfers and Jan Zilinsky identified several reasons why higher wages boost productivity: they motivate people to work harder, they attract higher-skilled workers, and they reduce employee turnover, lowering hiring and training costs, among other things. If fewer people quit their jobs, that also reduces the number of people who are out of work at any one time because they're looking for something better.[15] A higher minimum wage motivates more people to enter the labor force, raising both employment and output.† Finally, higher pay increases workers' buying power. Because poor people spend a relatively large proportion of their income, a higher minimum wage can boost overall economic activity and stimulate economic growth, creating more jobs. All of these factors vastly complicate the two-dimensional diagram taught in Economics 101 and help explain why a higher minimum wage does not necessarily throw people out of work.[16] The supply-and-demand diagram is a good

---

* In theory, if firms knew that higher wages would increase productivity, they would already be paying those higher wages, but in real life firms are not omniscient.
† The standard model says that if these people can get jobs at the higher minimum wage, they could have gotten the same jobs at the same wages under the lower minimum wage. But people don't necessarily know that, because they don't know their marginal productivity.

conceptual starting point for thinking about the minimum wage. But on its own, it has limited predictive value in our much more complex real world.

Even if a higher minimum wage does cause some people to lose their jobs, that cost has to be balanced against the benefit of greater earnings for other low-income workers. A study by the Congressional Budget Office (CBO) estimated that a $10.10 minimum would reduce employment by 500,000 jobs but would increase incomes for most poor families, moving 900,000 people above the poverty line. Similarly, a recent paper by the economist Arindrajit Dube finds that a 10 percent raise in the minimum wage should reduce the number of families living in poverty by around 2 percent to 3 percent.[17] The economists polled in the 2013 Chicago Booth study thought that increasing the minimum wage would be a good idea because its potential impact on employment would be outweighed by the benefits to people who were still able to find jobs.[18] Raising the minimum wage would also reduce inequality by narrowing the pay gap between low-income and higher-income workers.[19]

In short, whether the minimum wage should be increased (or eliminated) is a complicated question. The economic research is difficult to parse, and arguments often turn on sophisticated econometric details. Any change in the minimum wage would have different effects on different groups of people, and should also be compared with other policies that could help the working poor—such as the negative income tax (a cash grant to low-income households, similar to today's Earned Income Tax Credit) favored by Milton Friedman, or the guaranteed minimum income that Friedrich Hayek assumed would exist.[20]

Nevertheless, when the topic reaches the national stage, it is economism's facile punch line that gets delivered, along with its all-purpose dismissal: people who want a higher minimum wage just don't understand economics (although, by that standard, several Nobel Prize winners don't understand economics[21]). Many leading political figures largely repeat the central theses of economism, claiming that they have only the best interests of the poor at heart. In the 2016 presidential campaign, Senator Marco Rubio opposed increasing the minimum wage because companies would then substitute capital for labor: "I'm worried about the people whose wage is going to go down to zero because you've made them more expensive than a machine." Senator Ted Cruz also chimed in on behalf of the poor, saying, "the minimum wage consistently hurts the most vulnerable." Senator Rand Paul explained, "when the [minimum wage] is above the market wage it causes unemployment" because it reduces the number of employees whom companies can afford to hire. The former governor Jeb Bush also invoked Economics 101, saying that wages should be left "to the private sector," meaning companies like Walmart, which "raised wages because of supply and demand." For Congressman Paul Ryan, raising the minimum wage is "bad economics" and "will hurt the economy because it raises the price of labor."[22]

This conviction that the minimum wage hurts the poor is an example of economism in action. Economists have many different opinions on the subject, based on different theories and research studies, but when it comes to public debate, one particular result of one particular model is presented as an unassailable economic theorem. (Politicians advocating for a higher minimum wage, by contrast, tend to avoid economic models altogether, instead arguing in terms of fairness or helping the poor.) This happens partly because the competitive market model taught in introductory economics classes is simple, clear, and memorable. But it also happens because there is a large interest group that wants to keep the minimum wage low: businesses that rely heavily on cheap labor.

The restaurant industry has been a major force behind the advertising and public relations campaigns opposing the minimum wage, including many of the op-ed articles repeating the basic lesson of supply and demand.[23] For example, the CEO of a restaurant company explained in *The Wall Street Journal*, "Every retailer has locations that are profitable, but only marginally. Increased labor costs can push these stores over the line and into the loss column. When that happens, companies that want to stay competitive will close them." As a result, "broad increases in the minimum wage destroy jobs and hurt the working-class Americans that they are supposed to help."[24] A recent study by researchers at the Cornell School of Hotel Administration, however, found that higher minimum wages have not affected either the number of restaurants or the number of people that they employ, contrary to the industry's dire predictions, while they have modestly increased workers' pay.[25] Because restaurant closings do not increase, the implication is that paying employees more cuts into excess profits—profits beyond those necessary to stay in business. Or, as the financial commentator Barry Ritholtz put it, "raising the minimum wage works as a wealth transfer, from shareholders and franchisees, to minimum wage workers."[26] But instead of greedily demanding higher profits, industry executives can invoke Economics 101, which provides a simple explanation of the world that serves their interests.

The fact that this is the debate we are having already demonstrates the historical influence of economism. Once upon a time, the major issue affecting workers' wages and income inequality was unionization. In the 1950s, about one in every three wage and salary employees was a union member.[27] Unions, of course, were an early and frequent target of economism. Hayek argued that unions are bad both for workers, because "they cannot in the long run increase real wages for all wishing to work above the level that would establish itself in a free market," and for society as a whole, because "by establishing effective monopolies in the supply of the different kinds of labor, the unions will prevent competition from acting as an effective regulator of the allocation of all resources." For Friedman, unions "harmed the public at large and workers as a whole by distorting the use of labor" while increasing inequality even within the working class.[28] The changing composition of the U.S. workforce, state right-to-work laws, and aggressive anti-unionization tactics by employers—increasingly tolerated by the National Labor Relations Board, beginning with the Reagan administration—all contributed to a long, slow fall in unionization levels. By 2015, only 12 percent of wage and salary employees were union members—fewer than 7 percent in the private sector.[29] Low- and middle-income workers' reduced bargaining power is a major reason why their wages have not kept pace with the overall growth of the economy. According to an analysis by the sociologists Bruce Western and Jake Rosenfeld, one-fifth to one-third of the increase in inequality between 1973 and 2007 results from the decline of unions.[30]

With unions only a distant memory for many people, federal minimum-wage legislation has become the best hope for propping up wages for low-income workers. And again, the worldview of economism comes to the aid of employers by abstracting away from the reality of low-wage work to a pristine world ruled by the "law" of supply and demand. As Senator Paul said, "This is an economic argument. This is something that should be done in a rational way, not an emotional way."[31] Perhaps most important for a politician, this kind of rhetoric sounds better than saying that you are carrying water for the businesses and business owners that you rely on to finance your reelection. In the campaign to ensure cheap labor for America's restaurants and hotels, economism functions both as an effective debating tool and as a way of distracting attention from the real issues.

THE VIEW FROM THE TOP

Stagnant wages for the working class are only one reason for today's staggering levels of inequality in the United States, where the top 0.1 percent have as much wealth as the bottom 90 percent. The other reason is that the rich have been getting much, much richer. Rapid increases in labor compensation at the very top are a major reason why income inequality has soared in recent decades. Since 2010, the top 0.1 percent of households have taken home, on average, more than 10 percent of all income in the United States—up from less than 3 percent in the 1970s.[32] This explosion of rewards has mainly been concentrated among a few small groups of superstars: corporate executives, particularly CEOs; financial professionals, especially fund managers; and founders of public companies.

Since the late 1970s, the average total compensation (including salary, bonus, stock awards, and other perks) of large company CEOs has grown by more than 900 percent, after adjusting for inflation—to more than $15 million a year—while wages for frontline employees have gone up by only 10 percent. While CEOs of large companies made about twenty times as much as the average worker in the 1950s, today they make two hundred times as much.[33] At the high end, they can gain astronomical rewards. Robert Nardelli, for example, was paid more than $120 million for six years of work at Home Depot and then received a $210 million severance package when he resigned in 2007, even though the company's stock price was flat during his tenure (which included a raging housing boom).[34] Corporate CEOs, however, make a pittance compared to star hedge fund and private equity fund managers. In 2014 (which was not an especially good year), twenty-five fund managers made at least $175 million each, and three made more than $1 billion.[35] Technology start-ups, too, have their fair share of billionaires: the list of the eleven richest people in America includes the founders of Microsoft, Oracle, Amazon, Facebook, Bloomberg, and Google.[36]

America has always celebrated its winners and idolized the rich. Today, however, there is a widespread perception that society has become too unequal.* Surely something must be wrong

---

* This is the case even though most people have no idea just how unequal American society has become. On average, Americans think that the richest 20 percent of the population own 59 percent of all wealth, when in fact they own far more.[37]

with a world that pays one person more than $1 billion a year to manage other people's money.

PAY = PRODUCTIVITY

Or not. According to the principles of economism, the people raking in the big bucks are worth every penny. Remember, labor is bought and sold in a market. Let's say the market wage for factory workers is $20 per hour. If hiring one more employee would increase a manufacturing company's production by more than $20 per hour, it will hire that person. Conversely, if firing one worker would reduce the company's output by less than $20 per hour, one person will find herself out of a job. The company will adjust its workforce until adding or subtracting one person would increase or decrease its production by exactly $20 per hour. At that point, the workers' wages are equal to their *marginal product:* the amount of value that each person contributes to the company. In Henry Hazlitt's words, "The more [an individual worker] produces, the more his services are worth to consumers, and hence to employers. And the more he is worth to employers, the more he will be paid."[38]

There's nothing special about factory workers, so the same principles hold for everyone. The universal rule is that workers are paid the value of their marginal product; if that were not the case, companies would be better off hiring more employees or laying some off. So if Goldman Sachs's CEO, Lloyd Blankfein, made $24 million in 2014, that's because he was worth $24 million to his company.[39] In short, you make what you deserve based on your skills, effort, and productivity, in this fairest of all possible worlds.

Economism provides the perfect justification for the winner-take-all reward scale—at least from the winner's point of view. The competitive market model of Economics 101 rationalizes inequality by explaining it as the inevitable outcome of a system in which compensation is determined by the free exchange of labor. And it celebrates unequal outcomes as the best possible way to maximize social welfare. People must be paid the value of their output. If they are paid too much, labor costs will be too high, and companies will cut back on production; if they are paid too little, they will work less and take more leisure time. Milton Friedman summarized this key principle in *Capitalism and Freedom:* "Payment in accordance with product is therefore necessary in order that resources be used most effectively."[40]

So whenever people raise questions about whether top executives are paid too much—whether, say, Michael Ovitz deserved the $140 million parting gift he received from Disney when he was fired after a little more than a year on the job[41]—economism's adherents remind us of the fundamental law of supply and demand. According to *The Wall Street Journal*'s editorial page, CEO pay isn't exorbitant, because it's set by the market; people who claim otherwise are simply seething with "executive envy." In the wake of the recent financial crisis, Mark Calabria of Cato argued that executive compensation "could simply reflect the efficient outcome of market processes." In *Forbes,* the economist Jeffrey Dorfman reiterated that "employees get paid what employees are worth." As for top executives, "CEO pay may or may not be too high, but until somebody compares their pay to the marginal profit they have brought to their companies, we won't know." The liberal economist Robert Reich claimed that CEOs, like movie stars, make "mammoth sums" because "they're still small compared to the money these stars bring in and the profits they generate."[42] The former senator Phil Gramm took this logic even further, saying of Ed Whitacre, who retired from AT&T with a $158 million severance package, "If there's ever been an exploited worker . . . the man added billions of dollars of value. He was exploited. It was an outrage."[43]

HOW THE RICH GOT THAT WAY

However, the simple principle that pay equals marginal product has little to do with how the world actually works. It certainly isn't true for the economy as a whole. In the United States, growth in wages closely tracked increases in productivity from the late 1940s until the early 1970s; since then, however, wages have risen much more slowly than productivity.[44] This divergence highlights the possibility that pay levels are determined by negotiating power, not pure productivity.

Nowhere is this more true than in the executive suite. The idea that good CEOs are entitled to enormous rewards is based on the belief that the success or failure of a company depends on one person—what historian Nancy Koehn calls the business version of the Great Man theory of history. Instead, business is a team sport: not only is it impossible to quantify a single leader's marginal product; it's hard even to describe it clearly.[45] Because no one knows what a CEO is worth, her pay is whatever she can convince her corporation's board of directors to give her. This is hardly an arm's-length negotiation, however. The CEO is usually the most powerful person on the board to begin with. In half of Fortune 500 companies, the CEO serves as the chair of the board. Even without that title, a CEO still has disproportionate influence because of her knowledge, her relationships, and the fact that she is difficult to replace quickly. A savvy CEO can recruit allies and place them on the compensation committee, which recommends her compensation package, typically based on an analysis of similar companies—a comparison group that can be weighted toward those with highly paid CEOs. The committee invariably proposes to pay at least as much as the median comparable company, because no board wants to admit that its company has a below-average leader. Some portion of the package will be linked to certain performance targets, but the CEO can encourage the committee to select metrics that will be easy to satisfy.[46] Finally, as Warren Buffett puts it, "When the compensation committee—armed, as always, with support from a high-paid consultant—reports on a mega-grant of options to the CEO, it would be like belching at the dinner table for a director to suggest that the committee reconsider." The economist John Kenneth Galbraith described it perfectly: "The salary of the chief executive of the large corporation is not a market reward for achievement. It is frequently in the nature of a warm personal gesture by the individual to himself."[47]

As with the minimum wage, there is a serious debate among economists about whether CEOs' pay is related to the value they provide their companies. While leaders matter, says the management professor Sydney Finkelstein, "luck also plays a much bigger role than anyone wants to talk about." A 2001 study by Marianne Bertrand and Sendhil Mullainathan found that high CEO pay is often the result of dumb luck. For example, they found that heads of oil companies were paid more when profits increased, even when those profits were simply due to rising oil prices.[48] Lucian Bebchuk and several co-authors have argued that corporations that pay their CEOs the most are poorly governed and fare no better than other companies in general. Other economists, however, have defended CEO pay practices. Steven Kaplan and Joshua Rauh have found that CEOs' realized compensation—the amount they ultimately collect when they sell their stock—is highest at companies that do the best in the stock market, relative to their industries. Kaplan has also argued that boards actually do a good job at firing under-performing leaders and that, in the end, high compensation is simply the result of supply and demand in the "market for talent."[49]

The dynamics of high compensation are different on Wall Street, but here again the connection between pay and performance is murky at best. Many financial institutions pride themselves on tying individual compensation to marginal product. Traders' and investment bankers' bonuses are based on the profitability of their own deals: you eat what you kill, in banker-speak. But because a bonus can never be negative, individual employees can generate enormous payouts on bets that turn out well while sticking shareholders with the losses on bets that go bad. This dynamic was visible during the financial crisis that peaked in 2008. At AIG Financial Products (a division of AIG, the world's largest insurance company), for example, 30 percent of profits went into a bonus pool, from which the CEO, Joseph Cassano, received at least $38 million every year from 2002 to 2007.[50] But those "profits" were due to bets that went horribly wrong in 2008, leading to AIG's collapse and takeover by the U.S. government. With this kind of compensation system, seven- and eight-figure bonus checks can be a reward for outsmarting the markets, but they can also be the product of dumb luck—a big bet turning out right or at least not going bad before bonuses are paid.

The same principles apply in the world of high-end asset management, the most lucrative segment of the financial industry. The partners of hedge fund and private equity fund firms manage other people's money for "two and twenty"—2 percent of invested assets plus 20 percent of the investment returns. This means that if you manage $10 billion and earn a 10 percent return—not bad, but often not particularly spectacular—you earn $400 million: 2 percent of assets comes to $200 million, and 20 percent of the returns comes to another $200 million. That princely sum is a service fee paid by clients (the investors in the fund), so Economics 101 says it must be right—or else the clients wouldn't pay it.

But the economics of chance apply here as well as on Wall Street: given the way the markets work, some of the fund managers taking home big performance fees are simply the beneficiaries of luck. That said, the true superstars, like James Simons of Renaissance Technologies and Ray Dalio of Bridgewater, have delivered exceptional returns for decades—suggesting that talent may have something to do with it. Yet even these examples don't prove that we live in the best of all possible worlds. In the earlier example, a factory worker's marginal product is $20 per hour because she creates $20 of value—for example, taking raw materials worth $5 and turning them into a product that sells for $25 (because it provides $25 of value to a consumer). But buying low and selling high in the secondary securities markets doesn't produce billions of dollars' worth of tangible output that anyone can consume. In theory, there is economic value to this type of gambling, but its benefits are hard to quantify in meaningful terms. And in some cases, profitable trading strategies might have helped to perpetuate the subprime bubble and magnify the impact of the financial crisis[51]—just as AIG Financial Products' ill-fated bet on subprime bonds ended up freezing the financial system in September 2008. Seen from the perspective of their clients, maybe some star fund managers do earn their pay. From the perspective of society, however, it's not clear that it has anything to do with their marginal product.

The last group of winners in today's winner-take-all economy includes Bill Gates, Mark Zuckerberg, Jeff Bezos, Larry Page, Sergey Brin, and the late Steve Jobs—widely admired technology titans whose stock in their own companies became worth billions of dollars. A company's stock price reflects the future profits that it is expected to earn, and profits are certainly one measure of the value a company creates for its customers,* so perhaps the enormous riches of these start-up rock stars are warranted by their contributions to society. It's important to note first that, despite their fame, technology entrepreneurs are the exception, not the rule, among the economic elite; in 2005, a majority of the top 0.1 percent were corporate executives or financial professionals,

---

* Profits are the difference between revenues and costs, so you can think of them as the value that a company creates by taking a certain set of inputs (capital, labor, raw materials, and so on) and turning them into products that customers value more highly.

while only 3 percent were in technical fields.[52] Even for these modern heroes, it's not obvious that their wealth simply reflects their productivity. Consider Gates, the co-founder of Microsoft and the richest man in America. The key products that made Microsoft the world's largest software company included Windows, Office, and Internet Explorer—none of which was first to market in their category. Thanks in part to Gates's strategic acumen, Microsoft outmaneuvered its competitors and seized dominant positions in the markets for desktop operating systems, productivity software, and browsers, giving it a large share of the profits in those markets for decades. Without Gates and Microsoft, however, some other companies would have captured those profits, and some other people would be worth tens of billions of dollars. The same is true of Oracle, which was just one relational database among many in the 1980s, or Facebook, which was preceded by Friendster and Myspace, among others. In markets characterized by network effects—where having a large number of customers makes your product more attractive to other people—a small number of winners tend to reap a disproportionate share of the rewards.

And often what separates the winners from the also-rans is just a matter of luck. So many things can go wrong between founding a company and eventually going public that, even if an entrepreneur does everything right, success still depends on her company's ability to dodge the slings and arrows of outrageous fortune—cancellation of early customer projects, departure of key employees, economic recession, and so on. In a survey by the Kauffman Foundation, 73 percent of entrepreneurs agreed that good fortune was an important factor in their start-ups' success.[53] Founding technology companies is a little like playing the lottery—and no one would claim that lottery payouts are determined by the winners' marginal productivity. According to the Economics 101 labor model, Bill Gates's enormous wealth must be the result of his superhuman productivity. Anyone familiar with the technology world, however, recognizes that it is largely owed to timing, good fortune, and mistakes by his competitors. In any case, we should question a model in which Gates's work was worth billions of dollars a year while the work of Tim Berners-Lee, the inventor of the modern Internet, was worth virtually nothing by comparison because he never founded a company.

When we look at the people making the big money—whether Fortune 500 CEOs, Wall Street masters of the universe, or Silicon Valley tycoons—it is questionable whether Economics 101 has anything meaningful to say about their compensation. In each area, pay has only a tangential relationship to marginal product, from society's perspective, and often depends simply on luck. (Hayek was well aware of this phenomenon; in *The Road to Serfdom*, he wrote, "in competition chance and good luck are often as important as skill and foresight in determining the fate of different people."[54]) It is also unclear that such huge paydays are necessary for the optimal allocation of labor. According to the model, if companies pay people less than their work is worth, they may choose to do something less valuable. But this is not how the richest executives, fund managers, and technology entrepreneurs seem to make decisions; the money they already make so far dwarfs the amount they could consume in a lifetime that they are free to choose whatever job or activity gives them the most personal satisfaction. The ones who continue to work do so because they enjoy it or because it gives them a feeling of accomplishment that they cannot realize through other means.

Why should ordinary people care about whether or not corporate CEOs and fund managers really deserve to make hundreds as opposed to tens of millions of dollars? First, poorly designed pay packages can have harmful effects both on the companies paying them and on the economy as a whole. Excessive compensation reduces profits for shareholders, a group that includes not just the wealthy but also ordinary people whose retirement funds are invested in the stock market. In addition, awards linked to short-term targets that can be manipulated by insiders can cause executives to make decisions that maximize their bonuses but harm the company in the long run. For example, if a CEO is evaluated based on her company's quarterly results, she may boost profits by reducing expenditures on research and development—investments that only pay off years later. More worryingly, the allure of massive bonuses was one reason why major financial institutions were so eager to take on risk in the years leading up to the recent financial crisis. From mortgage brokers whose commissions were based on the value of the loans they originated to CEOs whose stock awards were closely tied to their banks' stock price, people responded to these compensation plans by pumping up deal volumes and placing increasingly one-sided bets. This tremendous appetite for risk helped inflate the housing bubble and ensured that when it finally collapsed, some of the world's largest financial institutions collapsed along with it.

When anyone argues that excessive compensation is a problem, however, economism comes to the defense of the status quo. After the financial crisis, reforming compensation practices seemed to be one logical step toward building a safer financial system. However, the mere thought of government regulation provoked vociferous opposition from the usual suspects among think tanks and media outlets. David Mason of the Heritage Foundation, for example, opposed government intervention because market forces necessarily prevent excess compensation: "In a well-functioning market, firms that pay executives above their market worth eventually suffer."[55] The Dodd-Frank financial reform act ended up mandating only a few modest rules— most notably, that corporations solicit a *nonbinding* shareholder vote to approve the compensation of their top executives and that they disclose the ratio of pay between their CEO and their median worker. These provisions might modestly strengthen the hand of shareholders but are unlikely to have much impact on current pay practices.

Both at the bottom and at the top of the income distribution, economism explains that everything is fine just the way it is: a higher minimum wage would only hurt the working poor, while the riches of CEOs and fund managers are a mere side effect of their astonishing productivity. The simple model of the labor market taught in first-year classes—in which both fast-food restaurant workers and business superstars are paid what they deserve—provides the perfect conceptual framework to justify poverty at one end of the workforce and aristocratic excess at the other. According to economism, extreme income inequality is natural because it results from market processes; it is optimal because it ensures the most efficient allocation of labor; and it is moral because everyone receives her just deserts. The idea that the collective product of society should be distributed more equally can be dismissed as a fantasy of well-meaning but soft-headed reformers.

For centuries, who should get what has been a central political question. Economism removes the question from the political sphere to the abstract realm of theory, in which the competitive labor market provides the perfect, indisputable solution. In aristocratic societies such as eighteenth-century France or nineteenth-century Russia, wealthy noblemen who owed their riches to the accident of birth had to worry about the prospect of violent rebellion by the have-nots. In the United States today, by contrast, the wealthy are protected by the widespread belief that their extraordinary incomes—and the inequality that they generate—are simply the product of inescapable economic necessity.

5

Incentives Are Everything

To help the poor and middle classes, one must cut the tax rates of the rich.

—George Gilder, 1981[1]

Warren Buffett, one of the three richest people in the world, pays taxes at a lower rate than his secretary. That doesn't exactly seem fair; Buffett himself recommended raising taxes on people who make more than $1 million per year.[2] Collecting more from the very rich would also mitigate the extreme inequality that has resulted from the combination of stagnant wages for ordinary people and extravagant rewards for executives, fund managers, and entrepreneurs.

In theory, the United States already has a progressive tax system, which means that the wealthy are supposed to pay a higher percentage of their income than the middle class—but things don't always work out that way. The federal tax rate on income from work can be as high as 39.6 percent, but the rate that applies to income from investments is much lower: up to 20 percent for most *capital gains* (profits from selling something for more than it cost) and *dividends* (cash payments by corporations to their shareholders). Most income is also subject to a 15.3 percent payroll tax that funds Social Security and Medicare, but the bulk of that tax only applies to income up to $120,000, so it consumes a larger portion of pay for the working poor than for the well-off. The picture gets more complicated still when you consider things like tax-preferred savings accounts, carried interest, or fancy tax shelters. The bottom line is that although many rich people do pay a lot to the Internal Revenue Service, it's quite easy for someone like Buffett, who makes his money from investments, to pay a lower overall tax rate than ordinary working people. Inspired by his example, President Barack Obama proposed the "Buffett Rule": a minimum tax of 30 percent on any family making more than $1 million per year.

DEADWEIGHT TRIANGLES

Unfortunately, this will only make things worse for everyone—at least according to Economics 101. One of the core principles of economism is that taxes are very, very bad. As usual, you can make the argument easily using a supply-and-demand diagram. Let's

Figure 5.1: Impact of a Tax

say there is a $5 tax on the sale of each snow shovel. As we learned earlier, the market price without a tax is $15, but now if you pay $15 for a shovel, the seller only gets to keep $10 after passing $5 on to the IRS. What happens to the supply curve? Because suppliers' choices depend on the actual amount they get to keep after taxes, the quantity supplied is lower at any sale price: the supply curve shifts to the left, as in Figure 5.1. (The demand curve doesn't change, because consumers only care about the actual amount they have to pay.) The market reaches a new equilibrium with a higher total price and, unfortunately, a lower quantity of goods manufactured and sold.

This is no longer the best of all possible worlds. Without the tax, the entire area between the supply and the demand curves to the left of their intersection is "social welfare" (recall Figure 2.5): the difference between the manufacturing cost of snow shovels and their value to consumers. In Figure 5.2, we can see the impact of a tax. Consumer surplus is now the difference between the value people place on snow shovels (the demand curve) and the total price they pay, including the tax. Producer surplus is the dif-

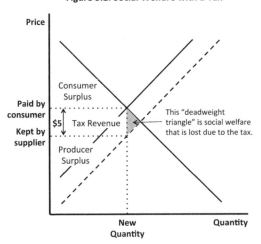

Figure 5.2: Social Welfare with a Tax

ference between the after-tax amount that suppliers get to keep and their costs of production (the original supply curve, shown by a dashed line). The rectangle in between is the government's revenue: the amount of the tax (the height of the rectangle) times the number of shovels sold (the width). But that last, shaded triangle represents value that is destroyed. The source of that value was the fact that companies could make and sell those shovels for less than consumers were willing to pay for them, leaving both sides better off. With the tax, however, those transactions will not occur, and there will be fewer shovels in the world. Since this argument applies equally to any market, a tax on anything causes the economy to produce less of it.*

That sad little triangle is a "deadweight triangle," and it is one of the abiding images of Economics 101. Long after students have forgotten the name of their professor or the assumptions behind the competitive market model, they remember that triangle and its lesson: taxes are bad. Granted, most textbooks recognize that the government must be funded somehow, because it is necessary to maintain a market system (by paying for police, courts, and national defense, at a minimum). They also concede that a tax may occasionally correct for a market malfunction; for example, making people pay a little more for gasoline, natural gas, and electricity could prevent them from burning too much fossil fuel. But the overriding lesson remains the same: taxes should be avoided whenever possible.

This is particularly true of the labor market. Income is the money that workers receive for selling labor; the supply curve shows how much people are willing to work for different amounts of money. Whatever your wage, an income tax reduces your take-home pay, the amount of goods and services you can buy, and

---

* Technically speaking, this welfare loss only occurs if there are no adjacent, untaxed markets that consumers can shift into. This detail, however, is usually forgotten except by economists and tax specialists.

therefore the utility you gain from working an extra hour; by comparison, an additional hour of leisure time becomes more attractive. On average, people will choose to work less and take more time off (or simply retire).* In other words, an income tax shifts the labor supply curve to the left, reducing the amount of work done in the economy. There is a deadweight triangle of transactions between workers and businesses (jobs) that no longer exist. More people are unemployed, and fewer goods and services are produced for everyone to consume.

THE ANTITAX CHORUS

The idea that higher taxes discourage people from working and therefore make society worse off is probably the single most deeply entrenched tenet of economism. The argument is a staple of the antitax movement that has strengthened its hold on the American political system over the past forty years. In the 1940s, Henry Hazlitt wrote, "[Income] taxes inevitably affect the actions and incentives of those from whom they are taken. . . . People begin to ask themselves why they should work six, eight or ten months of the entire year for the government, and only six, four or two months for themselves and their families." In *Capitalism and Freedom*, Milton Friedman bemoaned the effects of high taxes: "If present rates were made fully effective [that is, if people actually paid the rates set by law], the effect on incentives and the like might well be so serious as to cause a radical loss in the productivity of the society." More recently, Gregory Mankiw—the successful economics textbook author—explained that he routinely turns down moneymaking opportunities because of taxes.

---

* Some people may actually work more, especially if lower take-home wages mean they need to work longer just to make ends meet. However, the standard lesson on incentives in the labor market tends to emphasize the fact that work is less attractive if you make less money for it.

People with high incomes "respond to incentives," he concluded, and so "as they face higher tax rates, their services will be in shorter supply." In *The Wall Street Journal*, Holman Jenkins aptly summarized the party line: "America's well-being is determined by the incentives we allow our domestic citizens to work, save, invest and start businesses."[3]

Politicians have learned the lesson. When President Obama proposed the Buffett Rule in 2011, the House Speaker, John Boehner, responded, "Tax increases destroy jobs." Paul Ryan, then House Budget Committee chair, repeated the central Economics 101 principle: "If you tax something more, you get less of it." More recently, Ryan again donned his economics-teacher hat to add, "Growth occurs on the margin, which is a wonky way of saying, if you want faster economic growth, more upward mobility, and faster job creation, lower tax rates across the board is the key."[4]

In the 2016 presidential election, every proposal to cut taxes flew under the banner of higher economic growth. Senators Mike Lee and Marco Rubio announced a "pro-growth" tax plan that reduced rates for businesses and individuals, and the Heritage Foundation praised it in standard Economics 101 terminology: "Lower rates improve incentives for working, saving, investing, and taking entrepreneurial risk, the basic components of economic growth. They do so by lowering the tax-imposed bias against work, savings, investment, and entrepreneurship."[5] Senators Ted Cruz and Rand Paul each proposed a flat tax—applying a single rate to all households—an idea that Friedman had put forward in *Capitalism and Freedom*.[6] According to Paul, lowering all individual and business tax rates to 14.5 percent would be "an economic steroid injection" because it "rewards work, saving, investment and small business creation." Cruz went even lower in proposing a flat 10 percent tax rate on individual income. "The virtue of a single tax rate is that the rate doesn't rise as people work more and invest more," he reasoned. "This means better incentives to increase output, and fewer distortions." The *Wall Street Journal* editorial writer James Freeman cheered, "Every serious GOP candidate is proposing significant reforms to increase the incentives to work, save and invest," which promised "an end to years of stagnation in jobs and wages."[7]

TAX CUTS FOR JOB CREATORS

It's not too surprising that the historical party of big business and the wealthy should prefer lower taxes. However, the influence of economism explains two otherwise curious features of today's tax-cutting frenzy. One is the explicit emphasis on reducing the tax burden for the very wealthy. In terms of simply buying votes, benefits for the middle class make the most sense (and are favored by most Democrats) because there are more middle-class families than corporate CEOs or hedge fund billionaires. Yet current proposals to cut taxes shower a large proportion of their largesse on the very rich. Any flat tax—whether Paul's 14.5 percent, Cruz's 10 percent, or Herman Cain's 9 percent (from the 2012 presidential election)—is obviously most welcome to those paying the highest rates today and meaningless to the many families that don't pay income tax at all under the current system. The plans put forward by Rubio, Cruz, Jeb Bush, and Donald Trump all promised much larger benefits (in percentage terms, not just dollars) to the highest-earning 1 percent than to all other income groups; a staggering 44 percent of Cruz's proposed tax cuts would go to the top 1 percent.[8]

The second curious pattern is the particular zeal politicians have for reducing or eliminating taxes on investment income—money you earn by sitting around and watching your assets grow. In 2010, Paul Ryan's plan eliminated individual income taxes on all interest, dividends, and capital gains; in the 2016 election, both Marco Rubio and Ben Carson made the same proposal.[9]

Because most investments are owned by the wealthy—that's what makes them wealthy—this bias helps the rich much more than the middle class, which again seems to defy political logic.

Both of these anomalies, however, make perfect sense through the lens of economism. First consider the focus on alleviating the financial burdens of the rich. Higher tax rates reduce the incentive to work for everyone. According to the logic of economism, however, this effect is especially pernicious when applied to the highest earners. For one thing, low- and middle-income people may respond to a tax increase by working more, simply because they need the money to survive or maintain their lifestyle; only the wealthy have the option to simply pull out of the workforce. More to the point, the people who make the most money also contribute the most to society; remember that income equals marginal product. In the world of Economics 101, therefore, it is especially important that the rich participate in the economy, thereby helping everyone else.

In *Economics in One Lesson*, Hazlitt warned that high taxes would deter people from starting businesses: "Old employers do not give more employment, or not as much more as they might have; and others decide not to become employers at all. . . . The result in the long run is that consumers are prevented from getting better and cheaper products, and that real wages are held down." In *The Way the World Works*, Wanniski told a fable about the owner of a pin factory who suddenly faces a high tax rate: "The entrepreneur, who had been planning expansion, now plans contraction. He had been planning to leave the plant to his son, but his son will not work the same long hours to be rewarded by barely more than the skilled workers, nor will anyone else's son." The sad tale ends with the factory closed and the workers unemployed. Today the stories are the same, except their heroes are called "job creators." A *Wall Street Journal* op-ed criticized even the Lee-Rubio tax plan for not reducing top rates enough: "The highest tax bracket is especially important as top earners produce the most and innovate the most. Incentivized by a low top rate, they will increase earnings more than those further down the income scale."[10] Raise taxes too much, in other words, and Steve Jobs and Steve Wozniak never build a computer in Jobs's garage.

The argument for reducing taxes on investment income also flows directly from Economics 101. In theory, there are two things you can do with money: spend it or save it. Spending it on goods and services is called *consumption:* if you buy a sandwich, you get to enjoy eating it, but it gets used up in the process. Saving money, however, means that it gets *invested* somewhere else in the economy. If you skip lunch and put your money in a bank account, the bank will lend it out—maybe to an entrepreneur starting a sandwich shop. If you buy stocks or bonds, the money will (indirectly) go to companies that are building factories and discovering new medicines. Those sandwich shops, factories, and pharmaceutical patents are all forms of *capital:* the assets that enable businesses to operate and hire workers. If we spent all of our money on sandwiches and saved none of it, there would be no money left over for *capital formation,* and the economy could not grow.*

In short, we need people to save, which means we need rich people to save—because they are the ones who have money left over after buying sandwiches (and clothes, and housing, and other necessities). If taxes on investment income are too high, the story goes, people won't bother putting their money in banks, stocks, or private equity funds. Instead, they'll just spend it on the upper-class equivalent of sandwiches. In 1976, Friedman explained that Rolls-Royces were common on London streets because rich people would rather buy luxury goods than save their money and pay high taxes on the returns. Friedrich Hayek, in *The Constitu-*

---

* Businesses could charge higher prices and reinvest part of their profits in capital goods. To an economist, however, that counts as savings by businesses. The key point is that savings are good.

tion of Liberty, warned of "the very serious effect of progressive taxation on the supply of savings." The columnist George Will echoed Hayek half a century later: "Progressive taxation reduces the rewards of investments and the real rate of return on savings, thereby encouraging consumption over saving and hence over capital formation."[11]

This is why economism preaches that taxes on investments should be as low as possible. In 2005, the Federal Reserve chair, Alan Greenspan, told a government tax reform panel, "Many economists believe that a consumption tax [which does not tax investments] would be best from the perspective of promoting economic growth . . . because a consumption tax is likely to encourage saving and capital formation." The same theme resonates through the budget proposals put forward in recent years by Paul Ryan's House Budget Committee: "Tax reform should promote savings and investment because more savings and more investment mean a larger stock of capital available for job creation. That means more jobs, more productivity, and higher wages for all American workers."[12] Democrats have occasionally sung a similar tune. In 1988, for example, the presidential candidate Bruce Babbitt argued for a national consumption tax because it would increase savings: "Unlike an income tax, this would apply only to what we spend, not what we save. That might encourage us all to save a little more, which would be good for our families and for the economy."[13]

The bottom line is that the key to economic growth is reducing tax rates on very high incomes and on investments. These are the core principles of "supply-side economics"—so named because these policies are supposed to encourage more people to work and to start businesses, boosting the overall supply of goods and services. (Supply-side economics was not originally taught in introductory classes, but it was derived directly from Economics 101 principles—specifically, the impact of tax rates on the labor market and on savings.) The doctrine was popularized by Wanniski, but it was also favored by the corporate sector. Organizations such as the Business Roundtable, a lobbying group made up of the CEOs of many large corporations, successfully pushed for reductions in capital gains taxes in the 1970s.[14] The adoption of supply-side ideas by Jack Kemp and then Ronald Reagan produced a lasting shift in U.S. tax policy. Describing his major 1981 tax cut, which reduced the top rate from 70 percent to 50 percent, Reagan said, "We have significantly restructured [the tax system] to encourage people to work, save, and invest more."[15] Wealthy investors won even greater victories in the George W. Bush administration, including lower rates on capital gains and dividends and a large reduction in the estate tax (levied on large fortunes when left to heirs). And the idea that tax cuts will unleash the entrepreneurial energies of job creators remains popular today because it provides useful cover for politicians who want to cater to their billionaire super PAC contributors while reassuring ordinary people that they are only thinking about overall economic growth. It is also equally convenient for rich people who prefer lower taxes but don't like to think of themselves as greedy.

SAVINGS, LABOR, AND GROWTH

But is it true? Take Warren Buffett, who made his vast fortune through investments. This is what he thinks:

> I have worked with investors for 60 years and I have yet to see anyone—not even when capital gains rates were 39.9 percent in 1976–77—shy away from a sensible investment because of the tax rate on the potential gain. People invest to make money, and potential taxes have never scared them off.[16]

On its face, this seems obvious. If you can buy something— a house, a share of stock, a company, whatever—for $100 when you think it is worth $200, why wouldn't you? A higher tax rate reduces your expected profit, but we're talking about people who can already consume anything they want to and still have large amounts of money left over. At the very high end of the wealth distribution, people invest most of their money because there's virtually nothing else they can do with it.

Or, on a much smaller scale, take me. In 2001, five friends and I founded a software company. At the time, I didn't even know what the tax rates on labor income and investment income were, and I doubt any of my colleagues bothered to check. We started the company because that's what we wanted to do, not because the tax system encouraged us to do it.[17]

Anecdotes cut both ways, of course. Gregory Mankiw, as mentioned earlier, says he turns down moneymaking opportunities because of taxes. As with any economic issue, it's more valuable to look at real-world data than to rely solely on theory or individual opinions. First, let's ask whether taxes on investments really do reduce savings and therefore economic growth. Looking at historical data, this seems unlikely. As Figure 5.3 shows, taxes on investment income have fallen precipitously in the United States

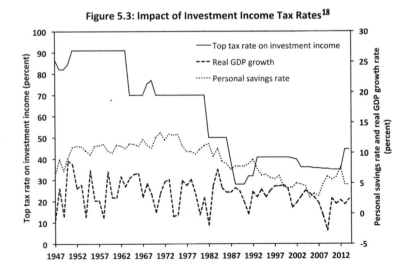

Figure 5.3: Impact of Investment Income Tax Rates[18]

over the past seventy years, with no obvious increase in either savings or growth. On average, the economy expanded most rapidly in the 1950s and 1960s—a period when the tax rates on most investment income were 70 percent or higher—and most slowly in the first decade of the twenty-first century, despite much lower tax rates. Personal savings rates have also been declining steadily since the early 1970s, even as taxes on investments have fallen.*

Simply comparing patterns of numbers across time can be misleading, however. This is why professional economists analyze many variables together to try to isolate the impact of tax policy. Even then, the evidence in favor of lowering taxes on investments is mixed at best. According to the Congressional Budget Office, "existing empirical studies provide a bewildering range of estimates." In a 1978 paper, the economist Michael Boskin found that a tax cut that increases investment returns by 10 percent (today, this would require reducing tax rates by about one-third) tends to result in 3–4 percent more savings.[19] Later studies, however, have shown that such estimates depend heavily on complicated methodological details. In a recent review of existing research, Eric Toder and Kim Rueben concluded, "Statistical studies find little evidence of a positive relationship between saving and the after-tax return." A Congressional Research Service report put it similarly: "Studies that examined the savings rate over time found results that were small in magnitude, but uncertain in direction, with a central tendency suggesting no response."[20] Leonard Burman, a prominent tax expert, has found that tax rates on capital gains have had little impact either on savings or on economic growth.[21]

According to Economics 101, this should be impossible: of course people will consume less and invest more if they get to keep more of their returns. But there are many reasons why taxes

---

* Figure 5.3 shows tax rates on investment income other than capital gains (and dividends after 2003). A chart using capital gains tax rates tells a similar story, except that there has been less variation in capital gains rates over time.

have less impact on savings and capital formation than predicted by the model. First, many people are like I was: they are blissfully unaware of their tax rates, which therefore cannot affect their savings decisions. Second, higher taxes on investments may cause middle-income families to save more, because now they have to put away more money to build up the same retirement nest egg. Third, behavioral economists have revealed that most human beings' financial decisions are based not on sophisticated calculations involving rates of return but on primitive rules, such as "save whatever is left over after expenses" or "save 10 percent of the amount on my paycheck," which are not affected by tax rates. Fourth, when it comes to the very rich, many seem to want to amass as much wealth as possible, so higher taxes will not motivate them to save less and consume more.[22] Finally, even if cutting taxes on investments did increase personal savings, lower tax revenues increase the amount of money that the government has to borrow—reducing the capital available to the private sector.[23] In short, the simple model saying that lower investment taxes will increase savings and growth doesn't hold up to scrutiny.

Next let's look at economism's other prediction: that lower income taxes will cause people—the wealthy in particular—to

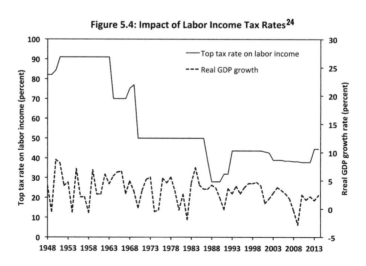

Figure 5.4: Impact of Labor Income Tax Rates[24]

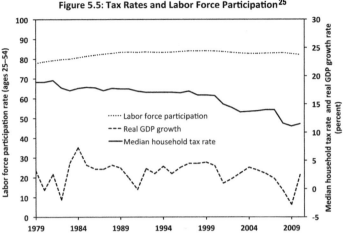

Figure 5.5: Tax Rates and Labor Force Participation[25]

work more, stimulating the economy. Figure 5.4 tells essentially the same story as Figure 5.3: the top tax rate on labor income has been falling over the long term with no corresponding increase in overall economic growth. Contrary to the theory, letting people keep more of their salaries does not always motivate them to work more. As shown in Figure 5.5, the average federal tax rate for middle-income households has been drifting steadily down, from around 19 percent in 1979 to less than 13 percent in 2010. However, the percentage of working-age adults in the labor force—either employed or looking for jobs—has not risen as a simple model would predict. Instead, we see only a modest increase in the 1980s followed by a steady plateau.

Alternatively, instead of looking across time, we can compare different states that have different tax policies. Here, too, the economists William Gale, Aaron Krupkin, and Kim Rueben have found no consistent relationship between state tax rates and either employment or economic growth, and only a small impact on the rate at which businesses are started.[26] The American Legislative Exchange Council regularly ranks states by their tax rates (lower is better, according to ALEC) and the size of their public sectors (smaller is better); states that receive top marks, however, do not grow any faster than other states. In Kansas, for example, since conservative politicians slashed taxes in 2011, economic growth and job gains have lagged the rest of the country.[27]

More detailed empirical research confirms that tax rates have at most a minor impact on people's willingness to work. According to a recent review by the economists Emmanuel Saez, Joel Slemrod, and Seth Giertz, the impact of a change in tax rates on working-age men is "close to zero," although it is higher for married women. In other words, men work basically the same amount in any case, but married women are more likely to look for jobs if taxes are lower. Another review by Robert McClelland and Shannon Mok of the Congressional Budget Office estimates that a 10 percent increase in tax rates would reduce the total supply of labor by anywhere from 0 percent to 3 percent. The Congressional Research Service report also concluded, "Empirical evidence has generally found small and uncertain labor supply effects from higher wages."[28]

In particular, the very rich—the "job creators"—are not more likely to respond to higher taxes by spending less time in the office. When Robert Moffitt and Mark Wilhelm studied the impact of the 1986 tax reform—which slashed rates on labor income—they found no change in actual hours worked by high-earning men. The CBO review also finds little support for the idea that the rich are more likely to abandon the workforce than the middle class because of higher taxes. Burman even concludes of the superrich, "Evidence suggests that their labor supply is insensitive to tax rates."[29] The wealthy do report less income when rates go up, but they don't actually work any less; instead, they put more effort into avoiding taxes, for example by becoming more strategic about when they recognize income.[30] Summarizing his analysis, the economist Thomas Hungerford concluded,

> Changes over the past 65 years in the top marginal tax rate and the top capital gains tax rate do not appear correlated with economic growth. The reduction in the top statutory

tax rates appears to be uncorrelated with saving, investment, and productivity growth. The top tax rates appear to have little or no relation to the size of the economic pie.[31]

Overall, the latest economic research indicates that raising tax rates will not suddenly push CEOs and hedge fund managers to take early retirement, nor will cutting taxes cause them to start working harder immediately. This shouldn't be too surprising. People who already make tens of millions of dollars per year clearly don't need to work in any meaningful sense, so they make trade-offs between labor and leisure differently from most people. Perhaps they work because they enjoy it, or perhaps because income and wealth are ways to keep score in a long-running competition with each other, but in either case tax rates are largely irrelevant.

THE PRICE OF CIVILIZATION

The easy-to-remember lesson that higher taxes shrink the pie for everyone turns out to be less true in the real world than on a whiteboard. In addition, economism's exclusive focus on deadweight triangles and lost output is itself a shortsighted perspective cultivated by Economics 101 classes. In particular, it ignores the crucial question of what the government does with its money.

One thing the government can do is reallocate resources by taxing some people and providing either cash transfers or services to other people. The moral argument for redistribution is that it is fair: after all, why should some people who work hard and follow the rules make thousands of times more money than other people who also work hard and follow the rules?[*] There is

---

[*] This perspective is typically introduced in a first-year economics class as a tension between efficiency (allocation of resources to their most productive uses) and equity (promoting outcomes that accord with people's notions of fairness) but then quickly discarded because it doesn't lend itself to simple diagrams and equations.

an economic argument as well, however: that redistribution can increase the aggregate utility of society.

The key here is the concept of *diminishing marginal utility*, which is an intimidating name for a commonsense idea. People generally gain utility by having more stuff—more food, more clothes, more toys—or at least most people behave that way. But the more you have of a particular thing, the less you benefit from getting even more of it. For example, a family moving from a thousand-square-foot house to a two-thousand-square-foot house gains enormous utility from the added space, while a different family living in a twenty-thousand-square-foot mansion might not even notice an extra thousand square feet. Similarly, $100 matters a lot more to a working mother making minimum wage than it does to Warren Buffett. As you gain additional units of something, each unit increases your overall utility by a diminishing amount. This concept applies to most things—think about eating five pieces of pizza in a row—but in particular it applies to overall wealth: an increase in your net worth from $1 million to $1.1 million will never be as significant as going from $0 to $100,000.

Although diminishing marginal utility may appear in first-year economics classes (when explaining how consumers make choices across different goods), it is often forgotten by economism's adherents when it comes to tax policy. The fact that very rich people gain little utility from an additional dollar, however, implies that they should pay more in taxes so that ordinary families can pay less (or receive other government benefits). Taking into account both the disincentive to make money (the typical Economics 101 argument) and the diminishing marginal utility of income, the economists Peter Diamond and Emmanuel Saez estimate that the optimal tax rate on the very rich is 73 percent—far higher than current levels in the United States or just about anywhere else.[32] In other words, by raising top rates significantly, the government could augment the tax revenues available to improve the lives of ordinary people, increasing the aggregate utility of society. In this case, the benefits of redistribution outweigh the deadweight triangles created by raising taxes on the rich.

Redistribution is not the only thing that a government can do with tax revenues; it can also spend money on services for society in general. The abbreviated Economics 101 model assumes that public spending neither creates nor destroys value. (In Figure 5.2, the Tax Revenue rectangle represents money transferred out of the private sector as taxes, but that isn't a loss to society, because the government theoretically provides services worth an equivalent amount.) In the real world, however, government programs are rarely break-even propositions. Money can be squandered building bridges to nowhere, subsidizing companies that should never have existed, or fighting wars of choice, among other things. There is no doubt that the U.S. government can be induced to use its resources and power on behalf of special interest groups; *13 Bankers*, a book I wrote with Simon Johnson, tells one version of that story.[33]

Many commentators go further and claim that all government spending is wasteful by definition.[34] But there are also public programs that create value and that the private sector alone would not replicate. The basic research that made the Internet possible is one example. Some government services were supported even by the famous economists who laid the foundation stones of economism. Hayek, for example, expected the state to take responsibility for the monetary system, a system of weights and measures, surveying and land registration, road construction, and even sanitary and health services. Friedman, too, endorsed

a government which maintained law and order, defined property rights, served as a means whereby we could modify property rights and other rules of the economic game, adjudicated disputes about the interpretation of the rules,

enforced contracts, promoted competition, provided a monetary framework, engaged in activities to counter technical
monopolies and to overcome neighborhood effects [exter-
nalities] widely regarded as sufficiently important to justify
government intervention, and which supplemented private
charity and the private family in protecting the irrespon-
sible, whether madman or child.[35]

Many of these crucial services are clearly worth more than
the tax dollars necessary to pay for them; without law and order,
property rights, contracts, competition, and a monetary system,
there wouldn't be much of an economy to begin with. Of course,
even though virtually everyone agrees that some government
functions are more than worth their cost, there is no easy way
to draw the line between services that destroy value and those
that create it. Still, once we acknowledge that government spending is necessary, it's no longer possible to justify tax cuts merely
by pointing to the deadweight triangle, as many commentators
and politicians do. Any economic losses caused by taxes have to
be compared with the benefits of centralized programs chosen
and controlled by democratic processes, which requires a complicated and fact-intensive analysis, not the sweeping pronounce-
ments of economism.

None of this should be too surprising. Taxes are the cost of
organizing ourselves in a democracy rather than as a collection of
autonomous individuals. "I like to pay taxes," said the Supreme
Court justice Oliver Wendell Holmes Jr. "With them, I buy civi-
lization."[36] A government is simply a mechanism by which we
organize certain aspects of society that we do not trust the private
sector to look after effectively. And so the question of whether
taxes are worthwhile depends on what functions we expect from
our government and how well it fulfills them.

As taught in Economics 101, however, taxes are an artificial
imposition on markets composed of individuals and businesses—

a source of deadweight losses that reduce social welfare. By sapping the incentives to work and to save, they discourage rich people from starting companies and starve businesses of the capital they need to flourish. This rhetoric is the first line of ideological defense against proposals to reduce inequality and help ordinary families by raising taxes on the rich. Introductory economics has not simply served to defend the status quo, however. The tax cuts inspired by economism, particularly those passed in 2001 and 2003 under President George W. Bush, were most generous to households at the top end of the income distribution, helping fuel the growth of inequality.[37] By reducing tax revenues and thereby increasing budget deficits, both the Reagan and Bush tax cuts constrained the ability of the federal government to respond to the needs of ordinary people and created increasing political pressure to scale back popular programs such as Social Security, Medicare, and Medicaid. Since the New Deal of the 1930s, the fundamental bargain of American society has been that a modest safety net would cushion working people against the inequality created by a capitalist economy. But after another round of tax cuts, there may be no money left to patch the fraying safety net, leaving the poor to fend for themselves in an increasingly unequal society.

6

The Consumer Knows Best

When medicine appears to the user to be a "free" good, there is no limit to the amount demanded. . . . Inevitably, people who are well connected, hypochondriacs with time on their hands, and the simply persistent get an undue share.

—Milton Friedman, 1975[1]

The United States has a health-care problem. In 2014, total spending on health care amounted to more than one-sixth of the entire economy—more than $9,500 per person. That's twice as much, in dollar terms, as in the average developed country.[2] Yet we do not get particularly good medical care; according to most measures of quality, the United States falls in the middle of the pack. Nor are we unusually healthy. Life expectancy for Americans is 78.8 years, 1.7 years less than the average in the Organisation for Economic Co-operation and Development (OECD)—a group that includes both the world's advanced economies and some developing countries such as Chile, Mexico, and Turkey. In a recent evaluation of eleven rich countries by the Commonwealth Fund, the United States came in dead last in overall health outcomes and led all countries in inequality of access to care.[3] Life expectancy for the richest 1 percent of Americans is ten to fifteen years longer than for the poorest 1 percent—a gap that has been widening since the beginning of the century.[4] How can we spend so much money and get such dismal and unequal results?

TOO MUCH FREE STUFF

If you've taken a little bit of economics, the answer is obvious: Americans don't pay enough for their health care. Politicians may bemoan the fact that tens of millions of people are uninsured, but the real problem is that we have too much insurance of the wrong kind. With insurance, you don't pay the full cost of your care at the time that you decide to see the doctor, take a test, undergo surgery, fill a prescription, buy medical equipment, or check into the hospital. Depending on your plan and the service provider you visit, you might pay nothing, or a flat $30 co-payment for each service, or "co-insurance" equal to 20 percent of the price, or the full price up to a $1,000 annual deductible, or something else. As a result, most people don't know the full cost of their

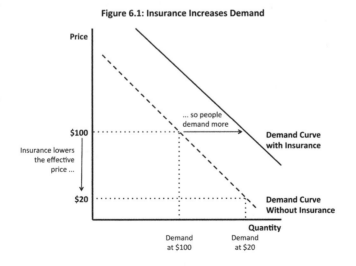

Figure 6.1: Insurance Increases Demand

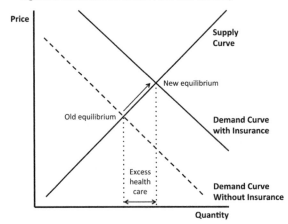

Figure 6.2: Insurance Increases Price and Quantity

health care—and they aren't really interested, because they pay just a fraction of it.

In Economics 101 terms, insurance increases the demand for health care. Let's say that you pay 20 percent of your medical bills and your insurer pays the other 80 percent. That means a $100 doctor's visit only costs you $20. Your demand for doctor's visits is based on your net price of $20, so you consume more than you would if you paid the total price of $100. Everyone behaves this way, so the demand curve shifts outward, to the right (Figure 6.1), and both the price and the quantity of health care go up (Figure 6.2).

Because insurance lowers the perceived cost of health care, people end up consuming services that provide less value than they cost to deliver. Let's say you are feeling just a little sick, so seeing the doctor is worth $30 to you.* You only have to pay $20, so you go, but the total price is still $100, because the insurer is paying $80—a cost ultimately borne by all of its customers in the form of insurance premiums. The net social welfare of this

---

* This may seem unrealistic, but Economics 101 assumes that you can estimate the dollar value to you of seeing the doctor.

appointment is negative because its cost exceeds its value to the consumer. Multiply this one example by all the people with insurance, and the economy ends up producing too much health care (as shown in Figure 6.2)—too many unnecessary tests, too many surgeries of dubious value, and so on—at too high a price. That's the problem with the American health-care system, according to economism.

If the problem is too much demand, the textbook solution is that people should bear more of the true costs of their consumption. Instead of those costs being shared across many people in insurance premiums—which you pay every month regardless of your behavior—you should face them every time you decide to go to the doctor, refill a prescription, or get an MRI. This way, you will only buy services when their value to you exceeds their cost to society. If you have to pay $100 to see the doctor, you will only go if it is worth $100 to you. This is how the rest of the economy works, after all: Apple produces exactly the right number of iPads because people buy them only if they will get more than $499 of value from them. Not only will exposing people to the full marginal cost of their health care solve the problem of overconsumption, but also it will stimulate competition among service providers, which will only be able to increase profits by lowering costs or providing more value to customers. In the terms that Ludwig von Mises used in *Bureaucracy*, consumer sovereignty will ensure that the health-care sector as a whole provides the services that consumers prefer, as efficiently as possible.[5] Making people responsible for their choices will make society as a whole better off.

CONSUMER-DRIVEN UTOPIA

Economism's preferred solution, therefore, is to apply the competitive market model to health care. As the economists John Cogan, Glenn Hubbard (chair of the Council of Economic

Advisers under President George W. Bush), and Daniel Kessler confidently asserted in a 2004 *Wall Street Journal* article, "Free markets are a proven way to discipline costs, encourage innovation and increase quality. The starting point to fixing the health-care system is recognizing that a handful of existing public policies prevent markets from working, and then changing them."[6] Economism's utopia goes by the name of consumer-driven health care: a system in which people behave like discerning shoppers because they bear the cost of their decisions, and their choices provide the incentives for businesses to offer superior services at lower prices.

The simplest way to make people recognize the real cost of their health care would be to eliminate insurance altogether. Without insurance, however, many people diagnosed with serious diseases would be unable to afford appropriate treatment. Most policy proposals take a less extreme form, featuring health plans that mandate greater *cost sharing:* mechanisms that require people to pay out of pocket for expenses as they incur them. Cost sharing can take the form of co-payments (flat fees per service), co-insurance (a percentage of the total price), or an annual deductible (an amount a participant must pay before receiving any benefits). Advocates of consumer-driven health care are particularly fond of "high-deductible" plans that require people to pay as much as $10,000 out of pocket before full coverage kicks in. The idea, as Cogan, Hubbard, and Kessler put it, is that "higher copayments will give consumers more 'skin in the game,' making them more cost-conscious and more willing to take greater control of health-care decisions."

All other things being equal, people tend not to like cost sharing. According to Economics 101, however, greater competition among insurers should shift the market toward consumer-driven plans. In a competitive market, people (or companies that provide health benefits for their employees) will shop around to find the cheapest acceptable insurance. Because plans with more cost sharing turn policyholders into smarter consumers (in theory), they reduce unnecessary consumption, which translates into lower insurance premiums. Therefore, individuals and employers will choose high-deductible and other consumer-driven plans. In the end, health care will become more like a textbook market in which consumers, by only buying what they are willing to pay for, ensure they are getting value for their dollar, which in turn encourages beneficial competition among service providers.

For the past quarter century, consumer choice and market competition have been central themes in health-care policy debates. As Stuart Butler of the Heritage Foundation said in 1993, "If people don't experience the actual cost of an item—or service or benefit—they tend to want as much as is available." Instead, the health-care system should be based on "the foundations of a market economy—consumer choice, competition, private contracts, and market prices." The CEO of CIGNA, a major insurer, said while promoting consumer-driven health care, "What didn't work in managed care [a system with little cost sharing, in which services are limited by health maintenance organizations] was that we separated the consumption of care from the cost of care. People didn't care what things cost anymore."[7]

"Choice" and "competition" have become magic words on *both* sides of the political aisle. On the campaign trail in 1992, Bill Clinton adopted the idea of managed competition, which an industry trade group called "a private-sector approach to health system reform that uses the marketplace and the power of informed consumer choice to achieve better coverage, while improving quality and cutting cost."[8] His 1993 health-care proposal was designed to allow individuals to choose among competing insurance plans offered through regional cooperatives—abandoning the universal government insurance model championed by Democrats for decades and embodied by Medicare, the federal health plan for seniors. For Republicans and some Democrats, however, the Clinton plan still involved too much government coercion, regulation, and bureaucracy. Under assault by politicians, industry groups, and talk radio hosts, it died an ignominious death without ever coming to a vote.

Clinton's successor, George W. Bush, promoted high-deductible plans coupled with health savings accounts—tax-sheltered accounts that can be used to pay for out-of-pocket expenses—because "empowering consumers is essential to improving value and affordability." In his ideal system, "competition and market forces . . . would be relied upon to improve the quality and efficiency of health care and to reduce the growth of health care costs." As Merrill Matthews, then head of a health insurer trade group, explained, "What the consumer-driven movement does is remove some of that insulation [from true costs], and give people the incentive to ask the question 'Where do I get value for my dollar?'"[9] Since getting a boost from President Bush, high-deductible plans have been growing in popularity among insurers and employers. In 2006, only 4 percent of workers were enrolled in high-deductible plans; by 2015, that figure had risen to 24 percent. Across all types of health plans, the average deductible has more than doubled since 2006.[10]

When Barack Obama became president in 2009, he was determined to expand health insurance coverage while avoiding the missteps of the Clinton administration. His signature legislative achievement was the Patient Protection and Affordable Care Act of 2010, better known as Obamacare—a reform package that sits politically to the *right* of the Clinton plan and that is similar to the program introduced in Massachusetts in 2006 by Governor Mitt Romney. (At the time, Heritage applauded Massachusetts's "consumer-driven marketplace" for increasing choice, stimulating competition, and lowering costs.[11]) Obamacare requires people to get health insurance from their employers or purchase it on an exchange, where private insurers compete for customers. By bringing buyers and sellers of insurance together in regulated, transparent exchanges, the system attempts to harness the power of markets to make everyone better off.

President Obama tried to lay claim to the principles of choice and competition with his health-care plan. According to his opponents, however, he didn't go nearly far enough, or he was simply lying. Since it was passed in March 2010, Republican politicians and conservative groups have been fighting to repeal the Affordable Care Act (with occasional support from Democrats opposed to specific provisions). When proposing alternatives to Obamacare, they typically assume that the health-care and health-insurance markets will behave according to the Economics 101 model. According to Heritage's experts, "When individual consumers decide how the money is spent, either directly for medical care or indirectly through their health insurance choices, the incentives will be aligned throughout the system to generate better value—in other words, to produce more for less." Their evidence for this claim is simply that this is how markets are supposed to behave: "In normal markets, consumers drive the system through their choices of products and services. . . . In response, the providers of goods and services compete to meet consumer demands and preferences by supplying products that offer consumers better value in terms of price, quality, and features." Researchers from the Hoover Institution and the American Enterprise Institute claim that, instead of Obamacare, "what's needed is a credible plan to reorient federal policy across the board toward markets and the preferences of consumers and patients."[12]

That plan includes not only repealing Obamacare but also rewriting Medicare according to Economics 101 principles. Since 2010, Republicans have been promoting the idea, first introduced by Paul Ryan, of converting Medicare into a voucher program: instead of simply being covered by a uniform government plan, seniors would get a voucher that they could use to buy insurance from private companies in a competitive market. "Putting patients in charge of how their health care dollars are spent will force providers to compete against each other on price and quality," the proposal predicted. "That's how markets work: The customer is the ultimate guarantor of value."[13]

The rhetoric of markets has been picked up and amplified by the media. *Wall Street Journal* op-ed articles, for example, regularly sing the praises of consumer-driven health care. A CEO and a Manhattan Institute researcher wrote,

> As millions of Americans move onto high-deductible plans, they will change their behavior—and the incentives of the market. . . . Providers will have to earn their business on the basis of quality, price and service, the way companies do in the other four-fifths of the U.S. economy. Competition has the potential to transform America's sclerotic, overpriced health-care system into something much more transparent and affordable.

The head of another conservative think tank claimed that, if Medicare were converted into a voucher system, "Insurers would have to compete for beneficiaries' business, and providers would have to compete to get on the most popular plans. Lower prices and better-quality care would be the result."[14]

In the 2016 presidential election, not only did all Republican candidates ritually pledge to repeal Obamacare, but most subscribed to the principles of market forces and consumer choice. Marco Rubio promised "modern, consumer-centered reforms that lower costs, embrace innovation in healthcare, and actually increase choices and improve quality of care," including "consumer-centered products like Health Savings Accounts." Rubio, Ted Cruz, and Rand Paul all signed the "Contract from America"—an initiative of FreedomWorks, Americans for Tax Reform, and other conservative groups—which called for replacing Obamacare with "a system that actually makes health care and insurance more affordable by enabling a competitive, open, and transparent free-market health care and health insurance system." Rick Santorum promised to expand health savings accounts "to give patients and doctors, not Washington bureaucrats, more freedom and control over their health care." Even Donald Trump, who in a prior life favored a universal health insurance system, has adopted the language of competition and choice: "We still need a plan to bring down health-care costs and make health-care insurance more affordable for everyone. It starts with increasing competition between insurance companies. Competition makes everything better and more affordable."*15

BAD CHOICES

It seems convincing. Of course health care should behave like any other market, so of course people should be required to pay the full cost at the point of care to ensure that they make smart decisions. In fact, however, health care does *not* behave like any other market (putting to the side the question of whether any market behaves the way it is supposed to in Economics 101)—something economists have known for decades.

Kenneth Arrow, one of the towering figures in modern economics, in 1963 wrote a canonical paper explaining why health care does not behave like a textbook market. The most obvious anomaly, he emphasized, is that we do not incur medical expenses regularly. In fact, we rarely need most forms of health care. When we do need them, we need them badly, however; illness itself can be costly, both in lost income and in reduced quality of life, even before the high cost of medical treatment. Because we are not regular consumers of health care, we lack both the knowledge and the experience necessary to be smart

* In the campaign, Trump endorsed a laundry list of standard Republican proposals based on "free market principles," including greater competition in the insurance market, health savings accounts, and tax deductions for individual insurance premiums.

shoppers. If you are diagnosed with a severe condition, you may have to choose among a variety of treatments that meant nothing to you the day before while facing a huge degree of uncertainty about their outcomes.[16] You can't rely on your friends' recommendations, because many medical situations are unique and even people who have recovered from similar illnesses are unlikely to know exactly why. If you do your own research on different treatments and providers, you will struggle to find useful information. As the health economist Uwe Reinhardt describes it, "The usual absence of reliable information on the quality and prices of health care available to consumers . . . effectively converts them into blind-folded shoppers in a bewildering shopping mall."[17] These are all reasons why people tend to put themselves in the hands of their doctors rather than trying to become experts themselves and why informed consumer choice is rare in the medical sphere.[18]

The inability of real people to make good medical choices turns out to be the Achilles' heel of consumer-driven health care. The landmark RAND Health Insurance Experiment, which followed close to three thousand families in the 1970s and early 1980s, showed that higher levels of cost sharing "reduced the use of effective and less-effective care across the board." Multiple subsequent studies have confirmed that "cost sharing is as likely to depress appropriate care as it is to depress inappropriate care," as the health law professor Timothy Jost concluded. A recent research paper found the same was true of high-deductible plans: when a company switched tens of thousands of employees from a traditional PPO (preferred provider organization) plan to a high-deductible plan, they reduced consumption of both valuable and wasteful procedures, with no evidence that they sought out lower prices for services.[19] In other words, higher cost sharing does get people to buy less health care in the short term but does not make them better at getting value for their money. In the words of the health economist Meredith Rosenthal, "[Consumer cost-sharing] will save money, but we have strong evidence that when faced with high out-of-pocket costs, consumers make choices that do not appear to be in their best interests in terms of health."[20] While people may buy too much health care under current insurance schemes, high-deductible plans present a different risk: that they will not buy enough care, or will not buy the right type of care, to their own detriment.

In the long term, the result can be worse health outcomes and higher total costs, particularly when people try to save money by cutting back on preventive care or medications for chronic illnesses. In his review of the empirical research, Jost found ample confirmation that "increased cost sharing can have adverse health effects." One study found that when people were switched into high-deductible plans, their primary response was to cut back on prescription drugs for chronic conditions; this was true even when prescriptions were *exempt* from the deductible (that is, such drugs were covered before participants reached the deductible), indicating that people are not the rational value maximizers that consumer-driven health care expects them to be.[21] In some cases, requiring people to pay more for medical care causes them to forgo valuable services or treatments. Higher levels of cost sharing make poor families several times more likely to skip seeing a doctor for their children's asthma and are also correlated with a higher frequency of asthma attacks among children. When retired state employees in California faced higher co-payments, they cut back on both office visits and prescription drug utilization, as predicted, but hospital visits went *up*, particularly among the very sick.[22] This implies that on the whole consumer-driven health care may not even achieve its goal of reducing total costs.

The Economics 101 model in which financial incentives turn people into discerning consumers turns out not to work in the real world. For Mises and Hayek, the crowning jewel of societal organization was the price system, which coordinates the activities of millions of people to deliver the most valuable goods and services to the most people. But in the market for health care, as Arrow said recently, "We talk about a price system, but that is not what we have. What we have is a system in which one buyer will pay ten times what other buyers will pay for similar medical devices, or services. So the idea of a price system as the source of efficiency fails at the most elementary level."[23]

BROKEN MARKET

The fact that our health-care needs are unpredictable and potentially costly also means that people want to insure themselves against future expenses. As a consequence, the market for health care is inseparable from the market for health insurance. But, as Arrow explained, the insurance market suffers from its own profound failings: "A great many risks are not covered, and indeed the markets for the services of risk-coverage are poorly developed or nonexistent."[24]

The private health insurance market is nearly fatally flawed. The goal of any insurance company is to predict how much a given person will cost in claims over the next year and charge a premium that more than covers those expected costs. The sicker the person, the higher the price. This is known in economics as *price discrimination*. In a competitive market, insurers will get better and better at figuring out how much you are likely to cost—by looking at your medical records, your genetic data, your purchasing patterns, and your online searches—so they can charge you the appropriate price. But if someone is likely to need $50,000 of health care, the appropriate price from the insurer's perspective is more than $50,000, which most people obviously can't afford. If you have a chronic illness, or your grandparents had expensive hereditary diseases, or you are simply old, the "correct" price could easily exceed your budget.[25]

If insurers set a profit-making price for each person, the poor and the sick will be left without any coverage at all. Ordinarily, we think that competitive markets maximize social welfare: remember, if people get something that they can't afford, the economy will produce too much of it. But this is not necessarily true of health insurance, which enables people to afford medical care that could be of great value to them and to society. If someone couldn't afford a needed heart transplant on her own, but her insurance policy pays for the operation, that's not an example of frivolous overconsumption; that's a benefit for society, particularly if she goes on to work productively for decades. The health economist John Nyman concludes,

> Because people value the additional income they receive from insurance when they become ill more than they value the income they lose when they pay a premium and remain healthy, and because everyone has in theory an equal chance of becoming ill, this national redistribution of income from the healthy to the ill is efficient and increases the welfare of society.[26]

If fewer people can afford insurance, society becomes worse off.

Most people are not prepared to say that poor people should go without health care, so there are various ideas about how to fix the insurance market. One way to prevent individuals from being priced out of the market is to prohibit price discrimination; Obamacare, for example, limits insurers' ability to set premiums based on people's medical status.[27] But if everyone pays the same amount, the problem of *adverse selection* appears: insurance becomes unattractive to healthy people (who are being charged "too much"), so they refuse to buy policies, driving up premiums for the sick people who remain in the insurance pool, causing the less-sick people to decline coverage as well, pushing up premiums even further. Limiting price discrimination, therefore, creates

the need for Obamacare's individual mandate; by forcing everyone to buy insurance, you can require the healthy to subsidize the
sick. Even then, the cost of insurance remains too high for poor
families. Remember, average health-care spending is more than
$9,500 per year, while a person earning the minimum wage only
makes about $15,000. For the working poor to afford insurance,
there must be explicit redistribution from richer families—such
as the Obamacare subsidies for low-income households. Finally,
if everyone pays roughly the same price, individual insurers have
the incentive to "cherry-pick"—to attract healthy people while
deterring sick people from applying. To make the system work,
Obamacare includes a complex risk adjustment mechanism that
shifts money between insurance companies based on how sick
their customers are.

In an ordinary market, the people who consume the most services should pay the most money; applied to health care, however, that principle would produce morally intolerable results.
Therefore, in the real world, the market must be hemmed in by
regulations that limit insurers' ability to maximize profits and
prevent individuals from opting out of the system. The point of
all these constraints is to separate the premiums charged for a
health insurance policy from the actual cost of underwriting that
policy so that poor and sick people can buy coverage that a textbook market would deny them. This is how we end up with a
barely tolerable system in which most people get some coverage
at a price that isn't too unaffordable.

Cost sharing, however, strengthens the link between the amount
of health care you use and the amount you pay. Indeed, for
advocates of consumer-directed plans, that's precisely the point.
Compared with other types of insurance, plans with high levels
of cost sharing transfer money from sick people, who pay more
out of pocket, to healthy people, who benefit from lower monthly
premium payments. And the increase in cost sharing over the
past decade has had a predictable impact on low- and moderate-

income families. About one in five people *with* private health insurance currently has difficulty paying medical bills. For the large majority of this group, the problem is not that evil insurance companies denied their claims but simply that their policies required them to pay too much out of pocket. Not surprisingly, people with high-deductible plans are much more likely to have trouble with medical costs than are people with other plans.[28] As the economist Jerry Green summarized, "It's equivalent to taxing the sick."[29]

The more you rely on the principles of the market, the more you have to accept its distributional consequences. This is the fundamental problem with consumer-driven health care. Higher cost sharing makes economic sense, at least in theory—*if* we think that health care should be delivered through a market. It makes sense that price signals would encourage people to make smarter choices (leaving aside whether they actually behave that way) and force service providers to be more efficient. But if we rely on a competitive market to provide health care, then everyone will get the care that she can afford. For people who are steeped in Economics 101, this is a good thing; how else could we maximize social welfare? But for many people with traditional moral sensibilities, the idea that the rich will have access to life-extending therapies, the middle class will scrape by, and the poor will go untreated except in an emergency is simply wrong. "Most of us think it's fine that some people can't buy fancy clothing or fast cars," the political scientist Jacob Hacker writes. "But most of us draw the line at basic health care."[30]

Perhaps the most fundamental lesson of Economics 101 is that competitive markets, in which prices are determined by supply and demand, are the right way to allocate resources and distribute goods and services. Even when there are specific market failures (such as adverse selection), the recommended solution is to correct for those discrete problems (for example, by requiring everyone to buy insurance), which will restore the market to its ideal state. One of the most sweeping triumphs of economism has been to convince both sides of the political debate that this fundamental lesson applies to health care. Virtually all Republican politicians favor deregulation and consumer-driven plans because they think that health insurance and health care can and should be delivered by a textbook competitive market. Most Democrats actually agree that health insurance and health care should be delivered by markets; they disagree only on the extent to which regulations should attempt to correct for predictable market failures. The result is Obamacare: a jury-rigged patchwork of mandates, regulations, taxes, subsidies, and risk adjustment mechanisms intended to force markets to produce a socially acceptable outcome—one in which most people can afford something approximating decent health insurance.

THE FORGOTTEN ALTERNATIVE

The current system provides widespread but not universal access to health care by (a) selling insurance in "competitive markets," (b) forcing everyone to buy it, (c) providing subsidies to people who can't afford it, (d) limiting the policies that insurers are allowed to sell, (e) restricting their ability to set prices, (f) subsidizing employer-sponsored plans because companies can get better deals than individuals, (g) penalizing people who get plans that we don't like, and (h) reshuffling money among insurance companies. Surely, there must be another way.

Not only is there another way; it's one that every other country in the developed world has chosen. The alternative is a universal health insurance system, paid for by taxes and either administered or overseen by the government, in which access to most health-care services does not depend on ability to pay. Different versions of this basic model exist around the world. In the United Kingdom, most services are provided for free or with minimal cost sharing by the National Health Service, which is mainly funded by general tax revenues. In Canada, most care is paid for by universal health insurance programs administered by provincial governments and financed by general tax revenues. In France, coverage is provided by nonprofit insurance funds and paid for mainly by payroll taxes. In the Netherlands, people must buy basic insurance from private companies (similar to Obamacare), but their policies are effectively financed by a payroll tax.[31] Although the role of the private sector varies from country to country, the unifying theme is that everyone is covered, mainly through taxes, with mechanisms to keep cost sharing at affordable levels. These systems are all based on the common principle of "mutual responsibility of citizens for the health care of each other," in the words of Daniel Callahan and Angela Wasunna.[32]

In the United States, the most common label for this type of system is "single payer," because one entity would pay for most health-care expenses. (The term is not entirely accurate, because some countries actually have multiple payers even for basic services, but they are so heavily regulated that they essentially behave the same way.) If the goal is to make health insurance affordable for everyone—something no politician would deny—the most direct solution is to have a universal, government-sponsored health plan with no up-front premiums, funded primarily by general tax revenues. Such a plan could have modest deductibles and co-payments intended to influence behavior at the margins, while still keeping out-of-pocket expenses manageable for everyone. It could also allow private insurance companies to sell supplemental policies to people who want additional coverage beyond the basic plan. In fact, the United States already has a single payer program: it's called Medicare, it serves fifty million people, and it's extremely popular.

Single payer, or a variant of it, will not magically solve all of our problems. In any system, there must be some mechanism to determine which people get what services—to "ration" health care, to use the dirty word. In a competitive market, it is prices, and therefore the rich live longer and more comfortably than the poor. In a government-run plan, it is statutes passed by legislators and regulations written by appointed officials and career civil servants. The question is which system can do a better job at delivering the most valuable health care to the largest number of people, in a morally acceptable way and at a reasonable cost.

There are reasons to be skeptical about single payer. The regulations necessary to implement such a system could end up enriching private interest groups with disproportionate influence over politicians (think about doctors, pharmaceutical companies, and medical device manufacturers) rather than improving the health of ordinary people. The bureaucracy that administers the system, unchecked by the pressure of competition, could impose its own layer of additional and excessive costs, as Friedman feared.[33] In addition, if a single payer plan is successful in reducing spending, that could result in fewer people wanting to become doctors and fewer health-care providers investing in new technologies.

Evidence from around the world demonstrates, however, that these challenges can be successfully overcome. Every other rich country in the world has a health-care system that is much closer to the single payer model than to the competitive market model, and they generally fare pretty well. Of the thirty-four countries in the OECD, only Chile relies more on private insurance and out-of-pocket spending to pay for health care than does the United States; in every other country, government spending, including social insurance systems, plays a larger role. On the whole, these countries enjoy health outcomes comparable to or better than those of the United States. Of the OECD countries, the United States ranks between twentieth and twenty-ninth on primary health status metrics, ranks in the bottom third for access to coverage, and has among the fewest doctors and hospital beds per capita.[34] As discussed above, we earn these dismal results despite spending by far the most money on health care. In this light, it seems quite possible that our high costs relative to the rest of the world are the result not of overconsumption but of a decentralized system organized around private profits rather than strong government spending controls.[35] Finally, contrary to Friedrich Hayek's dire warnings, public administration of health care has not led to an inexorable descent into totalitarianism.[36]

Competitive markets and single payer reflect two different ways of thinking about health. On the one hand, we can think of health-care services as discretionary consumer purchases that should be allocated via the forces of supply and demand, which will ensure that resources are directed efficiently toward those people who value them most (in dollar terms). On the other hand, we can think of illness and injury as unpredictable, expensive risks that all of us face and that we have an equal right to be protected against. The remarkable thing is that American political debates and policy discussions are dominated by the competitive market model, with one side saying it should be wholeheartedly embraced and the other saying that it should be redirected through judicious regulations.

This imbalance is a testament to the power of economism. Economic theorists and researchers have long recognized the unique characteristics of health care and the shortcomings of consumer-driven plans. As the economist Burton Weisbrod put it, "We cannot construct wise public policy on health care by applying elementary economic analysis. Competition does have a role to play. Yet the markets for health care and chocolate chip cookies *are* different."[37] Nevertheless, the basic idea that markets must know best has been accepted across most of the political spectrum. The result has been to drastically truncate the range of potential solutions to our current health-care problems, leaving the avowed socialist Bernie Sanders one of the few politicians willing to question the Economics 101 orthodoxy. The outcome is exactly what the health economist Thomas Rice warned against when he wrote,

> If analysts misinterpret economic theory as applied to health—by assuming that market forces are necessarily superior to alternative policies, and that other tools of the trade neatly translate to health care—then they will blind themselves to policy options that might actually be best at enhancing social welfare, many of which simply do not fall out of the conventional, demand-driven competitive model.[38]

With steady price increases making health insurance and medical care unaffordable for a growing number of families and businesses, one commonsense response would be to treat health care as a basic right that is collectively funded by all of society. Instead, policy proposals focus on making markets more efficient, which necessarily shifts costs onto the sick.[39] The result is "rationing by income," as Reinhardt puts it:[40] the rich can afford whatever they need when they fall ill, while the poor may have to choose between medications, utilities, car payments, and rent. High out-of-pocket costs increase the financial strain on families when they are least able to withstand it; about one-fifth to one-fourth of all household bankruptcies are primarily caused by medical expenses.[41] Our high level of income inequality may be more tolerable if all people can afford basic necessities, including health care. Today, however, low-income families are increasingly finding that even having insurance is not enough to pay for the services and medications they need, while the rich continue to enjoy the best care that money can buy.

The greatest power of a worldview is to set the boundaries of what people believe is even possible. In *The Problem of Unbelief in the Sixteenth Century*, the French historian Lucien Febvre demonstrated that the mental world of early modern Europe was so saturated with religion that it was essentially impossible to be an atheist in the modern sense.[42] Economism plays a similar role in contemporary American health-care debates, narrowing the window of possibility to different variations on the competitive market model taught in Economics 101—and blinding people to the lessons of the world around us.

7

Capital Unbound

The increasing sophistication and depth of financial markets promote economic growth by allocating capital where it can be most productive. And the dispersion of risk more broadly across the financial system has, thus far, increased the resilience of the system and the economy to shocks.

—Ben Bernanke, 2007[1]

In 2006, housing prices in the United States began to wobble. From 2007 until 2009, they fell more than 30 percent nationwide and more than 50 percent in some markets such as Las Vegas and Phoenix. The collapse in housing prices precipitated a tidal wave of foreclosures as millions of people were unable either to make their mortgage payments or to refinance houses that were now worth far less than their outstanding loans. By 2013, banks had claimed more than five million homes, with millions more in the foreclosure process or in default, leaving families with limited housing options and poor credit.[2] The crisis devastated entire neighborhoods, from old industrial cities in the Midwest to sprawling new subdivisions in the western desert, as concentrated foreclosures reduced property values, left buildings vacant, and encouraged vandalism.[3]

Defaults and foreclosures were particularly high among people who took out *subprime mortgages:* loans designed for borrowers who were considered risky because of limited incomes, poor credit histories, or houses of questionable value. Traditionally, these people would have been shut out of the housing market by banks unwilling to take on the risk that they would default. Beginning in the 1990s, however, a resurgent subprime lending industry enabled millions of aspiring homeowners to buy or refinance houses with innovative new mortgage products. In addition to high interest charges, these loans included several complicated features such as floating interest rates, multiple payment options, prepayment penalties, and even negative amortization, which causes the total amount due to go *up* over time. By 2009, a staggering 40 percent of subprime mortgages were delinquent (more than thirty days overdue), and more than 15 percent were in the foreclosure process.[4]

If the housing collapse had only shattered the dreams of millions of families, things would have been bad enough. In addition, it effectively bankrupted most of the world's largest financial institutions, which had placed massive bets on the housing market in general and on subprime borrowers in particular. On September 15, 2008, the storied investment bank Lehman Brothers filed for bankruptcy (following the emergency rescue of Bear Stearns in March and the government takeover of Fannie Mae and Freddie Mac in early September), paralyzing the global financial system over fears that several other megabanks would implode in its wake. The next day, the Treasury Department took over American International Group, the world's largest insurance company, which was itself on the brink of a collapse that would have blown holes in the balance sheets of many other financial institutions. Desperate measures by central banks and governments around the world prevented a complete meltdown of the financial system, but the damage was done. In the United States, more than eight million jobs evaporated in the Great Recession. From 2008 through mid-2015, the slowdown cost the American economy about $6 trillion worth of goods and services— about $20,000 per person.[5] The financial crisis sent shock waves around the European continent, nearly fracturing the eurozone (the group of countries sharing a common currency) as Greece, Portugal, Spain, and other countries struggled with large government debt burdens, high unemployment, and political unrest.

The tragedy is that none of this should have surprised anyone. We have known for over a century that financial instability can send severe shock waves through the economy. The United States suffered intermittent financial panics in the nineteenth century, but the object lesson was provided in the early 1930s, when a breakdown of the banking system brought on the Great Depression. Beginning in 1933, the federal government responded by building a comprehensive regulatory framework that constrained the activities that financial institutions could engage in and placed them under close supervision. The goals of these regulations were both to protect ordinary people's savings and to prevent banks from taking on excessive risks, because the collapse of multiple banks could endanger the overall economy. This regime successfully inoculated the financial system against damaging crises for half a century, including the three decades of sustained economic growth that followed World War II.

SUPPLY, DEMAND, AND CAPITAL

From the standpoint of economism, however, financial regulations simply prevent people from engaging in mutually beneficial transactions, discouraging innovation and constraining the free flow of capital. Let's go back to the basic supply-and-demand model. The demand curve shows how many people will choose to buy a product at each price; the supply curve represents the total cost to bring each product to market. A sale only occurs if a buyer values something at more than it costs a supplier to manufacture and sell it. That transaction increases social welfare, because it means that resources (materials, labor, and invested capital) are being turned into something more valuable (a finished product). If someone is willing to pay $15 for a shovel, and a company is willing to sell it for $15, then we want that sale to happen.

If a person does not think a snow shovel is worth $15, however, no one is forcing her to buy one. Buyers are protected from bad deals by their own self-interest; between $15 in cash and a shovel, they can individually decide which one they prefer. The lesson is simple: let people buy what they want. Consumers are the best judges of their own preferences, so they will only buy things that make them better off.

Similarly, if the market price of snow shovels is $15, but it would cost a firm $20 to manufacture and sell one more shovel, no one is forcing the company to make it. Businesses want to maximize their profits, so they only produce goods if they can sell them for more than they cost to bring to market.[6] If a company cannot deliver products for less than consumers will pay for them, it won't sell any; if it cannot make products for less than the price its competitors charge, it also won't sell any. Businesses, in short, are already regulated both by customers and by competitors. Just as individual consumers know their likes and dislikes better than anyone else, the executives running a company are best situated to know what products and services they can develop and market successfully. Again, the lesson is that we should let companies sell what they want. In *The Road to Serfdom*, Hayek emphasized "that the parties in the market should be free to sell and buy at any price at which they can find a partner to the transaction and that anybody should be free to produce, sell, and buy anything that may be produced or sold at all." The same principle was included in the draft statement of aims for the first meeting of the Mont Pelerin Society:

> The freedom of the consumer in choosing what he shall buy, the freedom of the producer in choosing what he shall make, and the freedom of the worker in choosing his

occupation and his place of employment, are essential not merely for the sake of freedom itself, but for efficiency in production. Such a system of freedom is essential if we are to maximize output in terms of individual satisfactions.[7]

Financial markets, the story continues, are just like any other markets. The product is the use of money; the lender sells the borrower the right to use money for a certain period of time (say, to buy a house). The price is the interest rate of the loan, along with any other fees. And the lender's cost of producing a loan is the interest rate it has to pay someone else to borrow that money. If this is confusing, the following example illustrates the basic concept: One group of people deposit money in bank savings accounts that pay 1 percent interest, and the bank then lends money to another group of people who pay 4 percent interest. The bank's cost is 1 percent, its sale price is 4 percent, and its profit is 3 percent.

Like in other markets, different people prefer different types of products. Imagine that all mortgages had the exact same terms— say, a fixed interest rate for a thirty-year term and a 20 percent down payment—and only had different interest rates (because some people have good credit and some have bad credit). This is analogous to a world in which you can only buy vanilla ice cream, which would clearly not be the best of all possible worlds. Instead, we want lenders to innovate in designing new loan products that better meet the needs of different borrowers. More variation in financial products increases the chances that buyers and sellers will be able to agree on transactions that are good for both sides. Borrowers don't have to take out mortgages if they don't like the terms, and lenders don't have to extend credit if they don't think the interest and fees are enough to compensate them for the risk they are taking on. In this context, restrictions on product features simply prevent the market from reaching its optimal equilibrium. Fancy subprime mortgages are good because they increase the total number of welfare-creating exchanges between borrowers and lenders.

Finally, although financial markets operate like other markets, they play a particularly important role in the economy. The product being bought and sold—the right to use money—is also known as *capital*. Capital is the money required to make up-front investments in things that produce value for years to come— houses, factories, industrial equipment, and so on.* Smoothly functioning financial markets ensure that capital flows to the people and companies who can put it to the best use. Let's say Company A wants to borrow $1 billion to build a factory that will generate profits of $200 million per year, and Company B wants to borrow $1 billion to build a factory that will generate profits of $10 million per year. If a bank has to choose between the two, Company A will get the money, because it will be willing to pay a higher interest rate than Company B. That's good, because we would rather have Company A's factory than Company B's in the best of all possible worlds. This is why it is particularly important that financial markets should not be encumbered by unnecessary regulation that neither borrowers nor lenders need.

INNOVATION UNBOUND

As economism became more influential in the three decades beginning around 1980, these core beliefs reshaped the financial landscape. They were eagerly adopted by financial institutions themselves, which were constantly seeking new ways to make money. Under constant pressure from industry lobbyists, Congress and regulators relaxed the rules governing the buy-

---

* "Capital" has many meanings. It can refer to money available for investment in value-producing assets or to those assets themselves. It can also denote the value of the shareholders' stake in a financial insitution, as discussed later in this chapter.

ing, packaging, and reselling of money, hoping that the pursuit of self-interest would extend the benefits of homeownership to millions of people, stimulate financial innovation, and lubricate the engine of capitalism.

Complicated subprime mortgages would not have been possible in the "boring banking" system that lasted from the 1930s to the 1970s. With a traditional mortgage, a borrower would pay 20 percent down and then make monthly payments at a fixed interest rate for thirty years, after which she would own the house free and clear of debt. Only in 1982, with the passage of the Garn–St. Germain Depository Institutions Act, were most banks allowed to offer virtually any mortgage features they wanted, including adjustable rates, interest-only payments, or negative amortization.[8] The Garn–St. Germain Act was in part an attempt to help savings and loan associations find additional revenues, because higher interest rates at the time were driving up their costs, but deregulating the mortgage market was also part of the Reagan administration's larger economic program.

Banks and other lenders responded by developing new mortgages with different durations, balloon payments due at the end of the loan period, and interest rates that "floated" up and down after an initial "teaser" period. These products became even more complicated during the subprime lending boom that began in the late 1990s. The most extreme was probably the option adjustable-rate mortgage, or Option ARM, which allowed the borrower to decide how much to pay each month: she could even pay less than the interest on the loan, in which case the total balance would go up from month to month. After a few years, the loan would convert into an ordinary adjustable-rate mortgage with a higher interest rate—at which point the monthly payment could easily double or triple, leading to default or, at best, the need to refinance.[9] Refinancing typically cost another round of fees and sometimes a penalty for paying off the original loan early.

For federal banking regulators such as the Office of the Comptroller of the Currency (OCC), innovative mortgages could only be good for borrowers. When several states barred various mortgage features that were most likely to lead to defaults, the OCC overruled those laws on the legal grounds that federal rules took precedence over state regulation.[10] The underlying economic principle behind those rules was that complicated, expensive loans could not harm anyone; if borrowers accepted the terms, that meant that they valued the loan enough to justify the price.

The Federal Reserve had the power to crack down on some abusive lending practices under the 1994 Home Ownership and Equity Protection Act. In 2000, Edward Gramlich, a member of the Fed's Board of Governors, argued for increased oversight of mortgage lenders. At the time, however, the central bank was dominated by Alan Greenspan, a committed proponent of economism, who refused to take action.[11] For Greenspan, the proliferation of mortgage products and the growth of subprime lending simply demonstrated that the market was expanding to offer more choices to more people: "Where once more-marginal applicants would simply have been denied credit, lenders are now able to quite efficiently judge the risk posed by individual applicants and to price that risk appropriately."[12] In other words, high-risk borrowers were now able to take out loans at prices they were willing to pay. Because more loans were being made, more people were able to buy houses, and society as a whole must be better off. And the fact that banks were willing to sell complex subprime mortgages was proof that they understood the risks they were taking on, so there was no need to worry that borrowers would start defaulting in droves.

Complicated mortgages were the financial innovation most visible to ordinary people, but they were certainly not the only one. In the new vocabulary of economism, financial institutions were not just in the business of borrowing and lending money; now their purpose was to distribute risk. People and institutions face different kinds of risks: the risk of a house burning down, a borrower defaulting, interest rates falling, oil prices rising, and so on. The purpose of financial markets, on this theory, is to facilitate the transfer of risk—from households and businesses who want protection to investors who want to place bets in order to earn higher returns.

Beginning in the 1980s, financial institutions developed dizzyingly sophisticated instruments for buying, repackaging, and distributing risk. The two most important were derivatives and securitization. Derivatives are essentially side bets in financial markets. A credit default swap (CDS), for example, is a bet that some company will or will not default on its debt. The buyer of the CDS makes a small payment to the seller every month; but if the company defaults, the seller makes a large payment to the buyer. Neither party to the CDS has to have any relationship to the company it is betting on. According to basic economic theory, derivatives are good for two reasons. First, the general rule of markets applies: two parties will only agree to a transaction if it benefits both sides. Second, derivatives expand the set of tools available for trading risk, making possible welfare-creating exchanges that could not exist otherwise.

As the derivatives markets expanded in the 1990s—and several companies and municipalities suffered huge losses taking bets they didn't fully understand—some legislators and regulators began to worry about the risks they presented. In 1998, for example, Brooksley Born of the Commodity Futures Trading Commission began to investigate the market for over-the-counter (individually customized) derivatives. The financial lobby mobilized in defense of its increasingly profitable business: at one point, the deputy Treasury secretary, Lawrence Summers, called Born to say (according to one of Born's lieutenants), "I have 13 bankers in my office and they say if you go forward with this you will cause the worst financial crisis since World War II."[13] Their argument for derivatives was the same as the one for complex mortgages:

innovative financial products make possible new transactions between willing buyers and sellers, in this case allowing them to trade risk. According to Greenspan, the sophisticated players in the derivatives markets could police themselves; "Professional counterparties to privately negotiated contracts also have demonstrated their ability to protect themselves from losses, from fraud, and counterparty insolvencies," he observed. Therefore, Greenspan concluded, "regulation of derivatives transactions that are privately negotiated by professionals is unnecessary."[14] Congress rallied to the derivative dealers' defense, and Born's proposal died a quiet death.

Securitization was the state of the art in repackaging and redistributing risk. Although just about any financial asset can be securitized, the most popular raw material was mortgages, particularly subprime ones. First, mortgage originators sold individual loans to investment banks (Merrill Lynch, Goldman Sachs, and so on).* The banks then created trusts—separate legal entities—which bought the loans. The trusts paid for them by selling mortgage-backed securities (MBSs) to a new set of investors (hedge funds, pension funds, mutual funds, and so on). MBSs, like bonds, are a promise to repay the investor at some point in the future, with periodic interest payments along the way. Each month, home-owners mail mortgage checks to the trust, which uses that cash to make the interest payments it owes to the MBS investors. Most important, these MBSs were *tranched* ("sliced," in a combination of French and English). Each trust issued bonds with different levels of seniority. For example, there might be three tranches, labeled AAA, BBB, and C. (AAA, BBB, and similar designations are used by credit rating agencies to denote the riskiness of different types of bonds.) As money came in from homeowners, it was

---

* When a bank sells a mortgage, the buyer pays a lump sum of cash—typically about the same amount as the balance of the mortgage—and gains the right to keep the monthly mortgage payments from the original borrower.

first used to pay interest on the AAA bonds; if all of that interest was paid, the next cash would go toward interest on the BBB bonds; and if there was anything left over, it would be paid to the holders of the C bonds. The most senior tranches were the least risky—bondholders were most likely to be repaid—and therefore offered the lowest interest rates; the least senior tranches offered the highest interest rates.

Mortgage lenders liked securitization because they received cash up front for the loans they had just made. This not only locked in their profits but allowed them to recycle the cash into new loans. Investment banks collected large fees for packaging and selling the MBSs. The buyers, primarily institutional investors like hedge funds and pension funds, were attracted to securities that had relatively high interest rates for the amount of risk that they seemed to present. Investment banks would also buy some tranches of their own MBSs and use them as raw material for a second round of securitization. Just as mortgages were transformed into MBSs, those MBSs could then be transformed into a new set of tranched bonds, now known as collateralized debt obligations (CDOs).*

The brilliant thing about securitization, according to economism, was that it created new markets for risk. Individual banks no longer had to worry that a downturn in local housing values could cause many of their borrowers to default at the same time. Securitization pooled together risk across the entire economy and carved it up into small pieces that were sold to investors who wanted them. Tranching created securities that carried different levels of risk and promised commensurate returns, offering more choices to investors. Any MBS was backed by loans to thousands of different borrowers; because it seemed unlikely that

---

* A CDO has the same relationship to its underlying MBSs as an MBS has to its underlying mortgages. Adding to the confusion, "CDO" can refer either to an entire deal that repackages MBSs into new securities or to the resulting securities themselves. Then there are CDO^2 and synthetic CDOs. . . .

many of them would default at the same time, even individually risky subprime mortgages could be used as the raw material for AAA-rated MBSs—supposedly as safe as U.S. Treasury bonds. The proliferation of MBSs and CDOs increased the volume of transactions in the financial markets, making it easier for capital to flow from investors around the world to aspiring homeowners across the United States. This was the best of all possible worlds.

Federal legislators and regulators, seduced by the idea that large, sophisticated banks had mastered the art of managing risk and were unerringly steering capital around the economy, cheered on this transformation of the financial sector. Investment banks were only allowed to securitize mortgages in the first place because of the Secondary Mortgage Market Enhancement Act, passed in 1984. In 1999, Congress approved the Gramm-Leach-Bliley Act, which allowed investment banks, commercial banks, and insurance companies to combine into single firms for the first time since the 1930s. Gramm-Leach-Bliley rejected the long-held belief that risk-taking activities by investment banks could threaten the financial system. A year later, Congress passed the Commodity Futures Modernization Act, which, among other things, enshrined into law the nonregulation of over-the-counter derivatives.

Regulators also relaxed some of the key rules designed to prevent financial institutions from failing. For a bank, *capital* represents the amount of money invested by shareholders, which the bank then supplements by borrowing from depositors and the bond markets. Minimum capital requirements historically limited the amount that banks could borrow, thereby reducing the chance that they would go bankrupt if their bets turned out badly. Those rules, however, limited the total volume of loans that they could make with the same amount of capital, restricting their ability to earn profits. During the heyday of financial innovation, regulators became convinced that securitization, derivatives, and sophisticated new modeling techniques enabled banks to calibrate and monitor their risk precisely, rendering traditional capital requirements unnecessary. In 2001, federal agencies gave banks new flexibility in determining how much capital they needed when investing in certain types of complex assets.[15] Then, in 2004, the Securities and Exchange Commission allowed the largest investment banks to use their own, internal models to calculate their capital requirements. The premise was that banks had an interest in measuring their risk accurately and had "developed robust internal risk management practices," so they could be trusted to regulate themselves effectively.[16]

In the worldview of economism, the deregulation of the financial system was a crucial step forward in unleashing the forces of supply and demand to deliver the most credit to the most people at the lowest possible cost. As economists Stephen Cohen and Brad DeLong describe it, "Junk bonds, subprime mortgages, securitization to pool and diversify risk, and the construction of financial derivatives to carve up and distribute risks . . . these were all seen as ways of broadening access to capital, potentially democratizing finance, and boosting upward mobility."[17] Deregulation also had more concrete benefits for the financial sector itself. Beginning in the 1980s, the profits of financial institutions skyrocketed compared to the rest of the U.S. economy, accounting for more than one-third of all corporate profits from 2001 to 2007. People employed in the industry benefited as well; from 1980 until the financial crisis, average incomes more than doubled relative to the rest of the private sector, while the bankers and traders designing and betting on new derivatives or CDOs often made millions or tens of millions of dollars per year.[18] Economism provided the perfect justification for this increase in inequality, however: higher compensation simply reflected the value that the modern financial system created for society as a whole and was necessary to attract the best and brightest to where they could do the most good.

Only . . . as we have seen, this story ended in a tidal wave of collapsing housing prices, defaults, foreclosures, and countless stories of financial ruin. The most sophisticated financial system in world history, boasting computer power previously available only to the national security establishment, manufactured hundreds of billions of dollars of loans that would never be repaid. In addition to putting families out on the street, those loans caused massive overinvestment in residential real estate, funding vast exurban developments that stood vacant years later—an irreversible waste of real resources.[19] As homeowners began missing mortgage payments across the country, the diversification promised by MBSs and CDOs turned out to be worthless: if borrowers are defaulting everywhere, the fact that an MBS is backed by mortgages from many different places isn't much help. It turned out that MBSs and CDOs were in fact a large bet on the U.S. housing market—a bet that most financial institutions and many investors suddenly discovered they had placed. The very banks that orchestrated the housing boom collapsed or nearly collapsed along with the housing market in 2008, while investors ranging from midwestern school districts to small towns in Norway suffered crippling losses.[20]

TOXIC MORTGAGES

Economism's rosy model failed to predict how both individuals and companies would behave in a world of ever-increasing financial complexity. In the real world, people cannot always predict how much products will be worth to them, especially when it comes to complicated instruments like mortgages. Because a mortgage is one of the most important products that a person will select in her lifetime, poor choices can have serious long-term consequences.

Consider the Option ARM, the emblematic mortgage of the subprime boom. In order to make a rational decision about an

Option ARM, you would need to understand how the product worked, how much interest rates might go up, and the potential range of future housing prices (which would determine whether or not you could refinance in the future). In retrospect, it is clear that many borrowers during the housing bubble had no idea how much risk they were assuming. Most people taking out ordinary adjustable-rate mortgages—not even the fancy Option ARMs—did not realize how much their interest rates could rise. As Option ARMs became more popular, the vast majority of borrowers were making only their minimum monthly payments and were therefore highly likely to default when the teaser period of low rates ended.[21]

And yet people signed up for Option ARMs, in increasing numbers—$255 billion worth of them by 2006.[22] From the borrower's perspective, these fancy mortgages made it possible to buy a relatively big house with a small income. This was the case because lenders approved loans by comparing the low, *initial* monthly payment with the borrower's income, which they often declined to verify independently. These "stated income" loans were thus issued to people who simply claimed to meet the required income thresholds—sometimes at the prompting of unscrupulous salespeople. At the extreme, an agricultural laborer with an income of $14,000 could even buy a $724,000 house with no money down.[23] According to an executive at Countrywide, one of the nation's largest lenders, anyone who could "fog a mirror" could get a loan.[24] So people tempted by the prospect of owning a house took out complex mortgages without asking questions.

Still, however, few people sought out Option ARMs. Instead, they had to be sold. Mortgage brokers actively pushed them onto customers by showing how low their initial monthly payments could be. Internal research by Washington Mutual, a large mortgage lender, indicated that people were more likely to buy an Option ARM if they knew less about the product; brokers often did their part by making sure that borrowers did not understand what they were signing up for. Common tactics included making up or doctoring information on applications, forging signatures, and pretending that adjustable-rate loans were actually fixed-rate mortgages.[25] Even if people could qualify for low-interest-rate loans, brokers would steer them toward higher-rate products that paid bigger commissions; in 2005, more than half of subprime borrowers could have qualified for prime loans.[26] Mortgage brokers were eager to sell Option ARMs because they received high commissions from banks and other lenders. Those banks were happy to lend money to risky borrowers with unverified incomes because it helped them meet their revenue targets and penetrate the subprime market, with its attractively high interest rates. Washington Mutual, for example, relied on the Option ARM and other high-risk mortgages to gain market share in the first decade of the twenty-first century.[27] Lenders could then pass the loans on to investment banks, which paid a premium for Option ARMs because their high interest rates made them the perfect input to the fee-generating securitization machine, which spit out mortgage-backed securities at the other end.

In short, Option ARMs were popular because the financial industry wanted them, not because well-informed borrowers thought they were a good deal. The people buying and refinancing houses were not the customers; they were a source of raw material. The fact that ordinary human beings could not understand the legal documents they were signing was a crucial feature of the entire system, not a bug. According to economism, an unregulated mortgage market will maximize the number of value-creating transactions between buyers and suppliers of credit. Instead, the lack of regulation made it possible for millions of borrowers—aided and abetted by mortgage brokers and lenders—to take out loans they had little chance of repaying. The capital that flowed into Option ARMs and similar mortgages increased the number of buyers in the housing market, forcing up prices everywhere in an unsustainable frenzy that eventually produced the largest economic collapse in more than seventy years.[28]

TOXIC BANKS

The irony, of course, is that when those ordinary human beings stopped making their monthly payments, it was the investment banks, staffed by some of the smartest graduates of the world's top universities, that collapsed along with the toxic securities they had been manufacturing for years. The theory was that financial innovation made it possible for any company or investor to construct exactly the portfolio of risks that it wanted to hold. The reality was that the enormous banks at the heart of the system lost track of the risks that they were buying and selling, only to discover, like a character in a television cartoon, that they were left holding the time bomb when it finally exploded.

Economics 101, remember, assumes that firms always rationally maximize their profits. In the financial context, this means that banks don't make loans unless they get enough interest and fee revenue to compensate for their losses on borrowers who don't pay them back. It also means that financial institutions don't hold on to large portfolios of assets that could suddenly become worthless; instead, they divide up those assets into small pieces and sell them to different investors. It is possible that a bank could misjudge its risks and end up losing money, but that's ultimately a good thing, because it will be forced out of the market by more efficient competitors that are better at allocating capital.

But anyone who has ever worked at a large company—or read *Dilbert*, for that matter—knows that corporations are not ruthlessly efficient profit maximization machines, but collections of fallible and often self-interested human beings. In economics, this is known as the principal-agent problem: the principal (company) can only act through agents (employees), who may not do what's best for their principal.* Wall Street investment banks in particular are populated by highly competitive bankers, most of whose pay comes in an annual bonus that depends heavily on the fees they generated in the previous year. For the people who packaged and distributed MBSs and CDOs, those bonuses were based on the size of the deals they closed, not what happened later when housing prices started to fall.

The immediate consequence of this compensation structure was apparent systematic fraud. Investment banks ignored problems with the loans they were buying from mortgage lenders, or failed to disclose those problems to the investors buying their MBSs and CDOs. As journalist David Dayen summarized, "The entire industry was assembled on a mountain of fraud" that began with mortgage brokers but continued on through the securitization chain.[29] The goal was to transform as many mortgages as possible into securities that could be sold to end investors, without stopping to ask inconvenient questions. At the end of the housing boom, when those investors were getting harder to find, that even meant selling toxic assets to their own bank.

Although investment banks generally claimed to be in the distribution business, buying mortgages at one end and selling highly engineered securities at the other, they did sometimes keep the most senior tranches of CDOs for themselves, thinking they were free from risk. In 2006, however, Merrill Lynch's bond traders, beginning to guess how the housing boom would end, balked at buying even the top-rated slices of the bank's own CDOs; without a buyer, the CDO team could not do any fee-generating deals in the first place. To solve this problem, Merrill created a new trading group that agreed to buy the hard-to-sell tranches. In exchange, the CDO team shared some of their prof-

---

* The principal-agent problem may show up in an introductory class but typically gets relatively little attention.

its with the new group, so everyone was happy—in the short term. Eventually, Merrill amassed a $32 billion portfolio of CDO securities, on which it took a loss of $26 billion during the financial crisis.[30] What was good for the bankers was not good for the bank.

Bankers also sometimes had the incentive to create CDOs that were likely to fail—meaning that their underlying mortgages were likely to default, so there would be no cash to pay investors in the CDO. In 2007, for example, JPMorgan Chase created a new CDO called Squared in collaboration with the hedge fund Magnetar, which bought some of Squared's securities while also placing a large bet that the CDO would fail. According to a *ProPublica* investigation, Magnetar pushed JPMorgan to pool together risky slices of existing CDOs, making Squared itself more risky. Those CDOs did end up in Squared, which generated $20 million in fees credited to JPMorgan's CDO team. JPMorgan the bank, however, ended up losing $880 million on its holdings in Squared when the market collapsed.[31] In short, one group of bankers engineered a deal that cost their employer almost forty times the fees from the original transaction. In both the Merrill and the JPMorgan cases, not only did the investment banks suffer enormous losses, but capital was funneled into the mortgage market even as the housing bubble was beginning to implode—not where it could do the most good for society.

The top executives of Merrill Lynch, JPMorgan Chase, and other investment banks were not simple dupes at the mercy of their employees. But as financial innovation became more sophisticated and the top banks became more complex, even insiders found it increasingly hard to tell just how much risk they were carrying. Executives were reluctant to cut back production of the MBSs and CDOs that were generating healthy revenues in the short term. The pressure of meeting quarterly financial expectations, combined with compensation packages that depended heavily on meeting those targets, made it difficult to prioritize anything other than short-term profits—even as some executives wondered how long the boom could be sustained. Charles Prince, the CEO of Citigroup, memorably admitted in 2007, "As long as the music is playing, you've got to get up and dance. We're still dancing."[32]

The lure of short-term profits seduced other key players in the securitization chain, including CDO managers, credit rating agencies, and institutional money managers. When an investment bank created a CDO, it hired a CDO manager to choose the securities for the underlying pool. In theory, the manager was supposed to protect investors by choosing securities that were unlikely to default. In practice, however, CDO managers depended on the investment banks for repeat business and were often suspected of doing their bidding. When a bank could not find enough investors for one of its CDOs, one solution was to pressure the manager of a different CDO to buy the unwanted tranches. As one CDO manager said, "I would go to Merrill and tell them that I wanted to buy, say, a Citi bond. They would say 'no.' I would suggest a UBS bond, they would say 'no.' Eventually, you got the joke."[33] In the words of the writer Michael Lewis, the CDO manager was "a double agent—a character who seemed to represent the interests of investors when he better represented the interests of Wall Street bond trading desks."[34]

Credit rating agencies such as Standard & Poor's, Moody's, and Fitch evaluate the riskiness of bonds, giving them grades like AAA, AA, A, BBB, BB, and so on, with the chance of default increasing as you move down the alphabet. These seemingly objective designations helped convince investors that MBSs and CDOs were safe investments. It was the investment bank managing a securitization, however, that chose the rating agency, which therefore had the incentive to keep the bank happy. According to one insider, the banks said, "Hey, if you don't [give me the rating I want], the guy across the street will. And we'll give him all the business."[35] That business was vitally important to the rating agencies, whose revenues grew rapidly during the housing boom. At Moody's, executives who thought the firm was giving overly generous grades found themselves out of a job. After the crash, however, those same ratings came back to haunt the agencies; Standard & Poor's, for example, later paid $1.4 billion to settle charges of grade inflation.[36]

Finally, institutional money managers placed the buy orders for MBSs and CDOs; without them, securitization could not have happened, and there would have been no cash to fuel the subprime boom. The money came from rich households and institutions such as insurance companies, pension systems, and universities, but it was largely invested by professional fund managers. Fund management firms mainly play with other people's money, from which they take an annual percentage. So one profit-maximizing strategy is to collect as much money to invest as possible, stick with the conventional wisdom, and not give your clients a reason to take their assets elsewhere. As long as housing prices continued rising, it made little sense to bet against the market and miss out on the party. Few fund managers looked carefully at what they were buying, trusting the investment banks' generic (and sometimes misleading) disclosures and the credit rating agencies' rosy reports. Instead, they kept putting their clients' money into complex securities that were dangerously dependent on the health of the U.S. housing market. When the crisis hit, however, it was their investors that absorbed the losses.

For investment banks, CDO managers, credit rating agencies, and institutional money managers, the most direct path to profits was to pretend that housing prices could only go up, even as the opposite became more and more inevitable. And so, most continued to play their appointed roles in the securitization process right until the end, helping funnel capital to increasingly speculative real estate developments. In the imagination of economism, a network of sophisticated, specialized firms collaborated to match loans with borrowers, manufacture securities with different risk-return profiles, and distribute those securities to buyers, efficiently allocating capital to homeowners and companies who could use it and transferring risk back to investors who wanted it. Instead, the modern financial system turned into a frenzied scramble to squeeze individual and company profits out of borrowers and investors, with consequences that few people understood.

In 2008, the firestorm that began with subprime mortgages and ultimately engulfed all of Wall Street demonstrated one final flaw in the Economics 101 model of the firm. In theory, companies should be allowed to take whatever risks they want; if their bets turn out badly, they go bankrupt, and life goes on. But when Lehman Brothers failed in September 2008, life did not go on; every other major investment bank teetered on the verge of collapse, while the money markets that ordinary companies rely on for their everyday operations suddenly froze up with panic. At that moment, we all found out that the world's biggest banks are *too big to fail:* if one of them suddenly goes out of business, the damage it does to other major financial institutions could bring down the entire economy. As the Federal Reserve chair, Ben Bernanke, said at the time, asking Congress to approve emergency measures, "If we don't do this, we may not have an economy on Monday."[37]

The fact that certain megabanks are too big to fail is not only infuriating to taxpayers forced to shoulder the costs of bailing them out. It also poses a serious problem for the economy. A financial institution that is too big to fail has the incentive to take on excessive risks. If its bets are successful, it will earn high profits for its shareholders (and its executives will be rewarded handsomely); if they go bad, however, the bank can count on being rescued by the government and shifting its losses to taxpayers at large. This asymmetric structure not only is unfair but also distorts the allocation of capital by increasing banks' appetite for risk. Once again, the pursuit of profit reduces social welfare and redirects capital away from its best uses.

In many sectors of the economy, the Economics 101 model

of the firm may be a reasonable enough approximation of the real world. If local restaurants are undermined by self-interested employees, or put short-term profits ahead of their long-term health, they may inflict bad food on their customers and eventually go out of business, but society will not be too much worse off as a result. With the financial system, however, the misguided belief that firms act rationally and are effectively regulated by competition has had disastrous consequences. In 2008, we relearned the lesson that a competitive market does not magically ensure that capital flows to its most productive uses. Instead, profit-seeking behavior leads both people and companies to maximize their individual gains in ways that distort lending decisions and waste resources—sometimes on a truly monumental scale.

ECONOMISM UNBOWED

Surveying the wreckage of the financial crisis, one finds it hard to imagine that anyone ever believed that rational consumers, relentlessly profit-seeking firms, and the magic of competition would provide just the right amount of credit to borrowers and allocate capital optimally across the economy. In 2008 and 2009, it seemed obvious that the financial system urgently needed to be reformed to reduce risk to ordinary families and to the economy as a whole. Instead, however, the simplistic beliefs that helped produce the crisis have remained both popular and influential. Perhaps this should not be too surprising. Because economism's arguments are rooted in pure theory, they can never be disproven by mere facts.

Even in the depths of the crisis, the idea that regulation would only interfere with the optimal workings of supply and demand quickly became the central argument against reforming the financial system. The campaign took economism's classic rhetorical form: if only people understood basic economics, they would realize that their well-intentioned proposals were doomed to backfire. A JPMorgan Chase research note mocked members of the Senate for "an unnerving ignorance of fundamental principles of market economics" and "a confusion about our market economy that is as fundamental as knowing that George Washington was the first president of the United States." This illiteracy, the author warned, meant that "financial reform will make credit more expensive and more difficult to obtain and businesses will find it more difficult to shed risk, harming the very people we are trying to help."[38]

As millions of borrowers faced the prospect of foreclosure, economism's champions argued vehemently that there was no need to protect consumers from dangerous financial products. Peter Wallison of AEI attacked the Obama administration's proposal for a consumer financial protection agency as "elitist protection consumers don't need," claiming that some people would be "denied the opportunity to buy products and services that are available to others." "Instead of actually helping consumers," David John of the Heritage Foundation argued, "the proposed CFPA [Consumer Financial Protection Agency] would more likely stifle innovation" and reduce the choices available in the market. Congressman Jeb Hensarling called the proposed agency "one of the great assaults on consumer rights."[39]

The belief that sophisticated, profit-seeking firms can do no wrong was another central theme of the campaign against financial reform. *The Wall Street Journal*'s editorial board claimed that proposals to regulate derivatives would make it more difficult for companies to hedge risk and thereby "needlessly suck cash out of productive parts of the economy." Wallison criticized a new regulatory regime aimed at the largest banks—those most likely to endanger the financial system because of their size—for interfering with free competition. The political action group Freedom-Works urged legislators to vote against the proposed reform bill because it did not "[allow] free-market mechanisms to set the right incentives for banks to make prudent lending decisions—where those who may profit are also the ones who will pay the cost of their own failure."[40] Indeed, the most prominent counternarrative of the financial crisis blamed the whole mess on government regulations that interfered with companies' freedom to pursue profits—supposedly, rules requiring government agencies and financial institutions to lend money to low-income households.[41] JPMorgan Chase's chief executive, Jamie Dimon, warned that if legislators picked on his industry too much, he and his colleagues would pack up their toys and pursue profits somewhere else: "When profits fall too sharply then capital will move somewhere else, where there is more money to be earned."[42]

In July 2010, the Obama administration and its allies squeaked through Congress the Dodd-Frank Wall Street Reform and Consumer Protection Act. This bill placed new restraints on the financial sector, although it failed to address some of the key factors that transformed a housing crisis into a global meltdown. The megabanks that nearly collapsed are larger and more complex than ever, and capital requirements are still too low to ensure that those banks will survive the next crisis intact.[43] As memories of 2008 continue to fade, however, critics argue that the Dodd-Frank Act violates economic common sense. The Consumer Financial Protection Bureau (CFPB) remains a prime target. A Heritage Foundation report argued that consumer protection is bad for the people it tries to help because it "constrict[s] the availability of financial products"—always a bad idea in Economics 101.[44] In July 2015, Senator Ted Cruz and Representative John Ratcliffe introduced a bill that would eliminate the CFPB altogether.

Repealing the entire Dodd-Frank Act has become a favorite cause among many conservatives, often for reasons that come straight from first-year economics. Senator Marco Rubio claimed that "Dodd-Frank cripples innovation and economic growth" and even asserted that "over 40% of small and mid-size banks that loan money to small businesses have been wiped out since Dodd-Frank has passed." The Senate Banking Committee chair, Richard Shelby, criticized Dodd-Frank's provisions addressing large, insolvent banks on the grounds that "failure is a part of capitalism and those businesses that take excessive risk should be allowed to fail." As usual, this is true in the abstract but fails to recognize that the sudden collapse of a megabank could still torpedo the global economy, and so the big banks have to be closely supervised.* In *The Wall Street Journal*, Hensarling concluded that the Dodd-Frank Act is "taking the power to allocate capital . . . away from the free market and delivering it to political actors in Washington."[45] Ultimately, what these tired clichés demonstrate better than anything else is the firm grip that economism has over a large segment of the political class, which has completely forgotten the hard lessons that we learned less than a decade ago.

As the stock market and the high-end real estate market roared back from their 2009 lows, it also became evident that the costs of those lessons were not shared equally across society. In the United States, the share of income earned by the top 1 percent surpassed its precrisis peak in 2012. Bankers have done well, too: average pay in the industry has climbed back above the levels of 2006 and 2007. For the population as a whole, however, things have turned out differently. As of 2014, the median household's income, after adjusting for inflation, was more than $3,000 *lower* than in 2007, and the proportion of working-age people with jobs was still well below 2007 levels.[46] Foreclosures and job losses had the most severe impact on people with limited assets and job skills, while high unemployment levels made it hard for new college graduates to enter the workforce, aggravating a growing stu-

---

* This is why, in *13 Bankers*, Simon Johnson and I argued that the largest banks should be broken up.

dent debt problem. One generation of policy makers, seduced by economism, deregulated the financial system and helped administer a tremendous shock to millions of ordinary working families. Today, another generation is once again promising that the secret to prosperity lies in competitive credit markets populated by profit-seeking financial institutions.

8

It's a Small World After All

That free trade is advantageous to both sides is the rarest of
political propositions—provable, indeed mathematically.

—Charles Krauthammer, 2015[1]

Campaigning in Michigan in March 2016, Senator Bernie Sanders blamed the "disappearance of the American middle class" on
international trade deals such as the 1994 North American Free
Trade Agreement (NAFTA), which facilitated the exchange of
goods and services between the United States, Canada, and Mexico. "Corporate America made the decision that they didn't want
to pay workers in this country a living wage," he argued. "What
they wanted to do was shut down plants in America, go to Mexico,
go to China . . . and then bring their products back into America." Sanders had an unlikely ally. "Michigan's been stripped,"
said the Republican presidential hopeful Donald Trump, describing the impact of trade. "You look at those empty factories all
over the place." Trump called NAFTA "a disaster for our country," and described the trade deficit with China (the fact that
China exports more goods and services to the United States than
vice versa) as "the greatest theft in the history of the world."[2] The
people of Michigan, once the home of the auto industry, agreed
with the two political outsiders. More than 50 percent of voters

in each party said that international trade costs the United States jobs, and Sanders and Trump won the state's primary elections.[3]

Michiganders may be particularly opposed to foreign trade, given the role of Japanese competition in the decline of the local auto industry, but the state is not an outlier. In a recent *Bloomberg* national poll, respondents favored more restrictions on imports ("to protect American jobs") by 65 percent to 22 percent (the remainder were unsure); 44 percent thought that NAFTA was bad for the U.S. economy, compared to 29 percent who thought it was beneficial.[4] The idea that imports force Americans out of work has intuitive appeal. Since the late 1970s, as foreign trade has grown, the United States has lost more than 7 million of the manufacturing jobs that enabled working families to join the middle class in the decades after World War II. In 2015, we imported more than $2.7 trillion worth of goods and services ranging from Chinese iPhones to German cars to Indian customer support. (At the same time, our exports totaled about $2.2 trillion, leaving a trade deficit of more than $500 billion.)[5] Many unemployed or underemployed Americans would be happy to make those products or take those phone calls. In today's climate of economic insecurity, the fear of getting laid off because of outsourcing or foreign competition has led many people to question the merits of international trade.

ORANGES AND BANANAS

In the sunny world of Economics 101, however, trade is always good. On one level, this follows directly from the basic model of supply and demand. If a company can make a snow shovel for $10 and a consumer would get $20 of value from that shovel, it doesn't matter whether or not they happen to be in the same country; trade will make them both better off, increasing social welfare—if "society" is defined to include the entire world.

Seen from a national perspective, there might appear to be a problem. If an American person buys a snow shovel from an American company, then both the consumer surplus and the producer surplus remain within the country. But suppose a Chinese manufacturer can make shovels more cheaply. If an American buys a Chinese snow shovel, the producer surplus—and the jobs making the shovel—are lost across the Pacific. The United States as a whole appears to be worse off. Now imagine that China can supply *everything* more cheaply than the United States, perhaps because its workers make less money. This might make you think that Americans would end up buying everything from Chinese companies, leaving no jobs in the United States.

Not to worry, however. The answer lies in the theory of *comparative advantage*, developed by the economist David Ricardo in the early nineteenth century. In Economics 101, this concept is usually illustrated with an idyllic example such as the following: Imagine two people living on neighboring tropical islands who can each plant orange and banana trees. If Mickey plants only orange trees, he can produce one hundred oranges per month; if he plants only banana trees, he can produce two hundred bananas

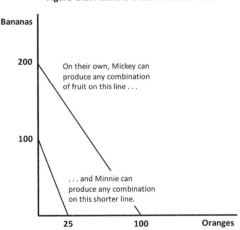

Figure 8.1: Possible Diets Without Trade

Bananas

200 On their own, Mickey can produce any combination of fruit on this line . . .

100

. . . and Minnie can produce any combination on this shorter line.

25   100   Oranges

per month. He can also plant some combination of the two, as shown in Figure 8.1; for example, if he covers half of the island with each fruit tree, he will grow fifty oranges and one hundred bananas per month. Minnie faces the same choices, except her island's soil is less fertile, particularly for orange trees. If she covers her island with orange trees, she can harvest only twenty-five oranges per month; if she plants only banana trees, she can harvest one hundred bananas per month; or she can plant some combination, also shown in Figure 8.1.

As Mickey is better at cultivating both oranges and bananas, you might think there is no reason for him to trade with Minnie. But here's the trick: Mickey is only twice as good at growing bananas as growing oranges (two hundred versus one hundred), while Minnie is four times as efficient (one hundred versus twenty-five). To produce two more bananas, Mickey has to produce one less orange; for him, the price of two bananas is one orange. If Minnie wants one more orange, she has to give up four bananas; for her, the price of an orange is four bananas. This makes possible a mutually beneficial deal: Mickey can trade one orange to Minnie for three bananas. Instead of producing one less orange and producing two bananas in its place, he trades the orange to Minnie for three bananas. Instead of growing four fewer bananas and growing one orange in their place, she trades three bananas to Mickey for an orange (and keeps the fourth banana). Both of them are better off than they would be on their own.

This works because Mickey has a comparative advantage over Minnie in oranges—he has to give up fewer bananas than she does to grow one orange—while she has a comparative advantage in bananas. Mickey has two ways to get bananas: he can grow them himself, or he can grow oranges and trade them for bananas. Because his comparative advantage is in oranges, he gets more bananas by choosing the latter. Substitute computers for oranges and clothing for bananas (Ricardo used English cloth and Portuguese wine), and you can see why international trade always makes both countries better off.

The principle of comparative advantage explains why, in the world of Economics 101, *protectionism*—limiting imports in order to shield domestic companies and workers from competition—is unequivocally bad. Restrictions on trade, such as tariffs (taxes on imports) or regulations that disadvantage foreign companies, prevent mutually beneficial cross-border transactions from occurring. Eliminating import barriers is even good for a country's residents—the people behind the barriers—regardless of other countries' trade policies, because the increase in consumer surplus due to lower prices outweighs the decrease in producer surplus caused by foreign competition.

The idea that the United States should open its borders to products from overseas, regardless of whether other countries reciprocate, seems counterintuitive. That might appear to harm American workers, who face competition from imports but are barred from exporting goods abroad. But international trade has to be seen as a complete system. When American consumers buy goods from overseas, we pay for them with U.S. dollars. The only thing foreign companies can do with those dollars is either buy American products (our exports) or invest in American assets, both of which are generally good for our economy, at least in theory.* The idea that we could buy everything from overseas, and that no jobs would be left for us to do, is simply self-contradictory. The lesson of comparative advantage is so compelling that most students leave Economics 101 with the conviction that free trade is indisputably good for everyone.

Milton Friedman was a lifelong advocate for free trade. In 1970, he dismissed as "utter nonsense" the idea that the United States should impose restrictions on Japanese imports because Japan did not open its markets to American companies. "Exports are the cost of trade, imports the return from trade, not the other

---

* For example, foreign purchases of U.S. financial assets lower interest rates for households and businesses; foreign direct investment, such as building factories, provides capital to U.S. business and employs American workers. In the real world, too much foreign investment can cause other complications.

way around," he wrote. Unlike on many other issues, however, conventional economic wisdom was already on Friedman's side. John Maynard Keynes also generally favored free trade, although he thought protectionist policies might have tactical usefulness, depending on the terms of the international financial system (a caveat with which Friedman agreed).[6] Indeed, compared with the other Economics 101 lessons discussed in this book, the idea that trade is generally good for both sides—not just in theory, but in the real world as well—is remarkably popular among professional economists. According to the commentator Matt Yglesias, "There is almost nothing in the whole wide world that economists like better than recounting David Ricardo's basic case for free trade." A panel of economists polled by the Chicago Booth School of Business was virtually unanimous in agreeing that the benefits of trade, in the form of efficiency and consumer choice, were "much larger" than the costs of any potential job losses and that U.S. citizens were made better off by NAFTA.[7] The economist and international trade specialist Paul Krugman, who sits at the opposite end of the political spectrum from Friedman on most policy issues, agrees with him on the merits of free trade. In *Capitalism and Freedom*, Friedman argued, "Our tariffs hurt us as well as other countries. We would be benefited by dispensing with our tariffs even if other countries did not." Four decades later, Krugman wrote, "A country serves its own interests by pursuing free trade regardless of what other countries may do."[8]

International trade is also one area in which policy makers seem to have listened to economists. After World War II, the United States generally sought to lower trade barriers—in part to ensure export markets for American companies, in part to accelerate our allies' redevelopment by giving them access to American customers, and in part to establish a network of peaceful co-dependence among countries outside the communist bloc. More recently, the United States has pushed for bilateral and multilateral trade agreements with many of our trading partners.

The long-standing consensus between economists and politicians that free trade is good for America is one reason that many commentators are horrified by Donald Trump's call for tariffs of 35 percent or 45 percent on imports from Mexico or China.[9]

WINNERS AND LOSERS

Despite this apparent unanimity among economists and the political elite, large segments of the public persist in questioning the wisdom of free trade. There are certainly bad reasons why someone might oppose free trade, such as xenophobia. But there are legitimate economic reasons as well—reasons that are often mentioned in Economics 101 but then overlooked or forgotten.

The key issue is that, within each country, foreign trade can often produce winners and losers. In our tropical island example, trade with Minnie causes Mickey to produce fewer bananas and more oranges. If Mickey is a country, and if oranges and bananas are two sectors of its economy, then the orange industry gains jobs at the expense of the banana industry. Ideally, people who used to work for banana companies find employment growing and selling oranges. In practice, the people losing jobs to foreign competition may differ from those gaining work because of increased exports; but things still balance out on the whole, because job increases in the orange sector should equal decreases in the banana sector.[10] As Friedman wrote in 1981, "Some jobs are certainly being lost to imports—jobs in industries especially affected. But other jobs are being created by imports—jobs in industries producing the exports that are purchased by the dollars foreigners earn from the goods we import."[11] Meanwhile, everyone benefits from cheaper bananas (thanks to imports from Minnie).

The same story reads differently from the perspective of the losers, however. When a rich country like the United States increases trade with a poor country, some industries will lose jobs because of competition from cheaper foreign labor. This can mean concentrated layoffs in specific sectors, as has happened to American manufacturing. Although those job losses may be balanced by gains in other parts of the economy, longtime assembly-line workers at automotive parts manufacturers in the Midwest cannot easily get hired by New Jersey pharmaceutical companies or Silicon Valley software firms. For them and their families, the direct impact of trade is long-term unemployment and financial hardship. The other losers from trade are workers in industries facing heightened overseas competition. Cheap imports, as well as the threat that American companies will send jobs overseas, reduce their ability to negotiate for higher pay, suppressing wages.

In a developed economy like the United States, then, foreign trade adversely affects low-wage workers who can be replaced by even cheaper workers in developing countries. Advanced economies' comparative advantage is not in labor-intensive sectors, but in those industries with the highest productivity levels and the most skilled employees—software companies, not banana farms. Companies in these industries enjoy higher revenues and profits because they can now sell to customers all around the globe, enriching their shareholders and employees. Within a rich country, in short, the primary winners are people who are already well-off, and therefore one result of increased trade with poor countries is greater inequality within the U.S. workforce.

In addition to people in high-productivity industries, the other group of winners from trade is American consumers, who gain access to a wider range of products and services, often with lower prices or higher quality. But their gains are relatively small, at least compared with the harm suffered by laid-off workers. People tend to notice when their jobs are eliminated or threatened by foreign competition; they tend not to notice that prices are lower than they would be without that same competition. If you were laid off from a General Motors factory, the fact that you can now buy a cheap, reliable Toyota is not particularly comforting. So it is understandable that free trade is less popular among ordinary people than it is among economists.

In theory, because trade makes the total pie bigger for everyone, both globally and within any one country, there should be a way to redistribute some of the gains from the winners (consumers and workers in export industries) to the losers (workers in industries exposed to foreign competition). In practice, however, this would require an increase in taxes to pay additional benefits to the long-term unemployed—something that is virtually inconceivable in the contemporary American political landscape. As a result, the likely effect of international trade is to force concentrated groups of families into poverty and suppress working-class wages in certain industries while boosting high-end incomes and making everyone else slightly better off—ultimately increasing overall inequality.

THE REAL IMPACT OF TRADE

In summary, Economics 101 teaches us two things about international trade. First, for any participating country, *seen as a whole*, the benefits of trade outweigh its costs; this simple principle has been absorbed into the worldview of economism. Second, and often forgotten, those costs and benefits are distributed unequally within each country, making some people better off and others worse off. But how well do these lessons apply to the real world?

Looking at the historical record, it's far from clear that open borders are better than trade barriers. In the nineteenth century, the United States became the world's leading economy not by pursuing free trade but by limiting imports. Alexander Hamilton, the first Treasury secretary, imposed high tariffs, which were maintained throughout the nineteenth century with the support of industrial interests. Those tariffs shielded U.S. companies from much more efficient British competitors until they were able to compete effectively. What the economists Stephen Cohen and Brad DeLong call the "Hamiltonian system" then inspired later-industrializing countries, including Germany in the late nineteenth century and Japan, South Korea, and China in the twentieth century. Each of the latter East Asian countries became an export powerhouse in part by protecting its infant manufacturing industries and carefully managing interactions with the outside world—not by allowing foreign companies free access to its markets.[12]

These history lessons may not apply to the contemporary United States, however, which is long beyond the initial stage of industrialization and has a large population of relatively affluent consumers eager to buy goods and services from around the world. In recent decades, increases in international trade have yielded mixed results for Americans—perhaps improving overall social welfare but certainly creating winners and losers. While the ongoing debate over NAFTA remains fierce, free trade with Mexico and Canada has had a relatively small impact on the U.S. economy as a whole. The Congressional Budget Office estimated that by 2001 NAFTA had increased exports to Mexico by 11 percent and imports from Mexico by 8 percent. Even so, the U.S. economy is so large that these additional imports only amounted to 0.1 percent of gross domestic product (GDP), implying that the trade deal's impact on jobs was small. Estimates by the Economic Policy Institute (generally anti-NAFTA) and the Peterson Institute for International Economics (generally pro-NAFTA) put net U.S. employment losses due to rising trade with Mexico in the range of fifteen thousand to forty thousand jobs per year—much less than one-tenth of 1 percent of the total labor market. Similarly, NAFTA's overall impact on the U.S. economy, including lower prices for consumers, has been small. Looking at multiple industry sectors, the economists Lorenzo Caliendo and Fernando Parro found that the United States experienced an overall welfare gain from NAFTA of just 0.08 percent.[13]

Although the impact of NAFTA on the United States appears to be relatively benign in aggregate,* the same is not true on the local level. As discussed above, many people "displaced" from jobs by foreign competition have difficulty finding work in other industries because they lack the necessary skills or cannot easily relocate. The economists Shushanik Hakobyan and John McLaren studied the impact of NAFTA on local labor markets and found that blue-collar wages in regions that were particularly vulnerable to Mexican competition grew significantly more slowly than in other areas. In summary, "the effect of NAFTA on most workers and on the average worker is likely modest, but for an important minority of workers the effects are very negative."[15] In a real-world labor market, trade agreements do create clear losers.

When it comes to international commerce, the major event of the past two decades has been not a free trade agreement with Mexico but the rise of China as a major exporter. In the United States, critics of free trade like to blame Chinese competitors for the decline in domestic manufacturing and the loss of well-paying, skilled jobs. There may be something to these claims. One group of economists separately measured the impact of Chinese trade on different industries and on local labor markets; they estimated that Chinese imports cost the American economy between 2 million and 2.4 million jobs from 1999 to 2011. Industries exposed to Chinese competition suffered job losses, as expected, but other industries did not see corresponding increases in employment.[16] This increase in imports from China did not result from an explicit free trade agreement. In

---

* There is another debate over whether NAFTA has been good for Mexico. Caliendo and Parro estimate a Mexican welfare gain of 1.31 percent (sixteen times as large as for the United States). Since 1994, however, Mexico's growth in per capita GDP has been among the lowest in Latin America.[14]

2000, however, the United States did grant permanent normal trade relations status to China, guaranteeing the maintenance of low tariffs; the economists Justin Pierce and Peter Schott have identified this policy change as the trigger for a rapid decline in U.S. manufacturing employment.[17]

That decline was concentrated in particular local labor markets. The economists David Autor, David Dorn, and Gordon Hanson analyzed the impact of increased imports across different geographic areas within the United States. Not surprisingly, the regions most exposed to foreign competition experienced the largest decline in manufacturing jobs. However, those regions saw no corresponding employment gains in other industries; instead, lost manufacturing jobs translated directly into higher unemployment or a decline in the workforce. The impact was greatest on workers who did not go to college—in general, those who were least well-off to begin with.[18] Another recent paper by the same team found that foreign trade reduced wages both in regions particularly exposed to import competition and in highly vulnerable industries whose workers were not easily able to shift to other sectors. The authors conclude,

> If one had to project the impact of China's momentous economic reform for the U.S. labor market with nothing to go on other than a standard undergraduate international economics textbook, one would predict large movements of workers between U.S. tradable industries, . . . limited reallocation of jobs from tradables [products that can easily be traded between countries] to non-tradables, and no net impacts on U.S. aggregate employment.

This optimistic forecast, however, has not been borne out in practice: "The reality of adjustment to the China trade shock has been far different. Offsetting employment gains either in export-oriented tradables or in non-tradables have, for the most part, failed to materialize."[19]

In summary, recent U.S. experience differs from the simple model of comparative advantage in two ways. First, the overall reallocation of capital and labor from products that are now being imported to products that can be exported—from bananas to oranges, for the island of Mickey—is not seamless and may never be complete. Otherwise, increased trade with China could not have resulted in the net loss of more than two million American jobs. On one level, this is not a surprise, because no one really believes that companies and workers can change what they are doing overnight. But the fact that the U.S. economy has adjusted to Chinese competition so slowly and imperfectly calls into question the simple case for free trade.

Second, individual workers and their families may never successfully adapt to the dislocation caused by lower-cost imports, especially if they live in areas dominated by industries vulnerable to foreign competition—such as the old industrial centers of Michigan and Ohio. This fact does not directly contradict the Economics 101 model, which recognizes that opening borders to overseas companies can create winners and losers. It demonstrates, however, that even if there are overall gains from trade in some aggregate sense—that is, comparing the benefits we all gain in the form of cheaper clothes, toys, and electronics with the harm suffered by laid-off workers—those gains come at the cost of increased inequality. Lower-skilled, less-educated people are most likely to lose their jobs or see their wages stagnate. As a practical matter, the United States has failed to help them share in the prosperity that is theoretically generated by increased international commerce. Meanwhile, corporations that can successfully export goods and services have become larger and more profitable, yielding even bigger paydays for their executives. According to the former Treasury secretary Lawrence Summers, "The view now is that trade and globalisation have increased inequality in the U.S. by allowing more earning opportunities for those at the top and exposing ordinary workers to more competition."[20] In this setting, free trade policies present a trade-off between modestly greater overall welfare (largely in the form of cheaper consumer goods) and worse outcomes for the working class, with the net result of increased inequality.

BAIT AND SWITCH

For a careful student of introductory economics, then, the case for free trade is nuanced. Lower tariffs should increase overall welfare in the long run, but the benefits for a developed country like the United States are relatively modest. This is especially true today, when import barriers are already low; as Krugman says, "Comparative advantage . . . suggests that once trade is already fairly open, the gains from opening it further are small."[21] At the same time, the dislocations inevitably caused by increased trade will hurt some low-wage workers and increase inequality. But when it comes to actual policy questions, many commentators and politicians on both sides of the aisle reflexively repeat the headline—free trade is good, full stop—while forgetting the details.

In the United States, the major trade issue in recent years has been the Trans-Pacific Partnership (TPP), an agreement signed in February 2016 by representatives of twelve Pacific Rim countries—Australia, Brunei, Canada, Chile, Japan, Malaysia, Mexico, New Zealand, Peru, Singapore, the United States, and Vietnam.[*] (This agreement is important not only because of its scope but also because it is expected to serve as a precedent for a future Transatlantic Trade and Investment Partnership between the United States and the European Union.) The TPP was one of President Barack Obama's top legislative priorities during his second term in office. The deal was politically controversial ever

---

[*] After signature, the TPP still required ratification by the governments of the participating countries.

since preliminary negotiations began in 2008; in 2015, Obama barely persuaded Congress to give him "fast track" authority— meaning that once the agreement was negotiated, it would get an expedited up or down vote with no amendments. Although the TPP is often described as a free trade deal, and one of its sections would lower tariffs on many goods, in reality it is a complex treaty covering everything from domestic regulations and labor and environmental standards to patents and dispute resolution processes.

Nevertheless, the primary argument by TPP supporters has been "Go read David Ricardo!" Jason Furman, chair of the Obama administration's Council of Economic Advisers, opened his case for the TPP with the theory of comparative advantage. The columnist Charles Krauthammer began this way: "That free trade is advantageous to both sides is the rarest of political propositions—provable, indeed mathematically. David Ricardo did so in 1817. The Law of Comparative Advantage has held up nicely for 198 years." The financial writer Roger Lowenstein similarly wrote, "Two hundred years ago, David Ricardo explained why foreign trade was beneficial; today's trade-deal opponents ignore him at their peril." He continued, "Hopefully, at some point before the TPP comes up for debate again, members of Congress will dedicate 10 minutes to learning about the man who, along with Adam Smith and Robert Malthus, virtually invented modern economics." The economist Gregory Mankiw reduced the TPP to a simple textbook question, asking, "If Congress were to take an exam in Economics 101, would it pass? . . . Among economists," he confidently asserted, "the issue is a no-brainer."[22] The common theme is one we've seen over and over again: people who oppose trade agreements just don't understand economics.

Simple invocations of David Ricardo, however, have little to do with the actual contents of the TPP. Because the United States already has trade agreements covering most goods with many TPP countries, the textbook comparative advantage benefits of eliminating the remaining barriers are relatively small. A Peterson Institute study estimated that the TPP would have the long-term effect of increasing average incomes in the United States by 0.5 percent in 2030 and would have no impact on total employment. However, a paper published by Tufts University using different modeling assumptions—in particular, that import competition could produce unemployment and that lower wages could reduce overall demand—concluded that the U.S. economy would shrink by 0.5 percent over ten years, with a net loss of 400,000 jobs.[23] While these numbers are not trivial, given the amount of uncertainty inherent in this type of forecast, they indicate that tariff reductions in the TPP will most likely have a relatively small impact on long-term economic growth. (As the economist Dean Baker put it, under the Peterson Institute's pro-TPP estimate, "we will be as rich on January 1, 2030 as we would otherwise be on March 15, 2030."[24])

Most of the action in the TPP is elsewhere. One component of the agreement requires participating countries to expand protection of intellectual property rights, such as patents and copyrights, to match existing U.S. law. Intellectual property rights, by definition, have nothing to do with free trade; instead, they *restrict* the ability of companies to produce or distribute certain types of goods and services. Stronger patents and copyrights benefit companies in sectors such as pharmaceuticals and the media, many of which are headquartered in the United States, by giving them longer monopolies on products like drugs and movies. Whether they are good for the world as a whole, or even for Americans, is less clear. For one thing, lengthening pharmaceutical patents would make it harder for drug manufacturers to introduce generic competitors, thus increasing prices and reducing availability in many countries.[25] More generally, if free trade is good, as assumed by TPP advocates, then strong intellectual property rights are actually bad, because they slow down the diffusion of technology from rich countries to imitators in developing countries who could make the same products at lower costs.[26]

Perhaps the most controversial aspect of the TPP goes by the obscure name of investor-state dispute settlement (ISDS). Under ISDS, an "investor," typically a corporation, can sue another country's government if it is harmed by that country's internal laws or regulations. The case will be heard not in domestic courts but in special-purpose tribunals whose decisions are not subject to appeal. Grounds for a suit include state policies that discriminate against a foreign company or that infringe on its ability to earn profits in the future.

ISDS was initially justified as a way to protect foreign investors from arbitrary or unfair treatment by domestic governments and courts. In practice, however, it has become a way for corporations to contest new regulations, particularly those protecting the environment and public health, that cut into their business. Canada has paid almost $200 million in fines and settlements resulting from ISDS cases under NAFTA. In one example, the Canadian government banned MMT, a potentially harmful gasoline additive; the U.S.-based Ethyl Corporation contested the ban and forced Canada not only to pay a $13 million settlement but also to repeal the prohibition on MMT. When Australia required that cigarettes be sold in plain packages with warning labels, Philip Morris sued under ISDS. Although the tribunal finally ruled against the company in 2015, the case cost the Australian government $50 million in legal costs and deterred Canada from pursuing similar legislation; a similar suit against Uruguay is still under way. In one of the largest ISDS cases to date, the Swedish energy company Vattenfall sued Germany for $6 billion in profits lost when the government, following the Fukushima nuclear disaster in 2011, ordered the closure of two nuclear plants. Closer to home, after President Obama rejected the expansion of the Keystone Pipeline, TransCanada responded by suing the United States under ISDS for more than $15 billion.[27]

For these reasons, many people, including prominent economists such as Jeffrey Sachs and Joseph Stiglitz, are deeply suspicious of ISDS. Noting that companies can contest even government actions "taken for a legitimate and important public purpose," Sachs and co-authors Lise Johnson and Lisa Sachs argue that ISDS "distorts the rules of the legal system and makes the economic interests of some foreign corporations much more powerful than the interests of domestic constituents."[28] There may be contexts in which ISDS makes sense; some developing countries, for example, may become more attractive to foreign investors by committing to resolve disputes under an international regime rather than in their domestic courts. The point, however, is that ISDS has nothing to do with free trade in goods and services. Instead, it is a mechanism for strengthening the rights of private businesses relative to more or less democratically elected governments.

The TPP is about trade, in the broad sense: economic interactions between households and businesses located in different parts of the world. But most of the agreement is not devoted to the elimination of protectionist import barriers. Instead, it regulates the relationships between workers, consumers, companies, and national governments. And the rules that it establishes were disproportionately influenced by business interests. Although negotiations were conducted in secret, the Obama administration sought advice from twenty-eight advisory committees—and 85 percent of the people on those committees were industry representatives.[29] It should be no surprise that the TPP's provisions appear to favor certain concentrated business interests, such as the pharmaceutical and entertainment industries in the case of intellectual property and the energy sector in the case of ISDS. "Whether the rules of the road favor the Lamborghinis or the Fords depends on who's writing them," writes the economist Jared Bernstein. "And on that point," he continues, "it's not the 'good U.S. guys' versus the 'bad Chinese guys'; instead, it is representatives of TPP-member multinational corporations versus workers and consumers."[30] From the outside, it certainly seems that large corporations are dictating the rules that will govern the global economy.

In short, whether the rules are good or bad, the TPP "is not about Ricardo," to quote the economists Simon Johnson and Andrei Levchenko. Economics 101 teaches that eliminating import tariffs is good, but offers no guidance on most of the complex provisions of the TPP. Yet the agreement's supporters like nothing better than to recite the lesson of comparative advantage. "There's a kind of bait and switch," writes Krugman, "in which people invoke Ricardo and the gains from trade to say 'free trade good,' then tell scare stories about how protectionism would destroy millions of jobs and cause a global depression, which doesn't make much sense."[31] Economism plays an unusually powerful role in discussions of international trade agreements. Not only do naive or disingenuous supporters of "free trade" forget the details that accompany the Economics 101 model—that overall welfare gains may be small, while displaced workers bear the brunt of the costs. In addition, they use that simple model, first developed using English cloth and Portuguese wine, to justify trade agreements that have nothing to do with comparative advantage and the benefits of specialization.

This does not mean that we should suddenly reverse decades of international trade policies and impose prohibitive tariffs on imports from lower-wage countries, as Donald Trump has proposed. The United States is no longer a developing country with infant industries to protect, nor should we be trying to shift our economy toward low-paying jobs. But the seductive mantra that free trade is always good drowns out the rest of the Economics 101 lesson: the benefits and costs of trade are unequally distributed, and in our case that means that the rich get richer and some of the poor get poorer. Instead of taking on faith that free trade produces the best of all possible worlds, we need to recognize that the more open our economy is to foreign competition, the more important it is to help displaced workers make the transition to new jobs. Because that transition is often difficult if not impossible, we need a more comprehensive safety net providing at least a minimum of protection from the hardships of long-term unemployment.

The rhetoric of comparative advantage also surreptitiously elides the distinction between trade and trade agreements. Much of the propaganda for the TPP obscures the fact that the actual deal does not just eliminate traditional import barriers, but also constrains the ability of national governments to pursue policies preferred by their citizens. Large corporations had a disproportionate influence on the drafting of the agreement, which effectively gave them a back-door mechanism to secure special favors that they could not obtain through ordinary domestic political processes. This is ultimately a question of political power—the power to dictate the rules of the economic game. There's nothing inherently wrong with that; in a democracy, we expect companies and industry associations to pursue their private interests. But the pretense that international agreements are just about the Economics 101 model of comparative advantage hides the crucial question—who wins and who loses—behind the veil of economism.

9

The Best Possible World–for Whom?

What rules the world is ideas, because ideas define the way reality is perceived.

—Irving Kristol, 1975[1]

The tone of *The Road to Serfdom* was one of resolute courage in the face of overwhelming opposition: "The important point is that, if we take the people whose views influence developments, they are now in the democracies in some measure all socialists. . . . It is because nearly everybody wants it that we are moving in this direction." Writing in England while the outcome of World War II was still in doubt, Friedrich Hayek had as his overriding objective to demonstrate that economic planning would lead inevitably to totalitarianism—"that democratic socialism, the great utopia of the last few generations, is not only unachievable, but that to strive for it produces something so utterly different that few of those who now wish it would be prepared to accept the consequences."[2] When he arrived in America to promote the book in 1945, he found a country where many people's "enthusiasm for the new kind of rationally constructed society was still largely unsoiled by practical experience."[3]

Since World War II, the intellectual and political climate in the United States has been completely transformed. Where Hayek was once a lone voice in the wilderness, now the argument that private competition is the best way of organizing human activity has virtually become a truism. So-called free-market capitalism has no serious rival. Politicians from across the ideological spectrum talk reflexively about strengthening incentives to work and to save, encouraging entrepreneurship, streamlining regulations to reduce the burden on businesses, and harnessing the power of the market. It was a Democratic president who announced the end of big government.[4] Liberals frame their policy proposals as technocratic solutions to specific market failures: an individual mandate to prevent adverse selection in the health insurance market, a carbon tax to correct for overproduction of greenhouse gas emissions, or renewable energy subsidies to balance existing support for fossil fuels. Socialism does not exist at the national level in the United States, with one debatable exception. In the 2016 presidential primaries, self-described socialist Bernie Sanders rocketed to prominence on a platform that would be so unremarkable in Western Europe (guaranteed universal health care, free college, and a higher minimum wage) that it would almost qualify as centrist—demonstrating just how unusual it is for Americans to hear anything other than the free-market orthodoxy.

The takeover of the political landscape by the competitive market model was due in part to experience: as living standards rose in the 1950s and strong unions enabled (some) workers to share in corporate profits, markets came to seem more friend than foe, even to many in the working class. To some extent, it is also consistent with developments in the field of economics itself, which has become more skeptical of many forms of government intervention: most professional economists, for example, doubt that rent control (a price ceiling) can improve on the market as a means of increasing the supply of affordable housing.[5]

The story of Hayek's triumph, however, is also the story of economism. Over the past seventy years, the fundamental principles of supply and demand in a competitive market have been drilled into millions of undergraduates—many of whom remember little else from their first-year classes—and reinforced through countless newspaper and magazine columns, radio and television talk shows, and Facebook and Twitter accounts. On the two-dimensional Economics 101 blackboard, the correct answer to any question is to allow supply and demand to reach their natural equilibrium, ensuring that we live in the best of all possible worlds. This simple analysis is often a useful first step toward understanding how things work in reality. On its own, however, it results in a blinkered worldview that leads to a preordained set of conclusions.

The great achievement of economism has been to repackage a political ideology as a lightweight, easy-to-use, seemingly neutral framework for seeing the world. The explicit political ideology has been called market fundamentalism or neoliberalism: the belief that competitive markets are the best way to organize economic activity, maximize material prosperity, and ensure political freedom; and that well-meaning interference in those markets at best will be counterproductive and at worst will lead down the path to tyranny. Hayek was willing to argue his case in *The Road to Serfdom*, as was Milton Friedman in *Capitalism and Freedom*. Both were well versed in the complexities of various markets, even if their political sensibilities constantly colored their economic assessments.

With economism, however, there are only implicit assumptions and asserted conclusions. When commentators and politicians say that a higher minimum wage will increase unemployment, or increased cost sharing will make the health-care system more efficient, or restrictions on the mortgage market will result in the misallocation of capital, they often do not realize that they are making contested claims about how the economy should be organized and how its output should be distributed. Instead, they are (unconsciously) assuming the premises of the standard Economics 101 model and automatically concluding that market forces will make society better off. One problem with economism, as seen throughout this book, is that these claims are often simply wrong: the effects of the minimum wage, cost sharing, and mortgage regulations are all complicated subjects on which the evidence is decidedly mixed. The other problem is that by claiming the status of absolute truth, economism denies that there is any debate at all, either empirical or normative. The world simply is the way it is; if you don't agree, you must not understand Economics 101. This is how an ideology can be most influential—by dressing itself up as insight into the true nature of things.

CUI BONO?

To understand the rise of economism, we have to ask the key question of any crime novel: Who benefits? Let's review. Economism helps suppress the minimum wage, lowering the wages of low-skilled workers and increasing the profits of restaurants, retail stores, and hotels. The argument that pay is based on individual productivity beats back efforts to constrain (or redistribute) the incomes of economic superstars such as corporate executives and fund managers. The idea that taxes are necessarily bad, and that taxes on high incomes and on investments are especially bad, has reduced the tax bills of the wealthy. At the same time, it has crippled the ability of the government to help ordinary families and created the budgetary pressure to scale back popular programs such as Social Security and Medicare. The fetishization of private markets has driven the idea of publicly funded health care to the margins of political debate, while the glorification of consumer choice has brought high-deductible health plans to the forefront—forcing poor families to make do with the coverage they can afford while allowing well-off, healthier families to benefit from lower taxes and tax-preferred savings accounts. The belief that credit markets should be as efficient as possible and that both individuals and firms can look after themselves brought large profits to financial institutions and unprecedented riches to their executives and employees but ultimately produced the most severe economic crisis since the Great Depression. The conviction that free trade makes everyone better off has diverted attention from the plight of working families "displaced" by foreign competition and camouflaged an international agreement that strengthens the rights of large corporations.

Economism's arguments usually favor the wealthy and busi-

Figure 9.1: Economism's Greatest Hits

	Economism's Claim	More Likely Reality
Labor Markets	The minimum wage causes unemployment and harms poor people	The minimum wage (around current levels) has little impact on unemployment and reduces poverty
	People's earnings are closely based on the value of their work	Earnings are very roughly related to productivity and highly dependent on bargaining power
Taxes	Reducing tax rates on labor causes people to work more, increasing economic growth	Lower tax rates have a small effect on work, primarily for married women
	Reducing tax rates on investments causes people to save more, increasing economic growth	Savings rates are not affected by tax rates (around current levels)
Health Care	Higher cost sharing causes people to make smarter choices, reducing waste and improving health	Cost sharing causes people to spend less on all types of care, sometimes harming their health
	Competitive markets are the best way to deliver high quality, affordable health care	Countries with universal, government-sponsored systems have lower costs and equal or better outcomes
Financial Markets	People only buy financial products that are good for them	Many people make poor choices about complex products such as Option ARMs
	Complex financial products improve the allocation of capital	Extreme complexity can produce excessive risk-taking and systemic instability
International Trade	International trade makes everyone better off	International trade may benefit people on average but makes some people much worse off
	Free trade agreements contribute to overall prosperity	Some "free trade agreements" have less to do with free trade than with corporate rights

nesses (which are largely owned by the wealthy), not ordinary families subject to the risks of unemployment, illness, or disability. In some of these cases, abstract economic arguments have had a causal impact: without the glorious simplification of supply-side economics, the Reagan and George W. Bush tax cuts might never have occurred; without Alan Greenspan's soft spot for self-correcting, self-policing markets, federal regulators could have done something about the subprime lending boom. In other cases, economism has served to defend the status quo by making particular outcomes look like the inevitable result of natural processes. Although Americans say we would prefer to live in a much more equal country, our unwillingness to do anything about inequality stems in part from the belief that there is nothing that can be done.[6]

A way of seeing the world, such as economism, does not become widespread and influential because it is more accurate or correct than the alternatives. Instead, worldviews become powerful because they reflect the beliefs and serve the purposes of an important interest group. While communism appealed to the downtrodden industrial working class of nineteenth-century Europe, in mid-twentieth-century America it was the owners of capital whose fortunes were at a historic low: in the 1950s and 1960s, the share of income received by the top 1 percent fell to only half the level reached early in the twentieth century.[7] The predominant ethos of the New Deal, formed amid the trauma of the Great Depression and strengthened by the shared sacrifice of World War II, conceived of society as a collective body with the obligation to protect its members against the risks of modern life. For intellectuals and businesspeople who found the postwar political climate to be toxic, economism was the perfect antidote. On one level, militantly conservative and libertarian thinkers—economists like Hayek and Friedman, journalists like Henry Hazlitt and William F. Buckley, and politicians like Barry Goldwater and Ronald Reagan—argued explicitly for lower taxes, smaller government, and lighter regulation. On another level, the Economics 101 model of competitive markets driven by supply and demand seeped into mainstream discourse, separating itself from explicit political ideology to become the Swiss Army knife of social and economic commentary.

Today, economism reflects the preferences and interests of the very rich more than those of ordinary citizens. Recent research by the political scientists Benjamin Page, Larry Bartels, and Jason Seawright shows just how much influence money has on people's beliefs about important issues. For example, 78 percent of Americans think that the minimum wage should be set so no full-time workers live in poverty, but only 40 percent of the wealthy; 46 percent think the government should reduce large differences in income, but only 13 percent of the wealthy; and 61 percent favor national health insurance, compared with 32 percent of the wealthy.[8] On each of these issues, the opinions of the very rich are consistent with their interests—but can also be justified by economism.

In a democracy, you might think that political outcomes would be determined by the preferences of the general public. You would be wrong. Considerable research has shown that when choosing between policies favored by ordinary people and those catering to the rich, the American political system sides with the money. According to an empirical analysis by Martin Gilens and Benjamin Page, average citizens' preferences have almost no impact on whether a bill is passed, while the priorities of the very wealthy are much more likely to become law. "[Ordinary citizens] have little or no independent influence on policy at all," they find. "By contrast, economic elites are estimated to have a quite substantial, highly significant, independent impact on policy."[9]

There are many reasons why the upper class has more political power than the middle class. Most obviously, they have the money: the richest 0.01 percent of households—that is, the top one-hundredth of the top one-hundredth of the income distribution—made more than 40 percent of all itemized political contributions in 2012.[10] As the law professor Lawrence Lessig has argued, our electoral system gives a tiny fraction of the population the power to decide who is able to run for office.[11]

Economism, however, also contributes to the domination of politics by the wealthy by providing an interpretive framework that justifies their preferred policies and the inequality generated by those policies. Our campaign finance system forces politicians to be sympathetic to the wealthy and to large corporations; lobbyists can then deploy the magic words of competitive markets to secure elected leaders' allegiances, with no need to stoop to naked bribery. Positions that benefit economic elites, filtered through the conceptual vocabulary supplied by economism, appear as necessary responses to the inexorable forces of supply and demand. This is not to say that politicians are cynically using Economics 101 to hide the favors they do for their wealthy benefactors, although it certainly comes in handy. Some may honestly believe the little bit they retain from their economics classes—or, more likely, the snippets they have gathered from hundreds of op-ed articles. Economism can have its strongest hold on people who think they are seeing the world clearly, not realizing that they are seeing it through a particular lens. Along with campaign contributions, social connections, and cultural prestige, it is one reason why the American political system is so responsive to the desires of the very rich.

WHERE ARE WE GOING?

Economism plays an important role in our contemporary political institutions, prioritizing certain types of analyses and arguments while pushing others to the margins. Ironically, the textbook world of Economics 101, populated by atomistic individuals and firms trading in idealized markets, has little use for institutions (corporations, markets, courts, governments, and so on), which typically appear as poorly defined abstractions. In this two-dimensional world, inequality is simply the natural result of competitive market processes, and so we face the textbook trade-off between *equality* and *efficiency* made famous by the economist Arthur Okun: policies that reduce inequality, such as progressive taxes and aid for the poor, will reduce the size of the proverbial pie for everyone.[12] Many proponents of economism go further; for them, inequality is a positively good thing, because it rewards the productive and motivates people to innovate and take risks.

Like so much of Economics 101, however, the trade-off between efficiency and equity is harder to see in the real world than on the blackboard. Economists at the International Monetary Fund studied the actual relationships between inequality, redistributive policies, and growth and found the opposite: when other factors are controlled for, higher inequality (*after* taking into account redistributive policies such as taxes and transfers) is associated with slower economic expansion, and redistribution itself seems to have no impact on growth. They conclude, "On average, across countries and over time, the things that governments have typically done to redistribute do not seem to have led to bad growth outcomes, unless they were extreme. And the resulting narrowing of inequality helped support faster and more durable growth."[13] The implication is that reducing inequality would actually make the pie bigger for everyone, as well as producing a division of wealth and income that most people would consider more fair.

To understand the relationship between inequality and overall prosperity, we have to leave the competitive market model and look at real-world institutions—one of the richest areas of recent economic study. In *Why Nations Fail*, the economist Daron Acemoglu and the political scientist James Robinson synthesize their decades of research (much of it in collaboration with my frequent co-author, Simon Johnson) into the crucial role of institutions in economic and political development. For a society to become rich, competitive markets are not enough; there must also be pluralistic, democratic political institutions that prevent elites from monopolizing power, suppressing competitors, and seizing an excessive share of resources. In this model, inequality is not a harmless by-product of a dynamic economy. Instead, inequality itself creates the risk that economic elites will dominate the political process and use their power to cement their position in society. Late medieval Venice, for example, was a hub of the Mediterranean economy and one of the richest cities in Europe. In the late thirteenth century, its semi-democratic political institutions were captured by a small group of wealthy families, who then used their power to monopolize long-distance trade. The city's economic growth stagnated; today it is a museum.[14] In short, economic outcomes are produced not by abstract markets, but by concrete institutions, and elites have every interest in using their unequal power to shape those institutions for their private benefit.

Today, the United States remains a democracy. We have a long way to go before we suffer the fate of Venice. But the gap between haves and have-nots is steadily widening, and our political leaders are becoming increasingly sensitive to the needs of their rich patrons rather than their ordinary constituents. As elite groups use their political influence to cement their position in society, economism comes to their defense: inequality, it argues, is a natural feature of the best of all possible worlds, and therefore need not concern us. As John Kenneth Galbraith said, a conception of economics that ignores the role of power "becomes, however unconsciously, a part of an arrangement by which the citizen or student is kept from seeing how he is, or will be, governed."[15] By veiling the operation of wealth and power behind the symbolic imagery of markets, economism protects the existing order from democratic challenge.

BEYOND ECONOMISM?

If we are to reduce the pernicious influence of economism in contemporary society, the first step is to call it out for what it is: a distorted worldview based on a misleading caricature of economic knowledge. One goal of this book has been to illustrate examples of economism in action, particularly for people who may pay undue respect to the logic of supply and demand. The competitive market model can be a powerful tool, but it is only a starting point in illuminating complex real-world issues, not the final word. The more that people understand the assumptions and limits of the model, the less likely they are to be swayed by its facile claims, which are incontrovertibly correct only on the Economics 101 blackboard. In the real world, many other factors complicate the picture, sometimes beyond recognition.

Still, the answer to economism is not to reject economics altogether. Rather, the immediate antidote to economism's simplistic model of reality is more and better economic analysis, which can help identify the fundamental drivers of social phenomena or select the most effective solutions to difficult problems. In this book, I have shown how richer theoretical models and careful empirical research can deliver a more nuanced understanding of the world than a simple supply-and-demand diagram. Statistical analyses of controlled or natural experiments can help untangle causal relationships and estimate the real impact of policy changes. Empirical research sometimes results in a long-running battle between competing experts, but that disagreement frequently reflects the genuine messiness of social reality. Recognizing that "economics" does not provide a single, simple answer to all questions is a crucial step in throwing off the blinders of economism.

Another valuable step would be to improve the way Economics

101 is taught, because that is where so many people are exposed to the discipline in the first place. According to a recent survey of undergraduate programs around the world, "Economics degrees are highly mathematical, adopt a single narrow perspective and put little emphasis on historical context, critical thinking or real-world applications."[16] Paying more attention to topics such as economic history, institutions, behavioral economics, common market failures such as asymmetric information, and empirical methods could help dilute the intellectual hegemony of the competitive market model. Even then, however, better economic training alone is not the answer, because most people absorb economism from the air of contemporary life, not from textbooks and professors.

Students who are more aware of the limits of their knowledge and a public that is more critical of facile arguments will help weaken the grip of economism on contemporary discourse. Ultimately, however, as Hayek, Friedman, and their allies understood, it will take a new worldview to do battle with the old. Many people have suggested specific policies that might slow down the march of inequality (some of which have been mentioned in this book): a higher minimum wage, single payer health care, expanded Social Security, universal pre-school, free public higher education, expanded job retraining, and even a universal basic income. These ideas all have merit. But as long as the overall terms of debate are set by economism, such incremental proposals will struggle to gain acceptance or will serve only to soften the hard edges of the inequality generated by supposedly free markets. Real change will not be achieved by mastering the details of marginal costs and marginal benefits, but by constructing a new, compelling narrative about how the world works.

What could that story be? Economism's appeal rests on its promise to give us, in the aggregate, the maximum possible amount of social welfare, defined as consumer surplus plus producer surplus. It assumes that the purpose of social organization is to increase overall material prosperity, and public policy in the United States largely adopts the same perspective. Why the overriding objective should be to have more and more stuff, however, does not have a simple answer. Many of the world's religions, including the one most practiced in the United States, teach that experiencing worldly pleasures and accumulating money and possessions are not our highest calling (although, according to some denominations, they may be signs of salvation). In recent decades, academic psychologists, as well as some economists, have been rediscovering and refining the ages-old idea that happiness is really what matters in life. Insofar as we can measure it, there is certainly more to being happy than simply having a lot of money.[17] As the economist Amartya Sen said, we should care about "the richness of human life," not just "the richness of the economy in which human beings live."[18]

Even one of the past century's most famous economists looked beyond the constraints of material scarcity. In 1930, John Maynard Keynes argued that, thanks to technological progress, the "economic problem" would be solved in about a century and people would only work fifteen hours per week—primarily to keep themselves occupied. With people freed from the need to accumulate wealth, the nature of human life would change profoundly:

> I see us free, therefore, to return to some of the most sure and certain principles of religion and traditional virtue—that avarice is a vice, that the exaction of usury is a misdemeanour, and the love of money is detestable, that those walk most truly in the paths of virtue and sane wisdom who take least thought for the morrow. We shall once more value ends above means and prefer the good to the useful. We shall honour those who can teach us how to pluck the hour and the day virtuously and well, the delightful people

who are capable of taking direct enjoyment in things, the lilies of the field who toil not, neither do they spin.[19]

Almost a century later, our productive capacity has grown about as much as Keynes predicted—in the United States, output per person is more than six times what it was in 1930—and robots are poised to do more and more of the work that human beings do today.[20] We have the physical, financial, and human capital necessary for everyone in our country to enjoy a comfortable standard of living, and within a few generations the same should be true for the entire planet. And yet our social organization remains the same as it was in the Great Depression: some people work very hard and make more money than they will ever need, while many others are unable to find work and live in poverty.

Millions if not billions of people today hunger to live in a world that is more fair, more forgiving, and more humane than the one that we were born into. Creating a new vision of society worthy of that collective yearning—one that goes beyond the false promises of economism—is the first step toward building a better future for our children. That is the story that remains to be written.

Acknowledgments

This book began as a bare glimmer of an idea back in 2010, when Simon Johnson and I were deciding what to do after writing *13 Bankers*. We chose instead to write *White House Burning*, a book about the politics and economics of deficits and the national debt—an issue unfortunately highlighted by the debt ceiling crises of 2011 and 2013. During the intervening years, however, I only became more distressed by the way that stylized economic lessons, typically drawn from the first chapters of an introductory textbook, are commonly held up as irrefutable descriptions of the real world—and more convinced that a book like this one needed to be written.

Because this is my first book without the safety net of a co-author, I have been fortunate to work with much of the old team from *13 Bankers* and *White House Burning*. Simon and I discussed various incarnations of the central idea over the years, and he provided advice and encouragement throughout the process. Rafe Sagalyn, my agent, once again provided invaluable suggestions on how to frame my various thoughts into a coherent book project. Erroll McDonald, my editor, helped me clarify some of the key conceptual issues raised by economism and oversaw the transformation of ideas into a finished book. Many people at Knopf Doubleday played important roles in that process, including Kristen Bearse, Catherine Courtade, Janet Hansen, Altie Karper, Lisa Montebello, and Nicholas Thomson.

I could not have written this book without drawing on the work of hundreds of scholars and journalists who have come before me, many of whom are acknowledged in the text or the endnotes. I have also discussed this book and the topics in it with more people than I can remember. Some of the people who provided helpful suggestions or encouragement, particularly as the overall argument was taking shape, included Jill Anderson, Anne Dailey, Seth Ditchik, Kaaryn Gustafson, Alexandra Lahav, John Mahaney, Niki Papadopoulos, and Holger Spamann. I am particularly indebted to the friends who read whole chapters (or the entire manuscript) and provided valuable feedback: Michael Ash, Simon Johnson, Nosup Kwak, Frank Pasquale, Peter Siegelman, Jennifer Taub, and Stephen Utz. For research help, I am grateful to Hilary McClellen and to the staff of the Thomas J. Meskill Law Library at the University of Connecticut School of Law, particularly Anne Rajotte and the research assistants Bryan Bowyer, Carolyn Child, and Thomas Eisenmann. Rachael Brown and Hilary McClellen painstakingly checked virtually all of the facts in the book, and Hilary assisted with proofreading as well. I've always considered myself a pretty good writer, but Laura Femino helped make everything better.

The University of Connecticut School of Law provided financial support (which Donna Gionfriddo helped me access). Dean Timothy Fisher also allowed me to take one semester of unpaid leave to work on this book.

Closer to home, I would never have been in a position to write this book without the upbringing and education I received from my parents, Nosup and Inkyung Kwak, and the friendship and support of my sister, Mary Kwak. Ed and Faydine Brandt, Adele Dowell, Melisa Fosberg, and Will Stamell all helped me find the time to escape up to the attic and write. My children, Willow and Henry, have been a constant inspiration and a reminder of why ideas matter. My wife, Sylvia Brandt, has supported and encouraged me through two decades, four careers, and now three books. I can never thank her enough.

Notes

1. Charles Baudelaire, "Le Joueur généreux," in *Œuvres complètes de Charles Baudelaire*, vol. 4 (Michel Lévy Frères, 1869), 80, translation by the author.

1. The Best of All Possible Worlds

1. Voltaire, *Candide: Or, Optimism*, trans. John Butt (Penguin, 1947), 20.
2. Gottfried Wilhelm Leibniz, *Theodicy: Essays on the Goodness of God, the Freedom of Man, and the Origin of Evil*, trans. E. M. Huggard (Routledge & Kegan Paul, 1951), 128. As one philosopher and Leibniz biographer writes, "All the evils of this actual world are logically necessary for the greater good of the best of all possible worlds." Maria Rosa Antognazza, *Leibniz: An Intellectual Biography* (Cambridge University Press, 2009), 486.
3. Voltaire, *Candide*, 20, 23.
4. Thomas Piketty, *Capital in the Twenty-First Century*, trans. Arthur Goldhammer (Belknap Press, 2014), 341.
5. Max Weber, *The Protestant Ethic and the Spirit of Capitalism*, trans. Talcott Parsons (Unwin, 1985).
6. Piketty, *Capital*, 349.
7. Quoted in Sidney Fine, *Laissez Faire and the General-Welfare State* (University of Michigan Press, 1956), 38.
8. Sumner quoted in Richard Hofstadter, *Social Darwinism in American Thought*, rev. ed. (Beacon Press, 1955), 58. See also Fine, *Laissez Faire*, 84–85.
9. Hofstadter, *Social Darwinism*, 5. The steel magnate Andrew Carnegie, for example, considered himself a follower of Spencer. Fine, *Laissez Faire*, 42.
10. Facundo Alvaredo et al., *The World Wealth and Income Database*, "United

States, Top 1% Income Share," http://www.wid.world; Caroline Freund and Sarah Oliver, "The Origins of the Superrich: The Billionaire Characteristics Database" (Peterson Institute for International Economics working paper 16-1, Feb. 2016), fig. 1.

11. "$3M Party Fit for Buyout King," *New York Post*, Feb. 14, 2007; Alexandra Stevenson and Julie Creswell, "Bill Ackman and His Hedge Fund, Betting Big," *New York Times*, Oct. 25, 2014.

12. Real median household income, averaged over 2011–13, was 8 percent higher than the corresponding figure averaged over 1971–73. U.S. Census Bureau, Historical Income Tables: Households, Table H-5: Race and Hispanic Origin of Householder—Households by Median and Mean Income: 1967 to 2013. Over that same period, the proportion of people aged twenty-five to fifty-four in the labor force increased from 72.4 percent to 81.3 percent—an increase of more than 12 percent. Federal Reserve Bank of St. Louis, FRED Economic Data, "Civilian Labor Force Participation Rate: 25 to 54 Years" (seasonally adjusted). Median income for men: Matt O'Brien, "A Stunning Stat About Pay Seems Impossible but Actually Is True," *Wonkblog* (blog), *Washington Post*, Sept. 22, 2015.

13. Elliot Blair Smith and Phil Kuntz, "CEO Pay 1,795-to-1 Multiple of Wages Skirts U.S. Law," *Bloomberg*, April 30, 2013; Carmen DeNavas-Walt and Bernadette D. Proctor, *Income and Poverty in the United States: 2013* (U.S. Census Bureau, Current Population Reports, P60-249, Sept. 2014), fig. 4.

14. See, for example, G. Warren Nutter, "On Economism," *Journal of Law and Economics* 22, no. 2 (Oct. 1979): 263–68; John Braithwaite, "The Limits of Economism in Controlling Harmful Corporate Conduct," *Law and Society Review* 16, no. 3 (1981): 481–504; Richard K. Ashley, "Three Modes of Economism," *International Studies Quarterly* 27 (1983): 463–96; Teivo Teivainen, *Enter Economism, Exit Politics: Experts, Economic Policy, and the Damage to Democracy* (Zed Books, 2002), 1–5; Des Gasper, *The Ethics of Development: From Economism to Human Development* (Edinburgh University Press, 2004), 80–81; Jonathan Wolff and Dirk Haubrich, "Economism and Its Limits," in *The Oxford Handbook of Public Policy*, ed. Michael Moran, Martin Rein, and Robert E. Goodin (Oxford University Press, 2006); Howard Brody, *The Golden Calf: Economism and American Policy* (CreateSpace, 2011).

15. Noah Smith, "101ism," *Noahpinion* (blog), Jan. 21, 2016.

16. Wanniski: Jude Wanniski, *The Way the World Works*, 4th ed. (Regnery, 1998), 89. Reagan: Jerold L. Waltman, *The Politics of the Minimum Wage* (University of Illinois Press, 2000), 44. Mankiw: N. Gregory Mankiw, "I

Can Afford Higher Taxes. But They'll Make Me Work Less," *New York Times*, Oct. 9, 2010. Ryan: John McCormack, "Paul Ryan: More Important to Cut Top Tax Rate Than Expand Child Tax Credit," *Weekly Standard*, Aug. 20, 2014.

17. Paul A. Samuelson, *Economics* (McGraw-Hill, 1948), 36.

18. Michael M. Weinstein, "Paul A. Samuelson, Economist, Dies at 94," *New York Times*, Dec. 13, 2009. Samuelson's textbook, first published in 1948, was the market leader until the 1970s.

19. Every introductory textbook includes chapters on monopolies and oligopolies, but those lessons are also highly stylized and tend to be forgotten sooner than the lesson about competitive markets.

20. Max Weber, "The Social Psychology of the World Religions," in *From Max Weber: Essays in Sociology*, ed. H. H. Gerth and C. Wright Mills (Routledge, 1991), 271.

21. William J. Baumol and Alan S. Blinder, *Economics: Principles and Policy*, 12th ed. (South-Western Cengage Learning, 2012), 5.

22. Actually, Marx never wrote those words. *The Communist Manifesto* concludes, "The proletarians have nothing to lose but their chains. They have a world to win. WORKING MEN OF ALL COUNTRIES, UNITE!" Karl Marx and Friedrich Engels, "Manifesto of the Communist Party," in *The Marx-Engels Reader*, ed. Robert C. Tucker, 2nd ed. (W. W. Norton, 1978), 500.

23. N. Gregory Mankiw, *Principles of Economics*, 5th ed. (South-Western Cengage Learning, 2008), 150.

24. Henry Hazlitt, *Economics in One Lesson* (Pocket Books, 1952), 181–82.

25. Bork: Sidney Blumenthal, *The Rise of the Counter-establishment: From Conservative Ideology to Political Power* (Times Books, 1986), 303. Hensarling: Joseph Guinto, "Jeb Hensarling: The GOP's Most Powerful Nobody," *D Magazine*, Nov. 2009. Carender: Michael Grabell, *Money Well Spent? The Truth Behind the Trillion-Dollar Stimulus, the Biggest Economic Recovery Plan in History* (PublicAffairs, 2012), 84.

26. On the shortcomings of neoclassical economics, see Julie A. Nelson, "Poisoning the Well, or How Economic Theory Damages Moral Imagination," in *The Oxford Handbook of Professional Economic Ethics*, ed. George DeMartino and Deirdre McCloskey (Oxford University Press, 2016).

27. Matthew Yglesias, "Sorry, Conservatives—Basic Economics Has a Liberal Bias," *MoneyBox* (blog), *Slate*, Feb. 4, 2014.

28. Dani Rodrik, *Economics Rules: The Rights and Wrongs of the Dismal Science* (W. W. Norton, 2015), 170.

29. Mark Thoma, "Yes, Nick Kristof, There Is a Conservative Bias in Economics," *Fiscal Times*, May 31, 2016.

30. Justin Fox, "How Economics Went from Theory to Data," *Bloomberg*, Jan. 6, 2016.

31. John Komlos, *What Every Economics Student Needs to Know and Doesn't Get in the Usual Principles Text* (M. E. Sharpe, 2014), 10–11; Noah Smith, "Most of What You Learned in Econ 101 Is Wrong," *Bloomberg*, Nov. 24, 2015.

32. Rodrik, *Economics Rules*, 174.

2. The Magic of the Marketplace

1. Irving Fisher, *The Rate of Interest: Its Nature, Determination, and Relation to Economic Phenomena* (Macmillan, 1907), 6. See "Teach a Parrot to Say 'Supply and Demand' and You Have an Economist," Quote Investigator, July 19, 2013.

2. Daniel Kahneman, Jack L. Knetsch, and Richard Thaler, "Fairness as a Constraint on Profit Seeking: Entitlements in the Market," *American Economic Review* 76, no. 4 (Sept. 1986): 728–41; Richard Thaler, *Misbehaving: The Making of Behavioral Economics* (W. W. Norton, 2015), 128; IGM Forum, "Price Gouging," University of Chicago Booth School of Business, May 2, 2012.

3. Clare Stroud, Lori Nadig, and Bruce M. Altevogt, rapporteurs, *The 2009 H1N1 Influence Vaccination Campaign: Summary of a Workshop Series* (National Academies Press, 2010), 15–16.

4. Matthew Yglesias, "When Supply Is Elastic, Gouge Away," *MoneyBox* (blog), *Slate*, Nov. 2, 2012.

5. Samuelson, *Economics*, 38.

3. The Long March of Economism

1. Karl Marx and Friedrich Engels, "The German Ideology: Part I," in Tucker, *Marx-Engels Reader*, 174.

2. John Maynard Keynes, *The General Theory of Employment, Interest, and Money* (Harvest, 1964), 383; F. A. Hayek, "The Intellectuals and Socialism," *University of Chicago Law Review* 16 (Spring 1949): 418.

3. Hayek, "Intellectuals and Socialism," 418, 432.

4. Karl Marx, "Marx on the History of His Opinions" (from the preface to

A Contribution to the Critique of Political Economy), in Tucker, *Marx-Engels Reader*, 5.

5. Adam Smith, *The Wealth of Nations*, ed. Edwin Cannan (Bantam Classic, 2003), 78–82.

6. Thomas M. Humphrey, "Marshallian Cross Diagrams and Their Uses Before Alfred Marshall: The Origins of Supply and Demand Geometry," *Federal Reserve Bank of Richmond Economic Review* 78, no. 2 (March–April 1992): 3–23.

7. Daniel T. Rodgers, *Age of Fracture* (Harvard University, 2012), 45.

8. Alfred Marshall, *Principles of Economics*, 9th ed. (Macmillan, 1961), vol. 1, bk. 5, chap. 13, § 5, 471–72.

9. See David A. Moss, *When All Else Fails: Government as the Ultimate Risk Manager* (Harvard University Press, 2002).

10. Keynes, *General Theory*, 249–50, 33–34.

11. Ibid., 129, 378–81.

12. Thomas Ferguson and Joel Rogers, *Right Turn: The Decline of the Democrats and the Future of American Politics* (Hill and Wang, 1986), 46–50.

13. Kim Phillips-Fein, *Invisible Hands: The Making of the Conservative Movement from the New Deal to Reagan* (W. W. Norton, 2009), 56–57.

14. Samuelson, *Economics*, 3; Jacob S. Hacker and Paul Pierson, *American Amnesia: How the War on Government Led Us to Forget What Made America Prosper* (Simon & Schuster, 2016), 168–69.

15. John F. Kennedy, "Commencement Address at Yale University" (June 11, 1962), American Presidency Project, http://www.presidency.ucsb.edu/ws/?pid=29661.

16. They included David Goodrich, president of the B. F. Goodrich Company; Jasper Crane, an executive vice president at DuPont Chemical; Harold Luhnow, who ran William Volker & Company and the William Volker Fund; Lewis H. Brown, the president of the Johns-Manville Corporation; and Harry Bradley, co-founder of the Allen-Bradley Company. Phillips-Fein, *Invisible Hands*, 27, 42, 61.

17. Ibid., 54, 61–65, 163; Ferguson and Rogers, *Right Turn*, 86.

18. These included the Lynde and Harry Bradley, Adolph Coors, Earhart, JM, Koch Family, Sarah Scaife, Smith Richardson, and John M. Olin Foundations. Alice O'Connor, "Financing the Counterrevolution," in *Rightward Bound: Making America Conservative in the 1970s*, ed. Bruce J. Schulman and Julian E. Zelizer (Harvard University Press, 2008), 152.

19. Quoted in Hacker and Pierson, *American Amnesia*, 232.

20. On the history of American conservative ideas, see, for example, Sidney

Blumenthal, *The Rise of the Counter-establishment: From Conservative Ideology to Political Power* (Times Books, 1986); George H. Nash, *The Conservative Intellectual Movement in America Since 1945* (Intercollegiate Studies Institute, 1996); Jonathan Schoenwald, *A Time for Choosing: The Rise of Modern American Conservatism* (Oxford University Press, 2001); John Micklethwait and Adrian Wooldridge, *The Right Nation: Conservative Power in America* (Penguin Books, 2005); Donald T. Critchlow, *The Conservative Ascendancy: How the GOP Right Made Political History* (Harvard University Press, 2007); Brian Doherty, *Radicals for Capitalism: A Freewheeling History of the Modern American Libertarian Movement* (PublicAffairs, 2007); Phillips-Fein, *Invisible Hands*; Angus Burgin, *The Great Persuasion: Reinventing Free Markets Since the Depression* (Harvard University Press, 2012); Daniel Stedman Jones, *Masters of the Universe: Hayek, Friedman, and the Birth of Neoliberal Politics* (Princeton University Press, 2012); Thomas O. McGarity, *Freedom to Harm: The Lasting Legacy of the Laissez Faire Revival* (Yale University Press, 2013).

21. Hacker and Pierson, *American Amnesia*, 172.

22. Ludwig von Mises, *Bureaucracy* (Yale University Press, 1944), 20–21, 26–27, 30–31.

23. F. A. Hayek, *The Road to Serfdom: Text and Documents*, definitive ed., ed. Bruce Caldwell (University of Chicago Press, 2007), 59.

24. Ibid., 59, 95–96.

25. McGarity, *Freedom to Harm*, 36.

26. Bruce Caldwell, introduction to *Road to Serfdom*, by Hayek, 19.

27. Bruce Caldwell, "The Chicago School, Hayek, and Neoliberalism," in *Building Chicago Economics: New Perspectives on the History of America's Most Powerful Economics Program*, ed. Robert Van Horn, Philip Mirowski, and Thomas A. Stapleford (Cambridge University Press, 2011), 303; Phillips-Fein, *Invisible Hands*, 42; Rob Van Horn and Philip Mirowski, "The Rise of the Chicago School of Economics and the Birth of Neoliberalism," in *The Road from Mont Pèlerin: The Making of the Neoliberal Thought Collective*, ed. Philip Mirowski and Dieter Plehwe (Harvard University Press, 2009).

28. F. A. Hayek, *The Constitution of Liberty*, definitive ed., ed. Ronald Hamowy (University of Chicago Press, 2011), pt. 3.

29. Corey Robin, "Nietzsche's Marginal Children: On Friedrich Hayek," *Nation*, May 7, 2013.

30. Quoted in Daniel Yergin and Joseph Stanislaw, *The Commanding Heights: The Battle for the World Economy* (Free Press, 2002), 89.

31. Stedman Jones, *Masters of the Universe*, 77; Phillips-Fein, *Invisible Hands*, 44, 49.

32. Nash, *Conservative Intellectual Movement*, 267; Stedman Jones, *Masters of the Universe*, 153.

33. Stedman Jones, *Masters of the Universe*, 98; Milton Friedman, *Capitalism and Freedom*, 40th anniversary ed. (University of Chicago Press, 2002), xv.

34. Friedman, *Capitalism and Freedom*, chap. 2.

35. Ibid., 91–96, 156–58, 124, 185–89.

36. Milton Friedman and Rose Friedman, *Free to Choose: A Personal Statement* (Avon, 1980), 5–12.

37. Underwriters included the Sarah Scaife Foundation, the John M. Olin Foundation, Getty Oil, *Reader's Digest*, Firestone Tire and Rubber, and the National Federation of Independent Business, for example. Free to Choose Media, "Underwriters," http://www.freetochoosemedia.org/broadcasts /freetochoose/underwriters.php.

38. Friedman, *Capitalism and Freedom*, xii.

39. Phillips-Fein, *Invisible Hands*, 19, 26, 54; Stedman Jones, *Masters of the Universe*, 155; Nash, *Conservative Intellectual Movement*, 18, 346. Early supporters included Harold Luhnow, Jasper Crane of DuPont, David Goodrich of B. F. Goodrich, Charles White of Republic Steel, and Donaldson Brown of General Motors.

40. Quoted in Phillips-Fein, *Invisible Hands*, 27.

41. Milton Friedman and George J. Stigler, "Roofs or Ceilings? The Current Housing Problem," *FEE Popular Essays on Current Problems* 1, no. 2 (Sept. 1946): 18–19.

42. Stedman Jones, *Masters of the Universe*, 155.

43. Phillips-Fein, *Invisible Hands*, 61–65; Critchlow, *Conservative Ascendancy*, 119–20; Micklethwait and Wooldridge, *Right Nation*, 80.

44. Lee Edwards, *The Power of Ideas: The Heritage Foundation at 25 Years* (Jameson Books, 1997), 26, 32, 53–54, 74.

45. James Allen Smith, *The Idea Brokers: Think Tanks and the Rise of the New Policy Elite* (Free Press, 1991), 221.

46. Roger Hertog and Lawrence J. Mone, preface to *Turning Intellect into Influence: The Manhattan Institute at 25*, ed. Brian C. Anderson (Reed Press, 2004), vi.

47. Edwards, *Power of Ideas*, 4–9; Smith, *Idea Brokers*, 220; Doherty, *Radicals for Capitalism*, 454, 478; John Blundell, "Hayek, Fisher, and *The Road to Serfdom*," introduction to "The Road to Serfdom," in Friedrich A. Hayek, *The Road to Serfdom, with The Intellectuals and Socialism* (Institute of Economic

Affairs, 2001), 28; Critchlow, *Conservative Ascendancy*, 122; Micklethwait and Wooldridge, *Right Nation*, 80; Manhattan Institute, *Manhattan Forums: The First Five Years*, http://www.manhattan-institute.org/pdf/mi_five.pdf; Rick Carp, "Who Pays for Think Tanks?," Fairness & Accuracy in Reporting, July 1, 2013.

48. Phillips-Fein, *Invisible Hands*, 176.
49. Jane Mayer, "Covert Operations," *New Yorker*, Aug. 30, 2010; Dave Levinthal, "Inside the Koch Brothers' Campus Crusade," Center for Public Integrity, March 27, 2014; Dave Levinthal, "Koch Brothers' Higher-Ed Investments Advance Political Goals," Center for Public Integrity, Oct. 30, 2015; Kris Hundley, "Billionaire's Role in Hiring Decisions at Florida State University Raises Questions," *Tampa Bay Times*, May 9, 2011.
50. Steven M. Teles, *The Rise of the Conservative Legal Movement: The Battle for Control of the Law* (Princeton University Press, 2008), 93–100.
51. Rodgers, *Age of Fracture*, 58.
52. Teles, *The Rise of the Conservative Legal Movement*, 105–8, 112–13, 115–17.
53. Quoted in ibid., 212.
54. Ibid., 211.
55. Hazlitt, *Economics in One Lesson*, vii.
56. Quoted in Blumenthal, *Rise of the Counter-establishment*, 64.
57. Quoted in Phillips-Fein, *Invisible Hands*, 163.
58. Daniel J. Arbess, "The Young and the Economically Clueless," *Wall Street Journal*, Feb. 19, 2016.
59. Elizabeth A. Fones-Wolf, *Selling Free Enterprise: The Business Assault on Labor and Liberalism, 1945–60* (University of Illinois Press, 1994), 40, 83–85.
60. Ibid., 40, 174–75.
61. Matthew C. Klein, "What Does It Mean to Be 'Economically Literate' Anyway?," *FT Alphaville* (blog), *Financial Times*, March 25, 2016.
62. Fones-Wolf, *Selling Free Enterprise*, 196–97, 201–5.
63. Bethany E. Moreton, "Make Payroll, Not War: Business Culture as Youth Culture," in Schulman and Zelizer, *Rightward Bound*, 55–61, 69.
64. Hazlitt, *Economics in One Lesson*, 5.
65. Ibid., 98.
66. Micklethwait and Wooldridge, *Right Nation*, 79.
67. Nash, *Conservative Intellectual Movement*, 134–40.
68. Stedman Jones, *Masters of the Universe*, 173.
69. William F. Buckley, *God and Man at Yale: The Superstitions of "Academic Freedom"* (Henry Regnery, 1951), 51; William F. Buckley, "Our Mission Statement," *National Review*, Nov. 19, 1955; William F. Buckley, *Up from Liberalism* (Honor Books, 1965), 201–2.

70. Wanniski, *Way the World Works*, xv–xvi.

71. Blumenthal, *Rise of the Counter-establishment*, 194.

72. Wanniski, *Way the World Works*, chaps. 7, 11.

73. Jude Wanniski, "It's Time to Cut Taxes," *Wall Street Journal*, Dec. 11, 1974.

74. Wanniski, *Way the World Works*, 346; Blumenthal, *Rise of the Counter-establishment*, 185–86, 201–2; Jonathan Chait, *The Big Con: The True Story of How Washington Got Hoodwinked and Hijacked by Crackpot Economics* (Houghton Mifflin, 2007), 16.

75. George F. Will, "Utah's Schools Showdown," *Washington Post*, Nov. 1, 2007; George F. Will, "Social Security: Opportunity, Not a Crisis," *Washington Post*, Jan. 20, 2005.

76. David Brooks, "The Center-Right Moment," *New York Times*, May 12, 2015; David Brooks, "The Minimum Wage Muddle," *New York Times*, July 24, 2015.

77. Kiron K. Skinner, Annelise Anderson, and Martin Anderson, *Reagan's Path to Victory: The Shaping of Ronald Reagan's Vision: Selected Writings* (Free Press, 2004), 24.

78. *The Rush Limbaugh Show*, Sept. 29, 2015, http://www.rushlimbaugh.com/daily/2015/09/29/trump_s_tax_plan_reaganesque_but; *The Rush Limbaugh Show*, Jan. 6, 2010, http://www.rushlimbaugh.com/daily/2010/01/06/state_run_media_has_cow_over_rush_s_hospital_press_conference; *The Rush Limbaugh Show*, Dec. 7, 2012, http://www.rushlimbaugh.com/daily/2012/12/07/a_16_year_old_rush_baby.

79. Annie Baxter, "Landlords Have the Upper Hand in Many Rental Markets," *Marketplace*, Feb. 17, 2015; Noel King, "Catching an Uber on New Year's Eve? It'll Cost You," *Marketplace*, Dec. 31, 2014.

80. Quoted in Jacob S. Hacker and Paul Pierson, *Winner-Take-All Politics: How Washington Made the Rich Richer—and Turned Its Back on the Middle Class* (Simon & Schuster, 2010), 189.

81. Barry Goldwater, *The Conscience of a Conservative* (Victor, 1960), 5, 12. The book was actually ghostwritten by L. Brent Bozell. Nash, *Conservative Intellectual Movement*, 192.

82. Goldwater, *Conscience of a Conservative*, 39–43, 99.

83. Blumenthal, *Rise of the Counter-establishment*, 39–40.

84. Phillips-Fein, *Invisible Hands*, 112–14; Micklethwait and Wooldridge, *Right Nation*, 48.

85. Ronald Reagan, "A Time for Choosing" (Oct. 27, 1964), Ronald Reagan Presidential Library & Museum, http://www.reagan.utexas.edu/archives/reference/timechoosing.html.

86. Stedman Jones, *Masters of the Universe*, 265.

87. Chuck's New Classic TV Clubhouse, "Ronald Reagan Political Ad #2, 1980," YouTube, May 11, 2015.

88. Blumenthal, *Rise of the Counter-establishment*, 120; Phillips-Fein, *Invisible Hands*, 261.

89. Quoted in Edward Cowan, "How Regan Sees the Budget," *New York Times*, Oct. 18, 1981.

90. Ronald Reagan, "Inaugural Address" (Jan. 20, 1981), American Presidency Project, http://www.presidency.ucsb.edu/ws/?pid=43130.

91. Ronald Reagan, "Remarks at the Annual Meeting of the Boards of Governors of the World Bank Group and International Monetary Fund" (Sept. 29, 1981), Ronald Reagan Presidential Library & Museum, http://www.reagan.utexas.edu/archives/speeches/1981/92981a.htm.

92. Quoted in Blumenthal, *Rise of the Counter-establishment*, 260.

93. Quoted in Phillips-Fein, *Invisible Hands*, 259.

94. William J. Clinton, "Address Before a Joint Session of the Congress on the State of the Union" (Jan. 23, 1996), American Presidency Project, http://www.presidency.ucsb.edu/ws/?pid=53091.

95. Richard K. Armey, *The Freedom Revolution: The New Republican Majority Leader Tells Why Big Government Failed, Why Freedom Works, and How We Will Rebuild America* (Regnery, 1995), 316.

96. George W. Bush, "Address Before a Joint Session of the Congress on the State of the Union" (Jan. 28, 2003), American Presidency Project, http://www.presidency.ucsb.edu/ws/index.php?pid=29645; George W. Bush, "Remarks in Aurora, Mississippi" (Jan. 14, 2002), in *Public Papers of the Presidents of the United States: George W. Bush, 2002*, bk. 1 (U.S. Government Printing Office, 2004), 64–69.

97. Mitt Romney, "Tax Deal, Bad Deal," *USA Today*, Dec. 14, 2010; Mitt Romney campaign website, archived at archive.org on Sept. 3, 2012; Mitt Romney campaign website, archived at archive.org on Sept. 11, 2012.

98. House Committee on the Budget, *The Path to Prosperity: Restoring America's Promise: Fiscal Year 2012 Budget Resolution* (April 5, 2011), 47, 51.

99. Stephen S. Cohen and J. Bradford DeLong, *Concrete Economics: The Hamilton Approach to Economic Growth and Policy* (Harvard Business Review Press, 2016), 107–8.

100. Rodgers, *Age of Fracture*, 76.

101. David M. Kotz, *The Rise and Fall of Neoliberal Capitalism* (Harvard University Press, 2015), 83.

4. You Get What You Deserve

1. Ray Dalio, *Principles* (Bridgewater Associates, 2011), 6.
2. U.S. Bureau of Labor Statistics, "A Profile of the Working Poor, 2013," *BLS Reports*, no. 1055 (July 2015). (For these purposes, the BLS includes people in the workforce for more than half the year.) U.S. Bureau of Labor Statistics, "Occupational Employment and Wages—May 2014" (press release), March 25, 2015. The median hourly wages for retail salespeople and cashiers are $10.19 and $9.17, respectively.
3. "McDonald's Helps Workers Get Food Stamps," *CNNMoney*, Oct. 24, 2013.
4. Drew DeSilver, "5 Facts About the Minimum Wage," Pew Research Center Fact Tank, July 23, 2015.
5. In September 1965, the minimum wage ($1.25) was almost half the average wage for frontline employees ($2.65); in 2015, the minimum wage ($7.25) was barely one-third the average wage ($20.81). Federal Reserve Bank of St. Louis, FRED Economic Data, "Average Hourly Earnings of Production and Nonsupervisory Employees: Total Private." The United States is tied with Mexico for the lowest ratio of minimum wage to average wage in the OECD. OECD.Stat, Labour, Earnings, "Minimum Relative to Average Wages of Full-Time Workers."
6. Baumol and Blinder, *Economics*, 5.
7. Hazlitt, *Economics in One Lesson*, 119; Friedman, *Capitalism and Freedom*, 180; Wanniski, *Way the World Works*, 89; Waltman, *Politics of the Minimum Wage*, 44.
8. For example, see Mark Wilson, "The Negative Effects of Minimum Wage Laws" (Cato Institute Policy Analysis No. 701, June 21, 2012); "Facts About the Minimum Wage" (Heritage Foundation Factsheet No. 136, Jan. 30, 2014); Douglas Holtz-Eakin and Ben Gitis, "Counterproductive: The Employment and Income Effects of Raising America's Minimum Wage" (Manhattan Institute issue brief 36, July 2015).
9. Richard K. Vedder, "The Transformation of Economics," *Wall Street Journal*, March 1, 2016; Tim Worstall, "Proof That Raising the Minimum Wage Will Increase Unemployment," *Forbes*, June 11, 2015; Jonah Goldberg, "Bernie and Hillary's Harmful Good Intentions on the Minimum Wage," *National Review*, April 20, 2016.
10. "The Real Minimum Wage," *The FRED Blog*, Federal Reserve Bank of

St. Louis, July 23, 2015; Federal Reserve Bank of St. Louis, FRED Economic Data, "Average Hourly Earnings of Production and Nonsupervisory Employees: Total Private."

11. David Card and Alan B. Krueger, "Minimum Wages and Employment: A Case Study of the Fast-Food Industry in New Jersey and Pennsylvania," *American Economic Review* 84, no. 4 (Sept. 1994): 792.

12. David Neumark and William Wascher, "Minimum Wages and Employment: A Review of Evidence from the New Minimum Wage Research" (NBER working paper 12663, Nov. 2006), 121; Hristos Doucouliagos and T. D. Stanley, "Publication Selection Bias in Minimum-Wage Research? A Meta-regression Analysis," *British Journal of Industrial Relations* 47, no. 2 (2009): 406–28; Dale Belman and Paul J. Wolfson, *What Does the Minimum Wage Do?* (Upjohn Institute, 2014), chap. 4.

13. Arindrajit Dube, T. William Lester, and Michael Reich, "Minimum Wage Effects Across State Borders: Estimates Using Contiguous Counties," *Review of Economics and Statistics* 92, no. 4 (Nov. 2010): 961; David Neumark, J. M. Ian Salas, and William Wascher, "Revisiting the Minimum Wage–Employment Debate: Throwing Out the Baby with the Bathwater?," *ILR Review* 67, no. 3 (May 2014) supplement: 608–48. For a detailed review of empirical minimum-wage research since the 1990s, see Belman and Wolfson, *What Does the Minimum Wage Do?* especially chap. 2.

14. IGM Forum, "Minimum Wage," University of Chicago Booth School of Business, Feb. 26, 2013. Thirty-four percent thought it would be harder for low-skilled workers to find jobs, while 32 percent did not (the rest were undecided or had no opinion). The same panel was also divided over whether an increase in the minimum wage to $15 would increase unemployment: 26 percent thought it would, and 24 percent thought it would not. IGM Forum, "$15 Minimum Wage," University of Chicago Booth School of Business, Sept. 22, 2015.

15. Justin Wolfers and Jan Zilinsky, "Higher Wages for Low-Income Workers Lead to Higher Productivity," in *Raising Lower-Level Wages: When and Why It Makes Economic Sense* (Peterson Institute for International Economics briefing 15-2, April 2015), 6–8.

16. See John Schmitt, "Why Does the Minimum Wage Have No Discernible Effect on Employment?" (Center for Economic and Policy Research, Feb. 2013), 11–13.

17. Congressional Budget Office, *The Effects of a Minimum-Wage Increase on Employment and Family Income*, Pub. No. 4856 (Feb. 2014); Arindrajit Dube, "Minimum Wages and the Distribution of Family Incomes," Dec. 30,

2013, http://arindube.com/working-papers/. Neumark has argued that a higher minimum wage does not affect the poverty rate. David Neumark, "Should Missouri Raise Its Minimum Wage?" (Show-Me Institute Policy Study No. 33, Sept. 2012). Dube, however, finds that data from Neumark's own empirical research show that a higher minimum wage does reduce poverty.

18. IGM Forum, "Minimum Wage." Forty-seven percent agreed that a $9 federal minimum wage would be desirable, while 11 percent disagreed.

19. Mike Konczal, "7 Bipartisan Reasons to Raise the Minimum Wage," *Boston Review*, March 3, 2014. In a recent review, all eight empirical studies on the topic found that higher minimum wages resulted in lower levels of inequality. Belman and Wolfson, *What Does the Minimum Wage Do?*, 336.

20. Friedman, *Capitalism and Freedom*, 191–92; Hayek, *Constitution of Liberty*, 424.

21. Peter Coy, "Seven Nobel Economists Endorse a $10.10 Minimum Wage," *Bloomberg*, Jan. 14, 2014.

22. Rubio, Cruz, and Paul: "Transcript: Freedom Partners Forum: Ted Cruz, Rand Paul and Marco Rubio in Conversation with ABC's Jonathan Karl," *ABC News*, Jan. 26, 2015. Bush: J. D. Lutz, "Jeb Bush on Raising Minimum Wage," YouTube, March 17, 2015. Ryan: Washington Free Beacon, "Paul Ryan Demolishes Case for Raising Minimum Wage," YouTube, Jan. 29, 2014.

23. Eric Lipton, "Fight over Minimum Wage Illustrates Web of Industry Ties," *New York Times*, Feb. 9, 2014. Campaigns for a higher minimum wage have their own supporting interest groups, but their arguments are generally not based on economic models.

24. Andy Puzder, "Killing the Working Class at Wal-Mart," *Wall Street Journal*, Feb. 4, 2016.

25. Michael Lynn and Christopher Boone, "Have Minimum Wage Increases Hurt the Restaurant Industry? The Evidence Says No!," *Cornell Hospitality Report* 15, no. 22 (Dec. 2015): 3–13.

26. Barry Ritholtz, "Historical Perspective on the Minimum Wage," *The Big Picture*, March 3, 2016.

27. Gerald Mayer, *Union Membership Trends in the United States* (Congressional Research Service Report, Aug. 31, 2004), app. A.

28. Hayek, *Constitution of Liberty*, 388–92; Friedman, *Capitalism and Freedom*, 124.

29. U.S. Bureau of Labor Statistics, "Union Members—2015" (press release), Jan. 28, 2016, table 3.

30. Bruce Western and Jake Rosenfeld, "Unions, Norms, and the Rise in U.S. Wage Inequality," *American Sociological Review* 76, no. 4 (2011): 532.

31. "Transcript: Freedom Partners Forum."

32. Emmanuel Saez and Gabriel Zucman, "Wealth Inequality in the United States Since 1913: Evidence from Capitalized Income Tax Data," *Quarterly Journal of Economics* (2016), table 1; Piketty, *Capital*, 315; Alvaredo et al., *World Wealth and Income Database*, "United States, Top 0.1% Income Share—Including Capital Gains," http://www.wid.world. Not counting capital gains, the top 0.1 percent income share grew from 2.0 percent in the 1970s to 7.6 percent since 2010. At the very high end, a large proportion of labor income is actually reported as capital gains, for reasons discussed below.

33. Elliot Blair Smith and Phil Kuntz, "CEO Pay 1,795-to-1 Multiple of Wages Skirts U.S. Law," *Bloomberg*, April 30, 2013.

34. Ylan Q. Mui, "Seeing Red over a Golden Parachute," *Washington Post*, Jan. 4, 2007.

35. Stephen Taub, "The 2015 Rich List: The Highest Earning Hedge Fund Managers of the Past Year," *Institutional Investor's Alpha*, May 5, 2015.

36. Forbes 400 (2015 Ranking), *Forbes*.

37. Michael I. Norton and Dan Ariely, "Building a Better America—One Wealth Quintile at a Time," *Perspectives on Psychological Science* 6, no. 1 (2011): 9–12.

38. Hazlitt, *Economics in One Lesson*, 122.

39. Peter Rudegeair, "Goldman Ties Leaders' Compensation to Performance," *Wall Street Journal*, April 10, 2015.

40. Friedman, *Capitalism and Freedom*, 166.

41. Laura M. Holson, "Ruling Upholds Disney's Payment in Firing of Ovitz," *New York Times*, Aug. 10, 2005.

42. "Executive Envy," *Wall Street Journal*, Jan. 21, 2006; Mark A. Calabria, "Regulating Executive Pay" (Cato Institute, Aug. 16, 2010); Jeffrey Dorfman, "The Wrong People Care About CEO Pay, and They Care for the Wrong Reasons," *Forbes*, July 18, 2013; Robert B. Reich, "CEOs Deserve Their Pay," *Wall Street Journal*, Sept. 14, 2007.

43. Tomoeh Murakami Tse, "Long-Serving AT&T Chief to Leave with Huge Payout," *Washington Post*, April 28, 2007; The Intercept, "Former GOP Sen. Phil Gramm: 'It Was an Outrage' That 'Exploited' AT&T CEO Only Got $75 Million at Retirement," Vimeo, July 29, 2015. Although Gramm said Whitacre received $75 million, his actual package was worth at least $158 million.

44. Susan Fleck, John Glaser, and Shawn Sprague, "The Compensation-Productivity Gap: A Visual Essay," *Monthly Labor Review*, Jan. 2011, 59.

45. Nancy F. Koehn, "Great Men, Great Pay? Why CEO Compensation Is Sky High," *Washington Post*, June 12, 2014.

46. Adair Morse, Vikram Nanda, and Amit Seru, "Are Incentive Contracts Rigged by Powerful CEOs?," *Journal of Finance* 66, no. 5 (Oct. 2011): 1779–821.

47. Buffett: John Komlos, *What Every Economics Student Needs to Know and Doesn't Get in the Usual Principles Text* (M. E. Sharpe, 2014), 127. Galbraith: John Kenneth Galbraith, *Annals of an Abiding Liberal* (Houghton Mifflin, 1979), 79.

48. Finkelstein quoted in James Surowiecki, "The Comeback Conundrum," *New Yorker*, Sept. 21, 2015; Marianne Bertrand and Sendhil Mullainathan, "Are CEOs Rewarded for Luck? The Ones Without Principals Are," *Quarterly Journal of Economics* 116, no. 3 (Aug. 2001): 901–32. See also Markus A. Fitzka, "The Use of Variance Decomposition in the Investigation of CEO Effects: How Large Must the CEO Effect Be to Rule Out Chance?," *Strategic Management Journal* 35, no. 12 (Dec. 2014): 1839–52.

49. Lucian Arye Bebchuk and Jesse M. Fried, "Executive Compensation as an Agency Problem," *Journal of Economic Perspectives* 17, no. 3 (Summer 2003): 71–92; Lucian A. Bebchuk, K. J. Martijn Cremers, and Urs C. Peyer, "The CEO Pay Slice," *Journal of Financial Economics* 102, no. 1 (Oct. 2011): 199–221; Lucian A. Bebchuk, Yaniv Grinstein, and Urs Peyer, "Lucky CEOs and Lucky Directors," *Journal of Finance* 65, no. 6 (Dec. 2010): 2363–401; Lucian Bebchuk and Jesse Fried, *Pay Without Performance: The Unfulfilled Promise of Executive Compensation* (Harvard University Press, 2004); Steven N. Kaplan and Joshua Rauh, "Wall Street and Main Street: What Contributes to the Rise in the Highest Incomes?," *Review of Financial Studies* 23, no. 3 (March 2010): 1004–50; Steven N. Kaplan, "Executive Compensation and Corporate Governance in the United States: Perceptions, Facts, and Challenges," *Cato Papers on Public Policy* 2 (2012): 99–164.

50. Financial Crisis Inquiry Commission, *The Financial Crisis Inquiry Report: Final Report of the National Commission on the Causes of the Financial and Economic Crisis in the United States* (PublicAffairs, 2011), 141.

51. Jesse Eisinger and Jake Bernstein, "The Magnetar Trade: How One Hedge Fund Kept the Bubble Going," *ProPublica*, April 9, 2010; Felix Salmon, "The Big Short," Reuters, March 15, 2010.

52. Jon Bakija, Adam Cole, and Bradley T. Heim, "Jobs and Income Growth of Top Earners and the Causes of Changing Income Inequality: Evidence

from U.S. Tax Return Data" (Williams College Economics Department working paper 2010-22, rev. April 2012), table 3.

53. Vivek Wadhwa et al., *The Anatomy of an Entrepreneur: Making of a Successful Entrepreneur* (Ewing Marion Kauffman Foundation, Nov. 2009).

54. Hayek, *Road to Serfdom*, 134.

55. David M. Mason, "Why Government Control of Bank Salaries Will Hurt, Not Help, the Economy" (Heritage Foundation Backgrounder 2336, Nov. 4, 2009).

5. Incentives Are Everything

1. George Gilder, *Wealth and Poverty* (Regnery, 2012), 256.

2. "The World's Billionaires," *Forbes*, March 1, 2016; Warren E. Buffett, "Stop Coddling the Super-rich," *New York Times*, Aug. 14, 2011.

3. Hazlitt, *Economics in One Lesson*, 25–26; Friedman, *Capitalism and Freedom*, 173; Mankiw, "I Can Afford Higher Taxes"; Holman W. Jenkins Jr., "Bad Days for Wal-Mart Americans," *Wall Street Journal*, Jan. 19, 2016.

4. Boehner and Ryan: David Jackson, "Obama, GOP to Revive Tax Debate," *USA Today*, Sept. 18, 2011. Ryan: McCormack, "Paul Ryan."

5. Curtis S. Dubay and David R. Burton, "The Lee-Rubio Tax Plan's Business Reforms Are Tremendously Pro-growth" (Heritage Foundation Backgrounder 3000, March 9, 2015).

6. Friedman, *Capitalism and Freedom*, 174–75.

7. Rand Paul 2016, "Rand Paul's Tax Plan Would Blow Up the Tax Code and Start Over," https://randpaul.com/issue/taxes; Ted Cruz, "A Simple Flat Tax for Economic Growth," *Wall Street Journal*, Oct. 28, 2015; James Freeman, "The End of the War on Business?," *Wall Street Journal*, Jan. 20, 2016.

8. Howard Gleckman, "How the GOP Candidates' Tax Plans Stack Up Against One Another," *TaxVox*, Tax Policy Center, Feb. 18, 2016; Joseph Rosenberg et al., "An Analysis of Ted Cruz's Tax Plan," Tax Policy Center, Feb. 16, 2016.

9. Paul D. Ryan, "A GOP Road Map for America's Future," *Wall Street Journal*, Jan. 26, 2010; Kyle Pomerleau, "Details and Analysis of Dr. Ben Carson's Tax Plan," Tax Foundation, Jan. 6, 2016; Elaine Maag et al., "An Analysis of Marco Rubio's Tax Plan," Tax Policy Center, Feb. 11, 2016.

10. Hazlitt, *Economics in One Lesson*, 25–26; Wanniski, *Way the World Works*, 89–90; Amity Shlaes and Matthew Denhart, "Where the Rubio Tax Plan Falls Short," *Wall Street Journal*, April 2, 2015.

11. Milton Friedman, "High Living as a Tax Shelter," *Newsweek*, Nov. 8, 1976; Hayek, *Constitution of Liberty*, 445; George F. Will, "The Nonexistent Case for Progressive Taxation," *Washington Post*, Dec. 4, 2015.

12. Alan Greenspan, "The Tax System" (testimony before the President's Advisory Panel on Federal Tax Reform, March 3, 2005); House Committee on the Budget, *Path to Prosperity*, 51.

13. James Risen and Robert A. Rosenblatt, "He Urges National Sales Tax: Economists Like Babbitt Plan—but Few Others Do," *Los Angeles Times*, Jan. 25, 1988.

14. Harland Prechel, *Big Business and the State: Historical Transitions and Corporate Transformations, 1880s–1990s* (SUNY Press, 2000), 167.

15. Ronald Reagan, "Message to the Congress Transmitting the Annual Economic Report of the President" (Feb. 10, 1982), American Presidency Project, http://www.presidency.ucsb.edu/ws/?pid=42121.

16. Buffett, "Stop Coddling the Super-rich."

17. As it turns out, there is a particular tax break for investing in small businesses that we did qualify for, but none of us knew about it until years later.

18. Citizens for Tax Justice, "Top Federal Income Tax Rates Since 1913"; U.S. Bureau of Economic Analysis, table 1.1.1, "Percent Change from Preceding Period in Real Gross Domestic Product"; table 2.1, "Personal Income and Its Disposition."

19. Congressional Budget Office, *The Economic Effects of Comprehensive Tax Reform*, July 1997, 25; Michael J. Boskin, "Taxation, Saving, and the Rate of Interest," *Journal of Political Economy* 86, no. 2, pt. 2 (April 1978): S16.

20. Eric Toder and Kim Rueben, "Should We Eliminate Taxation of Capital Income?," in *Taxing Capital Income*, ed. Henry J. Aaron, Leonard E. Burman, and C. Eugene Steuerle (Urban Institute Press, 2007), 127, 135; Jane G. Gravelle and Donald J. Marples, "Tax Rates and Economic Growth" (Congressional Research Service report R42111, Jan. 2, 2014), 6.

21. Leonard E. Burman, *The Labyrinth of Capital Gains Tax Policy: A Guide for the Perplexed* (Brookings Institution Press, 1999), 56–57, 81.

22. Christopher D. Carroll, "Why Do the Rich Save So Much?," in *Does Atlas Shrug? The Economic Consequences of Taxing the Rich*, ed. Joel B. Slemrod (Harvard University Press, 2002).

23. Cuts in capital gains tax rates can lead to onetime increases in tax revenues, but this effect is due to taxpayers' ability to time asset sales; in the long term, different capital gains tax rates have little or no impact on income from capital gains. Burman, *Labyrinth of Capital Gains Tax Policy*, 60–63.

24. Citizens for Tax Justice, "Top Federal Income Tax Rates Since 1913"; U.S.

Bureau of Economic Analysis, table 1.1.1, "Percent Change from Preceding Period in Real Gross Domestic Product."

25. Congressional Budget Office, *The Distribution of Household Income and Federal Taxes, 2010*, Pub. No. 4613 (Dec. 2013) (Supplemental Data); U.S. Bureau of Economic Analysis, table 1.1.1, "Percent Change from Preceding Period in Real Gross Domestic Product"; U.S. Bureau of Labor Statistics, "Labor Force Participation Rate, 25–54 Years."

26. William G. Gale, Aaron Krupkin, and Kim Rueben, "The Relationship Between Taxes and Growth at the State Level: New Evidence," *National Tax Journal* 68, no. 4 (Dec. 2015): 919–42.

27. Noah Smith, "Growth Fantasy of Tax Cuts and Small Government," *Bloomberg*, July 17, 2015; Menzie Chinn, "The Information Content of the ALEC-Laffer-Moore-Williams Economic Outlook Ranking," *Econbrowser* (blog), July 11, 2015; Menzie Chinn, "Kansas Relative Employment Performance since 2005," *Econbrowser* (blog), May 7, 2016.

28. Emmanuel Saez, Joel Slemrod, and Seth H. Giertz, "The Elasticity of Taxable Income with Respect to Marginal Tax Rates: A Critical Review," *Journal of Economic Literature* 50, no. 1 (March 2012): 3–4; Robert McClelland and Shannon Mok, "A Review of Recent Research on Labor Supply Elasticities" (Congressional Budget Office working paper, 2012-12, Oct. 2012), table 2; Gravelle and Marples, "Tax Rates and Economic Growth," summary.

29. Robert A. Moffitt and Mark O. Wilhelm, "Taxation and the Labor Supply: Decisions of the Affluent," in Slemrod, *Does Atlas Shrug?*; McClelland and Mok, "Review of Recent Research," 5; Leonard E. Burman, "Taxes and Inequality," *Tax Law Review* 66 (2013): 585.

30. Saez, Slemrod, and Giertz, "Elasticity of Taxable Income," 43.

31. Thomas L. Hungerford, "Taxes and the Economy: An Economic Analysis of the Top Tax Rates Since 1945 (Updated)" (Congressional Research Service report, R42729, Dec. 12, 2012).

32. Peter Diamond and Emmanuel Saez, "The Case for a Progressive Tax: From Basic Research to Policy Recommendations," *Journal of Economic Perspectives* 25, no. 4 (Fall 2011): 171. The optimal rate could be a little higher or a little lower, depending on how easy it is to avoid taxes through creative accounting.

33. Simon Johnson and James Kwak, *13 Bankers: The Wall Street Takeover and the Next Financial Meltdown* (Pantheon, 2010).

34. For example, see Andy Kessler, "The Capitalist as the Ultimate Philanthropist," *Wall Street Journal*, June 24, 2015.

35. Hayek, *Constitution of Liberty*, 332–33; Friedman, *Capitalism and Freedom*, 34.

36. As recollected by the Supreme Court justice Felix Frankfurter. See "Taxes Are What We Pay for Civilized Society," Quote Investigator, April 13, 2012.

37. The top 1 percent of households received more than 30 percent of the total tax cuts. Greg Leiserson and Jeffrey Rohaly, "The Distribution of the 2001–2006 Tax Cuts: Updated Projections, November 2006," Tax Policy Center, tables 7–12.

6. The Consumer Knows Best

1. Milton Friedman, "Leonard Woodcock's Free Lunch," *Newsweek*, April 21, 1975.

2. Centers for Medicare & Medicaid Services, "National Health Expenditures 2014 Highlights"; OECD, "OECD Health Statistics 2015—Frequently Requested Data."

3. Karen Davis et al., "Mirror, Mirror on the Wall: How the Performance of the U.S. Health Care System Compares Internationally, 2014 Update," Commonwealth Fund, June 2014, 7–9; OECD, "OECD Health Statistics 2015." The Commonwealth Fund's overall outcomes metric includes "mortality amenable to medical care, infant mortality, and healthy life expectancy at age 60."

4. Raj Chetty et al., "The Association Between Income and Life Expectancy in the United States, 2001–2014," *Journal of the American Medical Association*, April 26, 2016, 1750–66.

5. Mises, *Bureaucracy*, 21.

6. John F. Cogan, R. Glenn Hubbard, and Daniel P. Kessler, "Healthy, Wealthy, and Wise," *Wall Street Journal*, May 4, 2004.

7. Stuart M. Butler, "Why Conservatives Need a National Health Plan" (Heritage Lecture 442 on Political Thought, March 22, 1993); the CIGNA CEO is quoted in Wendell Potter, *Deadly Spin: An Insurance Company Insider Speaks Out on How Corporate PR Is Killing Health Care and Deceiving Americans* (Bloomsbury Press, 2010), 110.

8. Quoted in Potter, *Deadly Spin*, 127.

9. White House National Economic Council, *Reforming Health Care for the 21st Century*, Feb. 2006, 4. Matthews is quoted in Julie Rovner, "Bush Makes Push for Health Care Savings Plans," NPR, Feb. 1, 2006.

10. Kaiser Family Foundation and Health Research & Educational Trust,

Employer Health Benefits: 2015 Annual Survey (Kaiser Family Foundation and Health Research & Educational Trust, 2015), 79, 126.

11. Nina Owcharenko and Robert E. Moffit, "The Massachusetts Health Plan: Lessons for the States" (Heritage Foundation Backgrounder 1953, July 18, 2006); Robert E. Moffit, "State-Based Health Reform: A Comparison of Health Insurance Exchanges and the Federal Employees Health Benefits Program" (Heritage Foundation WebMemo 1515, June 20, 2007).

12. Edmund F. Haislmaier et al., "A Fresh Start for Health Care Reform" (Heritage Foundation Backgrounder 2970, Oct. 30, 2014); Merrill Matthews, "Ten Principles of a Market-Oriented Health Care System," *Human Events*, Jan. 27, 2014; Lanhee J. Chen and James C. Capretta, "Instead of ObamaCare: Giving Health-Care Power to the People," *Wall Street Journal*, Jan. 22, 2016.

13. House Committee on the Budget, *Path to Prosperity*, 47; see also Congressional Budget Office, "An Analysis of the Roadmap for America's Future Act of 2010" (letter to Paul Ryan), Jan. 27, 2010.

14. David Goldhill and Paul Howard, "An ObamaCare-Inspired Rebellion," *Wall Street Journal*, July 2, 2015; Sally C. Pipes, "Medicare at 50: Hello, Mid-Life Crisis," *Wall Street Journal*, July 30, 2015. See also Scott W. Atlas and John F. Cogan, "Two Essential Tools for Repairing the ObamaCare Damage," *Wall Street Journal*, Sept. 2, 2015.

15. Marco Rubio for President, "It's Time to Repeal and Replace Obama-Care," https://marcorubio.com/issues/repeal-obamacare-and-replace-it-with-this/; Contract from America, http://contractfromamerica.org; Rick Santorum, "A Flat Tax Is the Best Path to Prosperity," *Wall Street Journal*, Oct. 12, 2015; Trump, *Time to Get Tough: Making America #1 Again* (Regnery, 2011), 131; Donald J. Trump for President, "Healthcare Reform to Make America Great Again," https://www.donaldjtrump.com/positions/healthcare-reform.

16. Kenneth J. Arrow, "Uncertainty and the Welfare Economics of Medical Care," *American Economic Review* 53, no. 5 (Dec. 1963): 948–51.

17. Uwe E. Reinhardt, "Rethinking the Gruber Controversy: Americans Aren't Stupid, but They're Often Ignorant—and Why," *Health Affairs Blog*, Dec. 29, 2014.

18. For a more comprehensive discussion of the theoretical peculiarities of the health-care market, see Timothy Stoltzfus Jost, *Health Care at Risk: A Critique of the Consumer-Driven Movement* (Duke University Press, 2007), 96–108.

19. RAND Health, "The Health Insurance Experiment: A Classic RAND Study Speaks to the Current Health Care Reform Debate" (RAND Health

Research Highlights, 2006), 3; Jost, *Health Care at Risk*, 130; Zarek C. Brot-Goldberg et al., "What Does a Deductible Do? The Impact of Cost-Sharing on Health Care Prices, Quantities, and Spending Dynamics" (National Bureau of Economic Research working paper 21632, Oct. 2015).

20. Quoted in Robert Pear, "Harvard Ideas on Health Care Hit Home, Hard," *New York Times*, Jan. 5, 2015.

21. Jost, *Health Care at Risk*, 130; Peter J. Huckfeldt et al., "Patient Responses to Incentives in Consumer-Directed Health Plans: Evidence from Pharmaceuticals" (National Bureau of Economic Research working paper 20927, Feb. 2015).

22. Aaron E. Carroll, "People with Chronic Illness Fare Worse Under Cost-Sharing," *The Upshot* (blog), *New York Times*, May 19, 2014; Amitabh Chandra, Jonathan Gruber, and Robin McKnight, "Patient Cost-Sharing and Hospitalization Offsets in the Elderly," *American Economic Review* 100, no. 1 (March 2010): 193–213.

23. Asher Schechter, "There Is Regulatory Capture, but It Is by No Means Complete," *Pro-Market* (blog), Stigler Center at the University of Chicago Booth School of Business, March 15, 2016.

24. Arrow, "Uncertainty and Welfare Economics," 945.

25. Ibid., 963–64.

26. John Nyman, "Is 'Moral Hazard' Inefficient? The Policy Implications of a New Theory," *Health Affairs* 23, no. 5 (Sept.–Oct. 2004), 199.

27. Kaiser Family Foundation, "Summary of the Affordable Care Act," April 23, 2013.

28. Liz Hamel et al., *The Burden of Medical Debt: Results from the Kaiser Family Foundation/New York Times Medical Bills Survey*, Kaiser Family Foundation, Jan. 2016.

29. Pear, "Harvard Ideas on Health Care."

30. Jacob S. Hacker, *The Great Risk Shift: The New Economic Insecurity and the Decline of the American Dream* (Oxford University Press, 2008), 142.

31. Commonwealth Fund, *International Profiles of Health Care Systems, 2014* (Commonwealth Fund, Jan. 2015).

32. Daniel Callahan and Angela A. Wasunna, *Medicine and the Market: Equity v. Choice* (Johns Hopkins University Press, 2006), 90.

33. Friedman and Friedman, *Free to Choose*, 106.

34. OECD, *Health at a Glance 2015: OECD Indicators* (OECD, 2015), 171 and tables 1.1, 1.3, 1.5.

35. See Frank Pasquale, "The Hidden Costs of Health Care Cost-Cutting: Toward a Postneoliberal Health-Reform Agenda," *Law and Contemporary Problems* 77, no. 4 (2014): 174.

36. Hayek, *Constitution of Liberty*, 424.

37. Quoted in Callahan and Wasunna, *Medicine and the Market*, 210–11.

38. Thomas Rice, "Can Markets Give Us the Health System We Want?," *Journal of Health Politics, Policy, and Law* 22, no. 2 (April 1997): 422–23.

39. See Robert G. Evans, "Going for the Gold: The Redistributive Agenda Behind Market-Based Health Care Reform," *Journal of Health Politics, Policy, and Law* 22, no. 3 (April 1997): 447.

40. Reinhardt, "Rethinking the Gruber Controversy."

41. Daniel A. Austin, "Medical Debt as a Cause of Bankruptcy," *Maine Law Review* 67, no. 1 (2014): 1–23.

42. Lucien Febvre, *The Problem of Unbelief in the Sixteenth Century: The Religion of Rabelais*, trans. Beatrice Gottlieb (Harvard University Press, 1985).

7. Capital Unbound

1. Ben Bernanke, "Regulation and Financial Innovation" (remarks at the Federal Reserve Bank of Atlanta's 2007 Financial Markets Conference, May 15, 2007), https://www.federalreserve.gov/newsevents/speech /bernanke20070515a.htm.

2. Housing prices: Federal Reserve Bank of St. Louis, FRED Economic Data, "S&P/Case-Shiller 20-City Composite Home Price Index," "S&P/Case-Shiller AZ-Phoenix Home Price Index," and "S&P/Case-Shiller NV-Las Vegas Home Price Index." Foreclosures: Jennifer Taub, *Other People's Houses: How Decades of Bailouts, Captive Regulators, and Toxic Bankers Made Home Mortgages a Thrilling Business* (Yale University Press, 2014), 3; Bill McBride, "MBA: Mortgage Delinquency and Foreclosure Rates Decrease in Q3, Lowest Since 2007," *Calculated Risk* (blog), Nov. 14, 2014.

3. See Alyssa Katz, *Our Lot: How Real Estate Came to Own Us* (Bloomsbury, 2009), 78–81.

4. Bill McBride, "Mortgage Delinquencies by Loan Type," *Calculated Risk* (blog), Aug. 12, 2012.

5. Federal Reserve Bank of St. Louis, FRED Economic Data, "All Employees: Total Nonfarm Payrolls"; Menzie Chinn, "Closing the Output Gap," *Econbrowser* (blog), Nov. 19, 2015.

6. See, for example, Mankiw, *Principles of Economics*, 268.

7. Hayek, *Road to Serfdom*, 86; Dieter Plehwe, introduction to *Road from Mont Pèlerin*, ed., Mirowski and Plehwe, 23.

8. Financial Crisis Inquiry Commission, *Financial Crisis Inquiry Report*, 34.

9. Taub, *Other People's Houses*, 125–27.

10. Kathleen C. Engel and Patricia A. McCoy, *The Subprime Virus: Reckless Credit, Regulatory Failure, and Next Steps* (Oxford University Press, 2011), 158.

11. Greg Ip, "Did Greenspan Add to Subprime Woes? Gramlich Says Ex-colleague Blocked Crackdown on Predatory Lenders Despite Growing Concerns," *Wall Street Journal*, June 9, 2007.

12. Alan Greenspan, "Consumer Finance" (remarks at the Federal Reserve System's Fourth Annual Community Affairs Research Conference, April 8, 2005), http://www.federalreserve.gov/boarddocs/speeches/2005/20050408/default.htm.

13. Quoted in Manuel Roig-Franzia, "Credit Crisis Cassandra: Brooksley Born's Unheeded Warning Is a Rueful Echo 10 Years On," *Washington Post*, May 26, 2009. Summers declined to comment for the Roig-Franzia article. See also "Interview with Michael Greenberger," *Frontline*, July 14, 2009, transcript at http://www.pbs.org/wgbh/pages/frontline/warning/interviews/greenberger.html.

14. Alan Greenspan, "Government Regulation and Derivative Contracts" (remarks at the Financial Markets Conference of the Federal Reserve Bank of Atlanta, Feb. 21, 1997), http://www.federalreserve.gov/boarddocs/speeches/1997/19970221.htm; Alan Greenspan, "The Regulation of OTC Derivatives" (testimony before the House Committee on Banking and Financial Services, July 24, 1998), http://www.federalreserve.gov/boarddocs/testimony/1998/19980724.htm.

15. Johnson and Kwak, *13 Bankers*, 138–40.

16. U.S. Securities and Exchange Commission, "Final Rule: Alternative Net Capital Requirements for Broker-Dealers That Are Part of Consolidated Supervised Entities" (release 34-49830, June 8, 2004).

17. Cohen and DeLong, *Concrete Economics*, 184–85.

18. U.S. Bureau of Economic Analysis, table 6.16, "Corporate Profits by Industry"; Johnson and Kwak, *13 Bankers*, 115–16.

19. Alana Semuels, "The Unfinished Suburbs of America," *Atlantic*, Nov. 14, 2014.

20. Charles Duhigg and Carter Dougherty, "From Midwest to M.T.A., Pain from Global Gamble," *New York Times*, Nov. 1, 2008; Mark Landler, "U.S. Credit Crisis Adds to Gloom in Norway," *New York Times*, Dec. 2, 2007.

21. Financial Crisis Inquiry Commission, *Financial Crisis Inquiry Report*, 90, 108; Taub, *Other People's Houses*, 129.

22. Financial Crisis Inquiry Commission, *Financial Crisis Inquiry Report*, 108.

23. Ibid., 106; Michael Lewis, *The Big Short* (W. W. Norton, 2010), 97.

24. Taub, *Other People's Houses*, 141.

25. Financial Crisis Inquiry Commission, *Financial Crisis Inquiry Report*, 107; Taub, *Other People's Houses*, 129; Engel and McCoy, *Subprime Virus*, 30–32; David Dayen, *Chain of Title: How Three Ordinary Americans Uncovered Wall Street's Great Foreclosure Fraud* (New Press, 2016), 31.

26. Rick Brooks and Ruth Simon, "Subprime Debacle Traps Even Very Credit-Worthy," *Wall Street Journal*, Dec. 3, 2007.

27. Taub, *Other People's Houses*, 140–45.

28. *The State of the Nation's Housing, 2006*, Joint Center for Housing Studies of Harvard University, 2006, 3.

29. Dayen, *Chain of Title*, 31–32.

30. Jake Bernstein and Jesse Eisinger, "The 'Subsidy': How a Handful of Merrill Lynch Bankers Helped Blow Up Their Own Firm," *ProPublica*, Dec. 22, 2010.

31. Eisinger and Bernstein, "Magnetar Trade"; Securities and Exchange Commission, "J. P. Morgan to Pay $153.6 Million to Settle SEC Charges of Misleading Investors in CDO Tied to U.S. Housing Market" (press release), June 21, 2011.

32. Michiyo Nakamoto and David Wighton, "Citigroup Chief Stays Bullish on Buy-Outs," *Financial Times*, July 9, 2007.

33. Jake Bernstein and Jesse Eisinger, "Banks' Self-Dealing Super-charged Financial Crisis," *ProPublica*, Aug. 26, 2010.

34. Lewis, *Big Short*, 141–42.

35. Quoted in "The Watchmen," *This American Life*, WBEZ, originally broadcast June 5, 2009.

36. Kevin G. Hall, "How Moody's Sold Its Ratings—and Sold Out Investors," *McClatchy*, Oct. 18, 2009; Ben Protess, "S.&P.'s $1.37 Billion Reckoning over Crisis-Era Misdeeds," *New York Times*, Feb. 3, 2015.

37. Andrew Ross Sorkin et al., "As Credit Crisis Spiraled, Alarm Led to Action," *New York Times*, Oct. 1, 2008.

38. James E. Glassman, "Markets & the Economy/The Week Ahead," JPMorgan Chase, May 3, 2010.

39. Peter J. Wallison, "Elitist Protection Consumers Don't Need," *Washington Post*, July 13, 2009; David C. John, "The Lehman Brothers Collapse: Financial Regulation One Year Later" (Heritage Foundation WebMemo 2610, Sept. 14, 2009); Jeb Hensarling, "Punishing Consumers to 'Protect' Them," *Washington Times*, July 22, 2009.

40. "A Trillion Unintended Consequences," *Wall Street Journal*, July 6, 2010;

Peter J. Wallison, "Crisis and Ideology: The Administration's Financial Reform Legislation" (American Enterprise Institute Financial Services Outlook, April 2010); Matt Kibbe, "Key Vote 'No' H.R. 4173: Dodd-Frank Wall Street Reform and Consumer Protection Act," FreedomWorks (press release), July 14, 2010.

41. Peter J. Wallison, "Financial Crisis Inquiry Commission Dissenting Statement," in Financial Crisis Inquiry Commission, *Financial Crisis Inquiry Report*, 441–538.

42. "JPMorgan Chief Warns of Overregulation—Report," Reuters, April 18, 2010.

43. See Anat Admati and Martin Hellwig, *The Bankers' New Clothes: What's Wrong with Banking and What to Do About It* (Princeton University Press, 2013).

44. Diane Katz, "The CFPB in Action: Consumer Bureau Harms Those It Claims to Protect" (Heritage Foundation Backgrounder 2760, Jan. 22, 2013).

45. "Dodd-Frank Cripples Innovation and Economic Growth," Marco Rubio for President, https://marcorubio.com/news/dodd-frank-cripples-innovation-and-economic-growth/; Glenn Kessler, "Rubio's Fantasy Figure on Bank Closures Due to Dodd-Frank," *Washington Post*, Aug. 10, 2015; Guy Bentley, "Sen. Richard Shelby Slams Dodd-Frank and Takes Aim at CFPB," *Daily Caller*, July 21, 2015; Jeb Hensarling, "After Five Years, Dodd-Frank Is a Failure," *Wall Street Journal*, July 20, 2015.

46. Alvaredo et al., *World Wealth and Income Database*, "United States, Top 1% Income Share," http://www.wid.world; Peter Rudegeair, "Pay Gap Between Wall Street CEOs and Employees Narrows," *Wall Street Journal*, April 5, 2015; Federal Reserve Bank of St. Louis, FRED Economic Data, "Real Median Household Income in the United States."

8. It's a Small World After All

1. Charles Krauthammer, "Save Obama (on Trade)," *Washington Post*, May 14, 2015.

2. Michael Wayland, "Sanders: Bad Trade Policies Killing Middle Class Jobs," *Detroit News*, March 3, 2016; David Weigel and Lydia DePillis, "Voters Skeptical on Free Trade Drive Sanders, Trump Victories in Michigan," *Washington Post*, March 9, 2016; Binyamin Appelbaum, "On Trade, Donald Trump Breaks with 200 Years of Economic Orthodoxy," *New York Times*,

March 10, 2016; "Transcript: Donald Trump Expounds on His Foreign Policy Views," *New York Times*, March 16, 2016.

3. Dave Jamieson, "Why Bernie Sanders and Donald Trump Won the Michigan Primaries," *Huffington Post*, March 9, 2016.

4. John McCormick, "Free-Trade Opposition Unites Political Parties in Bloomberg Poll," *Bloomberg*, March 24, 2016.

5. Federal Reserve Bank of St. Louis, FRED Economic Data, "All Employees: Manufacturing"; U.S. Census Bureau and U.S. Bureau of Economic Analysis, "U.S. International Trade in Goods and Services, January 2016" (press release), March 4, 2016.

6. Milton Friedman, "Free Trade," *Newsweek*, Aug. 17, 1970; Friedman, *Capitalism and Freedom*, 71; Barry Eichengreen, "Keynes and Protection," *Journal of Economic History* 44, no. 2 (June 1984): 363–73.

7. Matt Yglesias, "Here's What Economists Cheering for the Pacific Trade Deal Are Missing," *Mother Jones*, April 30, 2015; IGM Forum, "Free Trade," University of Chicago Booth School of Business, March 13, 2012.

8. Friedman, *Capitalism and Freedom*, 73; Paul Krugman, "What Should Trade Negotiators Negotiate About?," *Journal of Economic Literature* 35 (March 1997): 113.

9. Appelbaum, "On Trade."

10. Daron Acemoglu et al., "Import Competition and the Great US Employment Sag of the 2000s," *Journal of Labor Economics* 34, no. S1, pt. 2 (Jan. 2016): S145.

11. Milton Friedman, "Do Imports Cost Jobs?," *Newsweek*, Feb. 9, 1981.

12. Cohen and DeLong, *Concrete Economics*, chaps. 1, 4.

13. Congressional Budget Office, *The Effects of NAFTA on U.S.-Mexican Trade and GDP*, May 2003, 19; Robert E. Scott, "Heading South: U.S.–Mexico Trade and Job Displacement After NAFTA" (Economic Policy Institute briefing paper 308, May 3, 2011); Gary Clyde Hufbauer, Cathleen Cimino, and Tyler Moran, "NAFTA at 20: Misleading Charges and Positive Achievements" (Peterson Institute for International Economics PB14-13, May 2014); Lorenzo Caliendo and Fernando Parro, "Estimates of the Trade and Welfare Effects of NAFTA," *Review of Economic Studies* 82, no. 1 (Jan. 2015): 3.

14. Caliendo and Parro, "Effects of NAFTA," 3; Mark Weisbrot, Stephan Lefebvre, and Joseph Sammut, "Did NAFTA Help Mexico? An Assessment After 20 Years," Center for Economic and Policy Research, Feb. 2014.

15. John McLaren and Shushanik Hakobyan, "Looking for Local Labor-Market Effects of NAFTA," *Review of Economics and Statistics* (forthcoming), 6.

16. Acemoglu et al., "Import Competition," S145–S147, S181.

17. Justin R. Pierce and Peter K. Schott, "The Surprisingly Swift Decline of US Manufacturing Employment," *American Economic Review* 106, no. 7 (July 2016): 1632–62.

18. David H. Autor, David Dorn, and Gordon H. Hanson, "The China Syndrome: Local Labor Market Effects of Import Competition in the United States," *American Economic Review* 103, no. 6 (Oct. 2013): 2144–45.

19. David H. Autor, David Dorn, and Gordon H. Hanson, "The China Shock: Learning from Labor Market Adjustment to Large Changes in Trade" (National Bureau of Economic Research working paper 21906, Jan. 2016), 31–35, 37.

20. Lawrence Summers, "A Trade Deal Must Work for America's Middle Class," *Financial Times*, March 8, 2015.

21. Paul Krugman, "TPP at the NABE," *The Conscience of a Liberal* (blog), *New York Times*, March 11, 2015.

22. Jason Furman, "Trade, Innovation, and Economic Growth" (remarks at the Brookings Institution, April 8, 2015), https://www.whitehouse.gov/sites /default/files/docs/20150408_trade_innovation_growth_brookings.pdf; Krauthammer, "Save Obama (on Trade)"; Roger Lowenstein, "TPP and Free Trade: Why Congress Should Listen to the World's Richest Economist," *Fortune*, June 22, 2015; N. Gregory Mankiw, "Economists Actually Agree on This: The Wisdom of Free Trade," *The Upshot* (blog), *New York Times*, April 24, 2015.

23. Peter A. Petri and Michael G. Plummer, "The Economic Effects of the Trans-Pacific Partnership: New Estimates" (Peterson Institute for International Economics working paper 16-2, Jan. 2016), 20; Jeronim Capaldo and Alex Izurieta, "Trading Down: Unemployment, Inequality, and Other Risks of the Trans-Pacific Partnership Agreement," with Jomo Kwame Sundaram (Tufts University Global Development and Environment Institute working paper 16-01, Jan. 2016), 11, 17.

24. Dean Baker, "Fools or Liars on the Trans-Pacific Partnership?," *Truthout*, March 21, 2016.

25. Jing Luo and Aaron S. Kesselheim, "The Trans-Pacific Partnership Agreement and Implications for Access to Essential Medicines," *Journal of the American Medical Association*, Oct. 20, 2015, 1563–64.

26. See Elhanan Helpman, "Innovation, Imitation, and Intellectual Property Rights," *Econometrica* 61, no. 6 (Nov. 1993): 1247–80.

27. Scott Sinclair, "Democracy Under Challenge: Canada and Two Decades of NAFTA's Investor-State Dispute Settlement Mechanism," Canadian Cen-

tre for Policy Alternatives, 2015, 32; Lori Wallach, "Public Interest Takes a Hit Even When Phillip [*sic*] Morris' Investor-State Attack on Australia Is Dismissed," *Huffington Post*, Jan. 5, 2016; Alexander Hellemans, "Vattenfall Seeks $6 Billion in Compensation for German Nuclear Phase-Out," *IEEE Spectrum*, Nov. 12, 2014; Todd Tucker, "TransCanada Is Suing the U.S. over Obama's Rejection of the Keystone XL Pipeline: The U.S. Might Lose," *Monkey Cage* (blog), *Washington Post*, Jan. 8, 2016.

28. Lise Johnson, Lisa Sachs, and Jeffrey Sachs, "The Real Danger in TPP," *CNN*, Feb. 19, 2016; see also Joseph Stiglitz, "The Secret Corporate Takeover of Trade Agreements," *Guardian*, May 13, 2015.

29. Christopher Ingraham, "Interactive: How Companies Wield Off-the-Record Influence on Obama's Trade Policy," *Wonkblog* (blog), *Washington Post*, Feb. 28, 2014.

30. Jared Bernstein, "Seeing Is Believing," *Democracy: A Journal of Ideas* no. 38 (Fall 2015).

31. Simon Johnson and Andrei Levchenko, "The Trans-Pacific Partnership (TPP): This Is Not About Ricardo," *The Baseline Scenario* (blog), May 21, 2015; Paul Krugman, "101 Boosterism," *The Conscience of a Liberal* (blog), *New York Times*, April 20, 2016.

9. The Best Possible World—for Whom?

1. Irving Kristol, "On Conservatism and Capitalism," in Irving Kristol, *Neoconservatism: The Autobiography of an Idea* (Free Press, 1995), 233.

2. Hayek, *Road to Serfdom*, 59, 82.

3. F. A. Hayek, "Foreword to the 1956 American Paperback Edition," in *Road to Serfdom*, 42.

4. William J. Clinton, "Address Before a Joint Session of the Congress on the State of the Union" (Jan. 23, 1996), American Presidency Project, http://www.presidency.ucsb.edu/ws/?pid=53091.

5. IGM Forum, "Rent Control," Feb. 7, 2012.

6. Norton and Ariely, "Building a Better America—One Wealth Quintile at a Time."

7. Alvaredo et al., *World Wealth and Income Database*, "United States, Top 1% Income Share," http://www.wid.world.

8. Benjamin I. Page, Larry M. Bartels, and Jason Seawright, "Democracy and the Policy Preferences of Wealthy Americans," *Perspectives on Politics* 11, no. 1 (March 2013): 57, 58, 63.

9. Martin Gilens and Benjamin I. Page, "Testing Theories of American Politics: Elites, Interest Groups, and Average Citizens," *Perspectives on Politics* 12, no. 3 (Sept. 2014): 572–73.

10. Adam Bonica et al., "Why Hasn't Democracy Slowed Rising Inequality?," *Journal of Economic Perspectives* 27, no. 3 (Summer 2013): 111.

11. Lawrence Lessig, *Republic, Lost: The Corruption of Equality and the Steps to End It*, rev. ed. (Twelve, 2015), 16–17.

12. Arthur M. Okun, *Equality and Efficiency: The Big Trade-Off* (Brookings Institution, 1975).

13. Jonathan D. Ostry, Andrew Berg, and Charalambos G. Tsangarides, "Redistribution, Inequality, and Growth" (IMF staff discussion note 14/02, Feb. 2014), 8–9, 26.

14. Daron Acemoglu and James Robinson, *Why Nations Fail: The Origins of Power, Prosperity, and Poverty* (Crown Business, 2012), 152–58.

15. John Kenneth Galbraith, "Power and the Useful Economist," *American Economic Review* 63, no. 1 (March 1973), 6.

16. "Economics Degrees Still 'Too Narrow in Focus,'" *Times Higher Education*, March 26, 2016.

17. People's day-to-day emotional well-being only tends to improve up to a level of family income around $75,000 per year; people's evaluations of their own lives, another measure of happiness, do continue to improve as they make more money. Daniel Kahneman and Angus Deaton, "High Income Improves Evaluation of Life but Not Emotional Well-Being," *Proceedings of the National Academy of Sciences* 107, no. 38 (Sept. 21, 2010): 16489–493.

18. Quoted in Hacker and Pierson, *American Amnesia*, 27.

19. John Maynard Keynes, "Economic Possibilities for Our Grandchildren," in *Essays in Persuasion* (Classic House Books, 2009), 201.

20. Louis Johnston and Samuel H. Williamson, "What Was the U.S. GDP Then?," MeasuringWorth, http://www.measuringworth.org/usgdp/.

Index

Page numbers in *italics* refer to figures.

About the Author

James Kwak is a professor at the University of Connecticut School of Law and the co-author, with Simon Johnson, of *13 Bankers* and *White House Burning*. He has a Ph.D. in intellectual history from UC Berkeley and a J.D. from the Yale Law School. Before going to law school, he worked in the business world as a management consultant and a software entrepreneur.

A Note on the Type

This book was set in Janson, a typeface long attributed to the Dutchman Anton Janson. However, it has been conclusively demonstrated that these types are actually the work of Nicholas Kis (1650–1702), a Hungarian. The type is an example of the sturdy Dutch types that prevailed in England up to the time of William Caslon (1692–1766).

Composed by North Market Street Graphics,
Lancaster, Pennsylvania

Printed and bound by Berryville Graphics,
Berryville, Virginia

Designed by M. Kristen Bearse

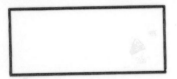

DATE DUE

This item is Due on
or before Date shown.

FEB - - 2017